Angling Library

VOLUME 3

SALMON

Angling Library

ISSN 0955–3827

Series Editors
Barrie Rickards and Martin Gay

VOLUME 1
PIKE
Martin Gay and Barrie Rickards

VOLUME 2
ZANDER
Barrie Rickards and Neville Fickling

SALMON

Neil Graesser

THE BOYDELL PRESS

First published 1991 by The Boydell Press, Woodbridge

The Boydell Press is an imprint of Boydell & Brewer Ltd
PO Box 9, Woodbridge, Suffolk IP12 3DF

ISBN 0 85115 273 2

British Library Cataloguing-in-Publication Data
Graesser, Neil
Salmon. – (Angling library)
I. Title II. Series
799.1
ISBN 0–85115–273–2

This publication is printed on acid-free paper

Printed in Great Britain by
St Edmundsbury Press Ltd, Bury St Edmunds, Suffolk

Contents

Introduction

Salmo salar, the Atlantic salmon, is one of the most valuable natural resources that any nation can have – not only because it has a very high nutritional value as a source of food, but also because of its amenity value as one of the game fish most sought after by the angling fraternity throughout the world. Because of this food value, commercial fisheries in the form of net and long line operators exploit salmon stocks at sea and in the estuaries. Their catch is marketed throughout the world, either as fresh salmon or smoked; some is also canned although this is more common in the case of Pacific salmon rather than Atlantic salmon. Rod fisheries on the freshwater rivers and loch systems draw many people from home and abroad to partake in angling for these sporting fish, often named the King of fish. Areas such as North America, Iceland, Norway, the United Kingdom and Eire are famed for their rod salmon fisheries.

The anglers not only swell the numbers of tourists drawn to such areas during the normal tourist season, but also at times of the year outside the tourist season. Salmon angling is a very valuable asset to the rural economy of these countries, and it also leaves a spin-off to the community at large, creating indirect employment in the hotel trade and many ancillary industries. Both the commercial and rod fishing industries provide direct employment on isolated coasts and valleys throughout these countries where other forms of employment are both scarce and difficult to find.

The Atlantic salmon is an anadromous species, depending on two separate and distinct environments for the fulfilment of its life cycle. It breeds in freshwater and spends the first few years of its juvenile life feeding in freshwater, before migrating to sea. While at sea, its main feeding phase takes place, during which rapid growth to the adult stage is rapidly achieved. It then has the uncanny ability to return to its river of origin, in order to regenerate the species.

The life of this fascinating migratory species has been studied by scientists from all over the world for very many years. Although much is now known about most stages of *Salmo salar*'s life in freshwater, far less is known of its sea feeding life. Indeed, it would be true to say that until the middle of this century little was known of the movements or whereabouts of this species during the time between the smolts' migration to sea and the return of the adult fish to freshwater. Only after some of their feeding areas at sea were discovered between 1950 and 1970 (which areas then became either net or long line commercial fisheries) were scientists able to track down their movements and time their homeward migrations.

Even today there are many, many unanswered questions about certain aspects of the life of this valuable resource.

I was born in the late 1920s, the youngest of a family of five boys and one girl, in the Vale of Llangollen in North Wales, close by the banks of the Welsh Dee. My parents were both very keen fishermen and, mainly because neither my brothers nor my sister showed a great interest in fishing, both my parents encouraged me to take up the sport at a very early age. Shortly after I was born my father bought a small estate in Rosehall, South Sutherland. Not only did this property have salmon fishing in the River Cassley, seatrout fishing on the Kyle of Sutherland and its own artificial trout lake, but also there was a wealth of fishing available close by in neighbouring salmon rivers and trout lochs.

I had the ideal opportunity, therefore, to study salmon and take part in fishing from the very start of my life, and literally took hold of this golden opportunity with both hands. If I could not fish myself, I accompanied others who were fishing or, alternatively, lay beside a burn, loch or river, merely watching and studying everything that went on beside, in, or on its surface. It would be true to say that water has always attracted me, from the earliest days of my life up to the present time.

I not only took to fishing at a very early age, but also studied everything I could learn about freshwater fish. Salmon fishing became my most favoured hobby. Salmon became first my life-study and then, while I was still in my twenties, my job, when I became a freshwater Fishery Consultant, specialising in Salmon and Salmon Fisheries. In recent years, I have become an author on both subjects.

Over the years many people have asked me from time to time what interests me most about salmon fishing and how I have the patience to work with, write about and talk about salmon day in and day out, and then spend my spare time on a river partaking in the sport of salmon angling. It is an interesting question and one that I have no difficulty in answering. In a nutshell, it is the peace and solitude of beautiful surroundings, with ever-changing light, scenery and vegetation, all according to weather and seasonal conditions. Nothing is ever boring because regardless of whether I am working on rivers, studying fish, or at meetings, wherever I go, whatever I do or whatever I discuss, no two problems are ever the same; something is always different, be it the setting, the light, or the topic under discussion.

When I am fishing, water flow, weather conditions and the scenery are always changing according to the time of day or season of the year. Sometimes I am frustrated by tricky wind conditions, by a rising river or, worst of all, by a horde of midges, while at other times my morale is boosted by the successful landing of a fish, or by the ability to place my fly where I want it or to time my cast perfectly. At all times, however, I am fully alert, waiting like a coiled spring to react when necessary: to counter a buffeting wind, to respond to a fish taking my fly, or to help an associate in trouble. Time passes very quickly; it seldom drags. Thus I have no time to dwell on problems and am relaxed. Can anyone who has been lucky enough to take up angling not agree that after his day out he may return weary with aches and pains, but he is always in a relaxed frame of mind with some interesting story to recount, either of his woe or joy, or perhaps of some animal, bird or plant he has seen during his excursion.

As a child and teenager I was taken by my parents to many famed beats and lochs throughout the UK. I also fished the Argoed beat of the Welsh Dee or the Rosehall beat of the Cassley, at will whenever I was at home. Later in life, as a guest, tenant or advisor, I have been lucky enough to fish countless rivers and beats in Scotland and many others elsewhere. I have found each to have its own fascinating peculiarities and interests and would find it hard to put any one in front of another; in the right conditions and on the right day, each and every one can be productive.

If I were asked what gives me, even today, my biggest thrill my answer would be either the sudden long elastic pull on my line as the fish makes its first contact with my fly, or helping a beginner to catch his or her first fish. Each is equally rewarding and satisfying.

Neil Graesser
1991

CHAPTER ONE

The Life Cycle of Salmon

OVA – ALEVIN STAGE

Once the salmon egg has been laid, fertilised and covered up by gravel some 6 to 9 inches beneath the river bed, it lies motionless nestled snugly in the crevices between the particles of gravel in the redd. Here it is adequately protected from the rigours of the buffeting current flows of widely varying velocities, as the river rises and falls above it. It must remain in its gravel enclosement for several months throughout the changeable winter months, until it hatches out some time later in the spring. The duration of the actual incubation period of the egg is almost entirely controlled by the mean average water temperature to which it is subjected wherever it resides in the river system. In a mean water temperature of 45°F the egg will hatch in about 80 days, whilst in a mean below 40°F the eggs will not hatch for 100 days or more.

Naturally, this can vary considerably from winter to winter according to the severity of the climatic conditions that prevail. During winters when there are either prolonged periods of hard frost or heavy snowfalls on the hills, or a combination of both, water temperatures fall quickly to the low 30°F and often remain low for a considerable period: not only through the duration of the cold snap, but often long afterwards until the deposits of snow on the high catchment have finally melted. Eggs subjected to these ranges of water temperature often do not hatch until late March or well into April, whilst during milder, more open winters, when snow falls and periods of frost last for shorter periods, some eggs will hatch out in late February or early March.

Obviously water temperature can vary considerably from river to river, according to where the water lies both geographically and topographically in the country, as well as varying fairly radically between high catchment and low catchment areas of the same river system. Therefore, there can be a considerable variation between when the eggs hatch out, both in differing parts of the catchment and also from river to river. It is possible that in some cases this difference could be as much as a month to six weeks. There is little doubt that the alliance between the incubation period of the egg and mean average water temperature is a precaution by nature to ensure that none of these eggs hatch out until there is sufficient food bloom in the river system to sustain the progeny once it hatches out.

Approximately twenty-four hours after the eggs have been fertilised and planted in the redd, they become extremely fragile and remain so for several weeks until they have reached the eyed stage, when the eye of the unborn fish is clearly visible in the egg. Once again, it is the mean water temperature to which the egg is subjected which determines when the eyed stage is reached, and this can vary from between 5 and 6 weeks to nearly twice that time. When the eggs reach the eyed stage, they become extremely robust and can withstand practically any abuse or movement. It is at this stage that eggs incubating in hatcheries are sold and despatched to their purchasers, or planted out in artificial redds made in the gravel, or placed in vibert plastic boxes and then covered by gravel in the river systems.

Before the eyed stage is reached, the eggs incubating in the redds in a river or in trays in the hatcheries are extremely prone to rupturing or destruction as a result of either undue movement or vibration. This is one of the main reasons why most experienced fishery managers are worried if they have more stock fish on their spawning fords than the spawning-grounds are capable of accommodating, as this can often result in later spawning fish over-cutting the redds made by the early spawning stock. This is because the act of spawning is a very vigorous activity, and if a female fish tries to cut its redd on top of gravel where eggs in the fragile stage are already incubating, then those eggs will almost inevitably be ruptured and destroyed by either the vibration or the movement created by the cutting operation. If, however, the eggs incubating in the gravel have already reached the eyed stage, no undue harm should be done provided they are not uncovered and washed away when the new redd is cut and finished. Eggs incubating in the river can also be lost due to natural causes, such as –

1. When eggs have been planted on loose unstable gravel, often washed into the river by flash floods following a thunder storm during the previous summer, and then subsequently washed on downstream in the heavy winter spates which often occur after spawning has taken place.
2. When eggs have been planted in insecure shallow gravel deposits lying on top of rocky foundations. Such eggs are often washed out along with the gravel they are in by high velocity flows during the winter months.
3. When sand, silt or sludge washed downstream by subsequent floods lodges on top of gravel where eggs are already incubating. These eggs are often smothered due to the fact that they cannot breath and are, therefore, lost, a common occurrence when landslides or serious bank erosion happens after high peak floods occur.

4. During periods of severe frost, when eggs laid in redds on the fringes of the river or in small tributaries can either be destroyed by the frost, encased in their redd in ice flows, or exposed and destroyed when the ice flows break up and tumble downstream once the thaw comes, ploughing up the gravel fords as they do so.

There is no doubt that all these natural hazards do, from time to time, take a significant toll of eggs incubating in our river systems over the long winter months, especially if abnormal weather conditions or peak floods happen to occur during the incubation period. These losses will obviously be far more marked in unstable watercourses than in spawning areas that have a stable regime. This is a matter I will deal with later.

LIFE IN THE RIVER: ALEVIN – SMOLT

Once the eggs hatch, the little fish that emerges from them is known as an alevin. This little creature, barely an inch in length, is almost transparent and has a yolk-sac attached to its under-belly. This is the alevin's food supply to sustain the little fish for the first three to four weeks of its life whilst it wriggles and wends its way slowly but surely upwards through the niches and crevices between the gravel of its redd, to the surface of the river bed above. The first stage of the alevin's life must be both wearisome and tedious as the yolk-sac will undoubtedly be cumbersome and is likely to both impede and restrict its freedom of movement as this little creature forces its way between the particles of gravel. As the alevin grows larger so the yolk-sac gets smaller until by the end of its journey it has been completely absorbed.

Once it has hatched in its comfortable haven within the gravel, the alevin has a fairly trouble free journey until it reaches the top layers of gravel some two inches below the surface. From here onwards, however, it encounters its first dangers in the form of predators lurking close to the river bed. These vary from the stone fly larva which can prick and burst the yolk-sac, whereup the alevin dies of starvation, to fish predators such as eels, which devour it.

Once they have emerged on to the surface of the river bed and their yolk-sac has been completely absorbed into their systems, the little fish are known as fry. Mainly black in colour and now just over an inch in length, they are generally shy at first having suddenly been introduced to light for the first time. As they slowly but surely become accustomed to their new environment, they hide beneath the particles of gravel and venture forth merely to forage for tiny morsels of food. At first they often remain in shoals, darting for cover whenever the least disturbance alerts them. If one is lucky enough to happen upon newly hatched fry feeding and they are suddenly alerted, what to the human eye seemed to be a mass of tiny fish one moment, disappears completely from sight as they merge with and seek cover in their hideouts under the gravel of the river bed.

As they grow stronger and get more used to their environment, they disperse both up and downstream from the redds and spread out over a wide expanse of the nursery areas and shallow sections of the river, in close proximity to the place where they were born. Here, they forage voraciously for tiny particles of fish fauna, plankton and various types of insects to sustain themselves daily, often vying with each other to secure their own patch of feeding territory.

Losses to the newborn fry stock are undoubtedly extremely high, due to fish and bird predators, to natural weaknesses and, even more so, to starvation because of the very limited food supply to be found in many sectors of freshwater rivers. In some of the poorer quality feeding areas, fry are partially or almost wholly reliant on terrestrial insects to provide the major part of their food supply.

Many fry, when they are first hatched, are caught up in fast current flows and swept downstream, often out of control, and those that are washed down into a deep pool are often quickly devoured by predatory fish lurking in the depths. Large hatches of fry can be quickly decimated in this manner before they have become acclimatised to their new environment. Planted fry, incubated in hatcheries, are particularly vulnerable and suffer significant losses by these means.

The pH value of the water largely determines the productivity of each individual feeding area within a river system, and this can vary considerably not only from river to river, but also throughout much of the catchment and, in some cases, from tributary to tributary within a river system. pH values of 6.5 upwards, can support fish fauna of high nutrient quality such as freshwater shrimps and snails. This category of feeding area is really comparable with the best arable land on a farm and is very productive and capable, therefore, of supporting large numbers of fry or parr through to the smolt stage; whereas nursery areas with pH values of 5.5 to 6.5 can be compared with marginal arable land. These areas are able to cultivate lower nutrient fauna and are, therefore, less productive, with fry and parr usually having a slower growth rate than those in the previous category. Feeding areas with 4.6 to 5.5 pH values can be termed as the poorest category. These are really poverty stricken areas with low productivity and a much slower growth rate, largely dependent on terrestrial insects to supplement the meagre low quality food chain. This type of nursery area is really comparable with hill or heath grazing in agricultural terms. Watercourses with pH values lower than 4.6 are unacceptable to salmonids and cannot support these species.

Another important aspect concerning feeding or nursery areas, is river bed or bank cover. These are of vital importance not only to afford protection against predators, but also to give shade against sunlight. At

Young salmon fry in a hatchery tank.

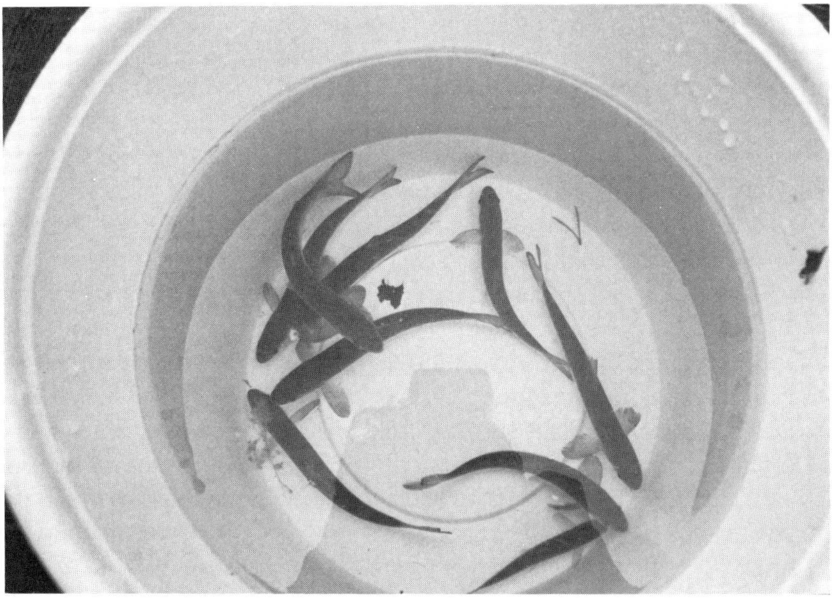

Good wild smolts caught in the Gruidie trap.

the same time, bank cover is a very valuable producer of the terrestrial food chain, with all types of insects being made available to drop or be blown on to the surface of the water from the lush undergrowth overhanging or cladding the adjacent banks. Banks that overhang or are undermined give an excellent haven affording shade or refuge against many different dangers. Bank cover also stabilises the river banks and helps to bind them with their root growth, which in many cases safeguards the banks against erosion during spate flows.

Areas of the river bed whose composition largely comprises either silt, sand or compacted gravel, afford little refuge or protection against either sunlight or predators, as there are few cracks and crevices for fry and parr to hide in when danger arises. Eroded banks also provide a constant source of sediment to silt up and destroy good spawning and feeding areas and are generally quite useless for food production, shade or protection. Only if weed growth becomes established on such silted river beds is any food productivity, shade or cover, returned to these areas and, even then, if this becomes too dense its value is often retarded.

Shallow, wide stretches of the river with a plentiful supply of open gravel and larger stones dotted around over the whole areas, flowing between stable banks well clad with undergrowth, bushes and the odd larger tree, probably afford the optimum habitat for feeding fry and parr. These shallow areas exclude easy access for large fish predators and at the same time are too shallow for mergansers, gooseanders and cormorants to dive or manoeuvre freely, whilst the many crevices and niches under the open gravel and larger stones afford a wealth of refuge if, perchance, danger does arise. The stable banks provide an ideal foundation for lush ground vegetation, bushes and trees become firmly established, and these in turn provide a useful source of terrestrial food. Both crevices under the stones and gravel and shade from the trees and overhanging vegetation, give these little feeding fish ample shelter from the relentless rays of sunshine and, at the same time, provide a cooler habitat if water temperatures rise to danger levels. If they rise to over 66°F then levels of dissolved oxygen in the water may be much reduced and often reach unacceptably low readings. At times, this can lead to fish losses, as fry and parr in their feeding areas can be at risk, either as a result of stress or due to suffocation. Sparsely watered burns or those affected by irrigation or other types of water abstraction, are among those most vulnerable, particularly during prolonged drought periods or extremely hot weather conditions.

Quite apart from feeding areas within the main river, there are those to be found in the larger tributaries and significant burns, and even more so in the numerous small side burns which flow both into these tributaries and into the main river. Even the smallest burn can, provided it has a clean gravel bed, afford adequate spawning facilities and often very productive feeding facilities. These watercourses of varying width and size often provide some of the most productive nursery areas within the entire river system. Those draining the lower slopes of the valley are often tree lined, with farm fences lining either side, thus protecting the vegetation, bushes and trees from being damaged by grazing stock. These burns are, therefore, well shaded and protected from many of the dangers which lurk so readily in the larger feeding areas of the main river system. Others, flowing off undulating open moorland, can also play an important part as they meander down gravelly bedded straths, often winding along the floor of long, kindly glens with a reasonably flat downward gradient. The beds of these watercourses often comprise of large areas of gravel intermingled with large stones and rocky pools with natural weirs, constituting ideal feeding and nursery areas for young salmonids. Provided the watercourses flowing through the lower slopes of arable valleys are not subjected to any form of pollution such as agricultural sprays, silage effluent or sheep dip, and they are not used for irrigation purposes, they usually have a high pH value. Therefore, in many cases they are likely to be amongst the most productive nursery areas, regardless of size, provided they are sufficiently watered at all times of the year.

Watercourses flowing off moorland or mountainous terrain on the higher catchment areas will also, provided they are stable and not too steep or torrential, play an important part in feeding young salmon stocks. However, although these are likely to be almost entirely free of chemical pollution, the pH values can vary considerably, with those flowing off peat land or hard rock deposits often having a relatively low value whilst those flowing off mountains with limestone or mineral outcrops may have a substantially higher value.

As the rivers descend and flow through the lower floors of the valleys and sometimes through the arable coastal plain, both the main river and its many tributaries and side burns still have an important role to play in feeding the progeny of the spawning stocks which propagate in these lower catchment areas. However, in the lower reaches, the increasing population densities, industry and more intensive agricultural activities all pose many differing problems to salmon conservation and in particular, to the health and protection of young feeding fish stocks. I will deal with these problems in later chapters of this book. But, by and large, it is sufficient to say at this stage that the requirements for productive feeding areas in this part of the catchment are no different from those in the higher parts of the system.

The growth rate of fry and parr during the summer months is almost entirely determined by the availability of their food supply and also by the density of the population this food has to support. In the autumn and winter months the food bloom in the rivers first retards, then remains dormant before beginning to increase once again in the spring. During autumn and winter, for the most part, fry and parr become languid and feed very little in water temperatures below 42°F, merely conserving their energy rather than expending it wastefully in search of food, which is at that time of year a very scarce commodity and usually insufficient to sustain them. In most cases, their growth rate is steady from the time they first become fry, in late March or April, right through to mid-September in high catchment areas and, in lower parts of the catchment, well into November or even further into the winter, entirely depending on the severity of the climactic conditions which prevail.

The duration of the feeding period can also vary considerably from river to river, and that of a river such as the Hampshire Avon, sited geographically in a warmer clime and lower altitude, would almost certainly be much longer than that of a river flowing off a high catchment, such as the Cairngorm area of Scotland, where early snow and frost would lower water temperatures quickly.

It is almost certain that it is size, and certainly not age, which largely determines when parr become smolts and migrate to sea. Rarely, if ever, do United Kingdom parr smolt at one year of age, with the possible exception of a few rivers in the south of England. Two to three years of age is acknowledged to be the norm, with probably the majority smolting at two years when milder winter periods prevail, and a large proportion smolting at three years when harder, longer winters are prevalent. This is due to the fact that when milder weather conditions prevail throughout the year, fry and parr gain almost an extra three month period of feeding that year, as they both hatch and begin to feed earlier, and then continue feeding for a longer period in the autumn; when severe winters prevail the majority probably do not hatch out for an extra month to six weeks, and they cease feeding very much earlier than they would in mild autumns.

Some parr in higher catchments or poorer quality feeding areas, do not smolt until they are four, or even five, years old. The numbers which do not smolt until they reach these ages will be few during mild weather cycles but they significantly increase during periods when very hard winter cycles prevail, as they did in the 1930–1950 era.

Because of the many variations – such as the duration of the annual feeding period, the quality of the nursery areas and the density of fry and parr to be supported, any of which can be liable to change literally from year to year – the numbers of parr of different age groups that smolt from a river system may not alter significantly each year. It is probable, therefore, that if there is a stock failure of a certain age class on the nursery areas the resultant lower density of feeding fry and parr will enable younger fry and parr to grow more quickly than they would normally have done and, therefore, they will smolt at an earlier age. This natural flexible type of stock adjustment levels out the overall numbers of smolts produced by each river system annually, and materially reduces the effect of a serious stock failure of any particular age class on a specific nursery area. There is little doubt that the fact that it is size rather than age which determines when parr become smolts, has enabled this species to overcome the pressures of both natural and unnatural disasters such as spawning failures or fish kills as a result of pollution incidents, because smolts can be recruited if necessary, from an earlier age class to make up for these losses. This naturally helps to regulate the overall salmon stocks returning to a river system annually and allows for a steady stocking rate, instead of one full of peaks and troughs, which would otherwise be the inevitable result.

As the fry grow stronger, they become easier to recognise because of a series of dark bars imprinted on the skin on either side of the body, often referred to as parr marks or 'thumb' prints. Less distinctive but similar marks are also to be found on young trout. It is really not clear when these little fish cease being called fry and become parr. Some refer to them as fry then fingerlings, and finally parr after the end of the first year's feeding. Others refer to them as parr once they have reached the size of a man's finger. Really, this specific point is not important and it should suffice to say that they are parr once they have settled down in their new environment and are feeding for themselves as individuals and no longer in shoals.

PARR – SMOLT

As the parr increase in size they are better able to forage more selectively for food, and are more aware of the many dangers with which they are faced. At this stage they generally move off the smoother, gravelly nursery areas, where they fed as fry, and take up station in the rougher, stoney riffles lying between the deeper pools. They also become more antagonistic amongst themselves and other species, and usually take up their own feeding territory which they zealously guard against intruders.

These little fish are by now quite sizeable, varying in length between three and five inches, and are voracious feeders, well able to devour much larger particles of food. Amongst their diet at this stage are species of water borne invertebrates, terrestrial insects, plankton, worms and smaller fry and parr, not only of their own species but also of any other freshwater fish that happen to come their way. As they lurk behind stones in the faster riffles they are well placed in the spring time to predate on newly hatched fry washed downstream from the spawning fords above. Throughout the summer, they enjoy a mixed diet of the many foods which vary in type considerably according to water flow. In high water flows worms and grubs washed off the land are plentiful, whereas in low flows terrestrial insects are more the norm. In the autumn, just before their winter period of dormancy, they get an added luxury to their diet. This is in the form of stray salmon and trout eggs that are washed out of the adults' redds during the act of spawning. These highly nutritious morsels are eagerly devoured by parr, and there is little doubt that these items in their food chain give a vital boost to their stamina and strength when it is most needed, immediately prior to their long period of fast. Even a few of these eggs suffice to sustain them.

Having moved into their new habitat in deeper, faster, riffling waters, the sizeable parr have to be constantly alert to danger from predators. Although by now they have grown sufficiently to avoid being preyed on by all but the largest fish predators, they are extremely vulnerable to bird predators like the heron and, even more so, the diving birds such as cormorants. These latter birds favour the fast flowing stoney riffles, where they have plenty of depth and width in which to dive and manoeuvre freely and where they can swim at speed underwater. By contrast, the heron stands stealthily, without moving a muscle, at the side of the river, often camouflaged by rushes or vegetation, eagerly waiting for the parr to come within his long reach before he pounces. This bird is also lethal on the nursery areas of small burns and tributaries.

It is at this time of their life that they are faced with yet another danger – that of the trout or coarse fisherman. Unfortunately, their new habitat may well be the favoured haunt of these fishermen using a fly, worm, maggot or some other tasty morsel. Naturally, the voracious parr eagerly foraging for food are easily tempted into taking one of these cunningly presented lures and often pay dearly for their simple error of judgment. At this stage in their life, salmon and trout parr are very similar and, for the amateur, very difficult to distinguish. There are, however, some subtle distinctions such as the shape of tail, the salmon parr having a deeply forked tail whilst the trout parr has a much shallower fork. The adipose fin of the salmon parr bears no reddish tinge on the upside edge, whereas the trout has. There is also a definite distinction between the alignment of the corner mouth hinge and the eye in the two species, the maxmilla being in line with the rear of the pupil in the salmon, and in line with the rear of the eye in the trout. A salmon parr also has more parr marks than a trout, ten to twelve instead of nine to ten. Finally, the wrist of the tail is much thinner in the salmon than in the thick wristed trout. None the less, to the inexperienced youngster a fish is a fish, and many parr lose their lives in this manner.

Once the winter months draw nigh and the water temperature drops to 42°F or below, these parr go into a stage of dormancy and feed languidly, if at all. For the most part they hide in rock crevices, beneath undermined banks or in crevices between stones, moving only when they have to in order to adjust their position as water flows constantly rise and fall in the river. The most important aspect of their winter life in the river is energy conservation: they must not weaken their physique unnecessarily in search of food which is either scarce or unobtainable. But even during this period they have to be constantly on the alert, as diving birds still scavenge the river in large numbers in search of unwary prey.

Once the spring arrives some of the large parr will take on their silver livery and migrate to sea as smolts, whilst those which are not large enough to smolt will remain in freshwater for a further year.

PRE-SMOLT PARR, SMOLTS

As the time draws near when the parr will turn into smolts and migrate to sea, some of those which inhabit the upper catchment areas or the top reaches of long tributaries make a local migration downstream during the early autumn of the year before that in which they become smolts. It is not known why some pre-smolt parr carry out this manoeuvre whilst others do not, nor is it easy to prove the real reason for this practice. Rightly or wrongly, it is deduced that these parr carry out this local migration in order to be better positioned in the river system when spring arrives, to enable a quick descent to the sea. There is little doubt that during the harder winters both water temperatures and flows will be more favourable for an early start to the journey in their new habitat than it would have been had they remained where they were in the higher catchment. Just how far down the river they actually go before taking up their new habitat is again unknown, but it is doubtful whether they reach the estuary as these autumn migrants are not dressed in their silver livery, which all smolts take on prior to migrating to sea. The very fact that there is an autumn downstream migration at all remained completely unknown for years until information was gleaned from monitoring parr and smolt movement by trapping certain tributaries of some river systems; this clearly showed that a significant number of parr did move out of these tributaries in the autumn.

In the early spring, the real seaward migration from the river systems begins in earnest. Parr take on a silver coat over the entire surface of their skin, completely obliterating any sign of the parr marks which identified them so clearly during their freshwater feeding period, and then become known as smolts. This covering is thought to play a critical role in protecting their skin and scales from erosion by sea water, as the specific gravity of the new environment they are about to enter is much different to that found in the river. Any serious damage to this coat can be fatal to these little migrants.

The earliest smolts begin to descend the river systems on the start of their seaward migration once the water temperature rises to around 45°F. This temperature is usually attained in some rivers, or parts of river systems, in March, and the migration continues throughout the months of April, May and June and, on occasions, into July. Although the 45°F water temperature level seems to be the trigger that starts the seaward migration, it is unlikely that it is the only control of the timing for all smolts leaving the river systems, as by late May or June temperatures throughout the river system are usually well in excess of 50°F. It is possible, therefore, that this staggering of the smolt descent to the sea may have some bearing on what feeding grounds these fish will journey to when they reach the sea.

Throughout their migration period smolts normally descend quietly downstream in sizeable shoals, much preferring to be in company rather than alone as they venture forth on the long journey to their feeding grounds. For the most part, the little silver fish descend downstream tail first, only swimming head first for short stretches whilst they negotiate the more difficult sections, such as dead water with little or no current, or when they are disturbed or impeded. The smolts usually take advantage of higher rates of water flow to aid them on their passage, the main movement generally occurring on the second or third day after a flood has peaked, when the river is settling down and dropping quietly with low turbidity levels prevailing. In lower flows, the main movement often occurs during the hours of darkness or just before dusk. As they descend, smolts feed voraciously and at times when there is a hatch of insects the surface of the water literally boils as the shoals pounce on them. Unfortunately, both this activity and their glinting and glittering as they negotiate sparsely watered shallows, alerts predators to their presence. Significant losses do, therefore, occur as gulls, terns and the other main bird predators all take their toll when the smolt shoals are caught in a confined space with little or no room to escape.

SALMON IN THE SEA

When the smolt shoals arrive at the estuary of their river they usually pause briefly whilst they adjust and become acclimatised to the significant change in specific gravity of their new environment. Often they use the tidal influence within the estuary to help with this adjustment, moving in and out with the tide in the zone where there is a mix of sea and fresh water in order to reduce the shock of this drastic change, before finally heading out to sea on the start of their long journey to the lush feeding grounds far from the shores of their native country.

In the estuary this precious component of a salmon stock is extremely vulnerable to predation from both birds and seals, because they are not only numbed by the shock of sea water but are also in an entirely different environment. Therefore, these shoals are at this stage easy prey for all and sundry, and can suffer substantial losses in consequence.

For many centuries very little was known about many aspects of *Salmo salar*'s life and movements at sea. Indeed, it can be said that it was not until commercial net fisheries began to exploit their feeding grounds off Greenland in 1957, and long line fisheries exploited similar grounds in the Norwegian sea in the mid–1960s and off the Faroes in the 1970s, that the movements of salmon stocks at sea became clearer. For many years scientists had presumed that the smolts did move far offshore and that they did not feed in the seas around the United Kingdom, purely because trawler fleets had never reported any sightings or catches of salmon in the North Sea, or in the Irish Sea or around the Hebrides, Orkney and Shetland to the north and west. Early in this century some of the most prominent of these scientists advised the Government not to mount research programmes at sea to try and establish where these fish were feeding, as they feared that once the feeding grounds were discovered they would be exploited commercially. Their fears turned out to be well founded because in 1957 a local inhabitant happened to set a net off the west coast of Greenland and caught numerous salmon in it, thereby positively establishing for the first time where some stocks of Atlantic salmon were feeding. Unfortunately, this chance discovery led to the setting up of a localised salmon fishery which quickly developed into an important autumn inshore salmon gill net fishery exploited mainly by the native Greenlanders. The catch of this fishery exceeded 1,500 tonnes by 1965. An offshore salmon drift net then developed and from 1969 to 1973 the combined catch of both these fisheries exceeded 2,000 tonnes.

Producing nations of Atlantic salmon stocks were naturally extremely worried at the advent of this fishery, which had obviously been established on a large salmon sea-feeding ground. Therefore, they sent teams of scientists over to the Greenland fishery zone in order to try and establish which nation's salmon stocks were present in this feeding area. In order to trace both their country and river of origin, many salmon caught in this fishery were tagged and released. As a result of the experiments it was positively established that salmon stocks from the United Kingdom, Eire, North America, Scandinavia and many other countries were using these feeding grounds. Once these facts had been verified, in order to prevent decimation of these valuable shoals of salmon, agreement was reached by the North West Atlantic Fisheries Commission to bring this fishery under stricter control and limit its annual catch to an agreed figure, to be reviewed from time to time.

Several years later, a further feeding ground was discovered off the Faroe Islands by the Faroese long-lining fleet. This new salmon feeding ground was again quickly exploited. Teams of scientists once again moved in to carry out tagging experiments to positively identify the origin of stocks present on these new grounds, and stocks of salmon from many rivers in the United Kingdom and other countries shown to use the feeding area. This was quickly followed by international meetings leading to an agreed quota being placed on the catch of the fishery, as well as strict controls pertaining to the management of the fishery by the Faroese government. Unfortunately, the problem is that as this is a long-line fishery in the main, where salmon are caught by hook and line and not by net, many immature fish are among those caught. Although there is a strict ruling on the size of fish which can be kept, all undersized fish having to be returned to the water, this causes much the same problem of wastage as occurs in the case of anglers catching parr and smolt in fresh water. The fact that these immature fish are voracious feeders means that when they are caught on hook and line many are badly hooked and do not survive when released. Therefore these fish die soon after release, only to become 'crab meat' on the bottom of the sea, surely a waste which no industry, no matter how strong, can possibly afford.

The discovery in recent years of these two salmon feeding areas so far apart in the oceans, and the knowledge that they are exploited by salmon stocks from many nations, has certainly added greatly to our knowledge of where our salmon stocks go when they leave our shores. There are still many questions which remain unanswered, such as how many more well stocked feeding grounds lie somewhere in the northern hemisphere? Or are these the only two which the world's Atlantic salmon depend on? Why do some of our stocks go to Greenland, and others to the Faroes? Is this partly determined by the month they migrate to sea, is it the age at which they smolt, or a combination of the two?

It is reasonable to suppose that those fish which will return to the United Kingdom as grilse will not go to the Greenland banks, because they will not have time to journey such a distance across the seas, feed for a sufficient period, and then return to their rivers of origin at the scheduled time. Therefore, is it our salmon which spend two or more winters at sea that exploit the Greenland grounds? Certainly some of our grilse and salmon exploit the Faroese banks. Or is it even more specific, with early run fish exploiting one of these banks and late run fish the other? Or do all salmon stocks exploit both banks, with the exception of United Kingdom grilse going to Greenland? There is scientific evidence to support the theory that the Greenland fishery did have a marked effect on stocks of early-run salmon returning to some of our rivers famed for their spring runs. The decline of the heavier, early-run class of spring fish, mainly of the three to four sea-winter age group, weighing from 15 to 40 pounds, coincided with the escalation of the commercial Greenland drift net fishery. It would seem probable, therefore, that the longer a salmon remained feeding on these banks in the danger zone, the less chance it would have of surviving. It could be argued that the Greenland fishery would take a toll of two sea-winter fish, a greater toll of those fish which would return after three sea winters, and an even greater toll of those which would have remained for four sea winters. Unfortunately, this theory can never be proved, and must remain entirely hypothetical.

There is absolutely no doubt that during their sea feeding life the fish are voracious feeders with a very high food/growth conversion ratio. Wild smolts which migrate to sea between March and May one year, at only a few ounces in weight and a mere four to six inches in length, often return as grilse from May to August in the following year weighing anything between 3 and 10 pounds. If they remain in the sea until the autumn of that same year some can be even heavier, up to between 12 and 16 pounds. Salmon which remain at sea for two or more sea winters can weigh anything from 6 to 40 pounds; thus fish over 25 pounds are more likely to be three or four sea-winter fish than two sea-winter fish. It is not known how long it takes smolts which have just entered the sea to journey out to their feeding grounds, nor is it known what determines which feeding grounds they head towards, nor whether they feed heavily on this outward journey. If, however, their feeding behaviour is similar once they reach the sea to that when they descend the river, they will feed voraciously on their outward journey, even though they are keeping on the move.

I know of no reports of smolt shoals having been intercepted on their outward journey by trawlers or other types of sea nets, although because of their size most of these nets would have too large a mesh to trap them. This may point to the fact that they are swimming deep, or it may just be that their route avoids any area where fishermen cast their nets. It is possible that these migrants take advantage of the warmer currents such as the Gulf Stream to help them on their way, and if this is so they may find a rich supply of suitable food available in these currents to sustain them on their long outward passage. The timing of their actual entry into the sea may be a vital factor in determining both their destination with regard to feeding grounds, and also be one of the factors prominent in determining whether they will mature as a grilse or a salmon. All these unanswered questions make us realise how little of the sea-life phase and life history of what is described as an anadromous species is really known even today.

Their main food on the lush feeding grounds is known to include many types of fish such as capelin, sprats, herrings and sandeels, various types of crustacea such as krill, and large zooplankton organisms. Salmon feed mainly in shoals and often follow their prey as they move inshore or offshore, or on their local migrations. In recent years concern has often been voiced by scientists and fishermen at the industrial fishing pressures on some of the salmon's favourite food such as sand eels, capelin and krill. The main fear is that this could well lead to a decline in the marine food chain, with unknown consequences which could affect the timing of the salmon's homeward migration, due to slower maturity.

With commercial net and long line fisheries established on at least two important feedings grounds, there are many serious questions which could have a significant effect on either a nation's or a specific river's stocks. These concern the fact that salmon feed in shoals, but what we do not know is whether our smolt shoals keep together once they reach their feeding grounds, or whether they join up with other smolt shoals migrating to sea from the same country, or from rivers whose estuaries are close together. If any of these things do happen, then shoals from one nation or part of a nation, or even from a single river system, could be decimated or completely lost when they happen to cross the path of either a drift net fishery or a long line fishing fleet. It could quite easily lead to the extinction of a large proportion of one of the seasonal stocks of a single river system, or even of a nation, often in the autumn prior to these fish returning to their rivers of origin. If, however, the fish congregate and do not feed in shoals belonging exclusively to one river or to a group of geographically close rivers then the danger may not be so great. The main problem is that we do not know whether these commercial high seas fisheries are taking a reasonable overall cull of every nation's feeding stocks, or whether during any one season only a few nations' stocks are badly affected whilst the stocks of other nations get off relatively lightly. In recent years scientific evidence in the United Kingdom has shown that although most rivers are producing a steady smolt run which varies little in strength from year to year, the numbers of grilse and salmon returning to these same rivers often fall far short of expectancy. This points to some loss occurring during the fishes' sea life. Exploitation by high seas commercial nets or lack of sufficient food could be two reasons for this. Another possibility could be that interceptory net fisheries are catching them in large numbers on their homeward migration, from their sea feeding areas to their rivers of origin.

It has always been accepted that the breeding nation should be allowed the biggest cull of stocks reared in their own river systems – both in the estuaries, in coastal and net fisheries, and up-river in rod fisheries. Similarly, nations that feed salmon stocks around their shores should be allowed a catch quota in lieu of grazing rights. It is very difficult, however, for any fishery manager to condone a drift net fishery intercepting salmon stocks on their homeward migration. This type of fishery can really be termed a pirate fishery, because it does not contribute in any way to the expense of breeding, rearing or feeding the fish which are caught in the fishery. Thus it reaps a rich reward at the expense of other countries.

Around the shores of the United Kingdom we not only have the Irish drift net fleet which fishes many miles out from the Irish shore and almost inevitably intercepts salmon stocks returning to numerous rivers in Northern Ireland, Scotland, Wales and England, but we also have legal drift net fisheries operating off the coast of England. The most intensive of these is that operated under licence in the Northumberland and Yorkshire water authority areas off the north-east coast of England. Scientific research, which entailed catching fish in this fishery, tagging them and then releasing them to find out their rivers of origin, has shown that 95 per cent of the fish caught on this fishery were destined for rivers in Scotland. The very fact that this important legal drift net fishery off the English coast has been neither banned nor more strictly controlled, may well have materially weakened the bargaining powers of the UK in negotiations within the North Atlantic Salmon convention. There is very little doubt that this fishery has also slowed down the recovery of salmon rehabitation in rivers such as the Tyne and the Forth, where fish stocks declined so drastically as a result of the Industrial Revolution during the last century, as well as weakening certain components of salmon stocks returning to other more productive rivers close by. The development of salmon ranching, a new industry that has been so successfully operated in Iceland and other countries in recent years, has been completely abandoned in both Scotland and England, almost entirely due to the presence of these interceptory fisheries. I will cover the subject of salmon ranching in another chapter.

For some considerable time it has been suggested that salmon and grilse on their homeward journey to their rivers of origin in the UK hit landfall in the area between the Butt of Lewis and Barra Head. Those destined for the north and east coast rivers then move northwards through the Pentland Firth, funnelling into their rivers as they pass along the north coast then down as far as the Moray Firth. However, those destined for the east coast rivers south of the Dee, seem to keep well out in the North Sea and turn shorewards off the south Yorkshire coast, before following the coastline northwards and funnelling into their rivers of origin as they come to them. It is thought that the reason for this manoeuvre is the fact that on the east coast the ebb tide flows south; thus fish destined for this area take advantage of the ebb tide and swim into it close to the shore, and then home into their native rivers as they come to them. This accounts for the fact that so many fish destined for the large Scottish river systems such as the Tweed, Forth, Tay and Esk, are caught in the English north-east coast drift net fishery. Fish tagged and then released have been recaptured as far north as the Aberdeenshire Dee, and even in the rivers flowing into the Moray Firth.

Fish destined for the west coast rivers of Scotland and the north-west of England move south from Barra Head and peel off into their native rivers as they come to them. It is not clear whether fish destined for the west coast of Ireland, south Wales, the West Country and the rivers flowing into the English channel home in on Barra Head or at some point on the west coast of Ireland, before swinging round the southern tip of Ireland to seek their rivers of origin. Whichever route they take there is no doubt that the fish destined for rivers in Ireland, and the west and south coasts of the UK, will be exploited by both the intensive Irish drift net fishery and the small drift net fishery operated off the coast of north-west England.

Our knowledge of the sea-life history and of the movements of the species by scientific evidence built up over the years through tagging fish in all the high sea and drift net fisheries has undoubtedly been considerably widened. However, much more research is needed before we fully understand the whole truth about this fascinating fish. This research would be extremely costly and difficult to undertake, with the added risk that if it were successful in identifying the whereabouts of feeding grounds at present unknown, further pressure would be brought to bear on salmon stocks because, almost inevitably, these would be exploited commercially.

During their sea life period, numerous predators pose a threat to the salmon's existence. Fish predators such as members of the Gadidae species take their toll of the smolt shoals at this stage of their life; cormorants, gulls, gannets and diving ducks such as mergansers and goosanders, predate heavily on the smolt shoals as they pause in the estuaries to acclimatise to their new environment. However, by far the worst predators on salmon, at sea, are the seals. These mammals not only devour smolts as they leave the rivers, but also take many grilse and salmon literally on the very last lap of their homeward journey, both along the coastline and within the estuaries. I cover predation at sea in a separate chapter.

Having reached the coastline in the proximity of their native rivers, salmon and grilse will try and ascend the river as soon as it is feasible. This very largely depends on the water flow in the river, but it is also influenced to some extent by the water temperature of the river. If there is ample flow in the river fish normally use the tide to take them up the estuary to the actual river mouth, and then enter the river as the tide turns to ebb. Under these conditions fish seldom hang about in the estuary. However, in the spring time low water-flow combined with water temperatures under 40°F often prevent fish entering the river, especially if there are shallow fords to negotiate in the bottom section.

Fish will then tend to hang about either within the estuary or off the adjacent coastline, until the flow in the river increases or spring tides occur. In either case, the shallows will become submerged, which enables fish to ascend more easily into the first large deep pool, where they can remain in comfort, ascending further upstream when conditions improve.

In late spring and summer, when water temperatures have increased to 45°F upwards, fish tend to enter the river in a much wider range of water flows, and are then willing to force their way upstream even in low ranges of flow, sometimes ascending the shallowest areas with part of their backs out of the water in order to negotiate sparsely watered fords.

For the most part, fish seem to prefer to move at dusk, and on through the night. This is particularly noticeable in the lower ranges of water flow, when water temperatures are high, but in the higher ranges of water flow fish will ascend freely throughout the twenty-four hour period.

In very low water, particularly during a prolonged drought, fish often congregate in the estuaries and off the mouths of the rivers in large numbers, waiting for an opportunity to ascend. This is the time when they are particularly vulnerable to predation by seals. In some of the worst drought periods fish that have been waiting to ascend for some considerable time tend to give up hope and move away to lie some distance off the coast until such time as the drought breaks and the rivers rise. Those fish which have net yet reached the coastline because they are later migrants often join the shoals waiting well offshore, and do not even bother to come into the estuaries under dire drought condition. It is impossible to establish whether this unusual behaviour is due to the scarcity of dissolved oxygen in the river water, caused by high water temperatures, or to something else. However, once the rains do come and the water rises to reasonable levels, the fish enter the rivers very quickly.

How salmon and grilse actually find their way back to their rivers of origin must still remain one of the many imponderables. The fact that a very large proportion of those fish do return to their rivers of origin is not disputed, and has been clearly shown by numerous tagging experiments carried out on migrating parr and smolts over many years. One of the first was reported by Isaac Walton in 1653, many more were reported in the eighteenth and nineteenth centuries, and more again during this century. Walton records tying a thread to parrs' tails. More recently, marked tags have been attached by silver wire in the proximity of the adipose fin of the fish, and now a favoured method is to insert a tiny micro tag into the nose of the fish. Few fish that have been tagged are found to have ascended the wrong river system, but many have been recaptured in the wrong estuary or on the coastline far from their rivers of origin. These fish may not have had any intention of entering these foreign river systems: they could have been trying to identify their own river or they could have joined a shoal of salmon homing to that particular river.

It is widely accepted that smell must play a large part in the final identification of the native river, and this is probably the reason why both salmon and grilse tend to hug the coastline once they hit landfall. It is thought this is the main reason why salmon returning to the major east coast UK rivers swim down the centre of the North Sea before swinging landwards off the Yorkshire coast and swimming northwards close inshore, facing the ebb tide. They then peel off into their rivers of origin as they come to them and recognise the smell of their chemical metabolism.

SALMON ASCENDING

Although salmon return to their rivers of origin for the prime and sole purpose of regenerating the species, it is interesting that some of these fish enter their river systems virtually twelve months before they are due to spawn, whilst other stocks enter some of the largest river systems almost every week, or even every day, thereafter with the last arrivals ascending within a few weeks of when they are due to spawn. Smaller river systems usually have fewer runs of fish with most of their stocks entering the river from June to October in the year in which they will spawn. The larger rivers are capable of accommodating more runs of fish with the earliest entering from October to December, although they will not spawn until October or November of the following year. These fish are quickly followed by the spring fish coming into the rivers from January to mid-May. The summer run, which includes a large proportion of grilse, comes in from mid-May to mid-September, with the autumn run finally coming in from mid-September to early December.

There is some overlap between the different runs of fish. Members of the spring, summer and autumn runs, including the grilse component of the latter two, will all spawn between November and January. They spawn during the same period as the fish which entered the river in the autumn of the previous year but which do not ripen to spawn for twelve months. In the past, this run of fish was known as the winter run but, for some strange reason only known to themselves, modern fishery scientists term these fish early run spring fish. Whereas it would be true to say that a proportion of these fish may have spent only two winters at sea, the fact is that many others have spent three or more winters at sea and are, therefore, usually a class of much heavier fish described by many in the past as the 'grey backs' or the winter run – probably a much more positive definition for this distinct run of fish.

Quite why nature spreads the return of the different runs of fish over such a wide period of the year must remain a mystery, especially in view of the fact that all these runs will spawn over the same three to four month period, regardless of where their parent river is geographically situated in the country. It may well be nature's way of assuring that a rich food supply is available to feed the population of those countries where the Atlantic salmon are indigenous over a long period of the year; otherwise it is difficult to see how this long stay in fresh water actually benefits the welfare of the species, or why it is necessary.

Salmon populate the river from the upper reaches downwards, with the early run fish occupying the upper reaches and its tributaries, the summer run the central body of the river, and the autumn run mainly the lower reaches, or the area of the river which is devoid of any formidable natural or man-made obstacles which might pose a problem for these gravid fish.

Grilse will return to their appropriate section of the river, depending on the run of which they are a component. In many cases, particularly in the shorter, smaller river systems, there can be significant overlapping of the various runs, which may lead to overcrowding of some sections of a river.

It is not entirely clear what governs the speed at which salmon and grilse ascend a river system, nor is it clear why nature has given some of the early runs of fish such an incredibly long space of time to reach their spawning grounds which, by comparison with the distances they travel at sea is a surprisingly short journey, even on the longest of our river systems. What is clear, however, is that they enter fresh water for the sole purpose of regenerating the species. It has also been fairly conclusively proven that, provided nothing untoward prevents them from doing so, they will return to the area of the river system where they themselves were born or spent their early freshwater feeding period as fry and parr.

It has also been established that water flow and water temperature do have a definite part to play in determining both when the fish can and cannot ascend the river, and at what speed they do so. In the case of natural obstructions such as falls, and man-made obstructions such as weirs and mill dams, fish can be held back and temporarily curtailed in their free ascent when either water flows or water temperatures are unfavourable. Company is another factor which very often has a bearing on fish movement within a river, as members of this gregarious species are seldom found alone.

It is interesting to note that once water temperature levels rise to over 50°F, a level at which formidable falls can be ascended, fish move far more quickly upstream. It is possible to make a reasonably accurate guess as to how long a fresh fish has been in a river provided it has sea lice on its back or underbelly or on its outer gill casing, because these parasites die and fall off after being subjected to fresh water for a short duration of time. The distance such a fish has travelled in fresh water can be equated to how far upriver it has been caught. On many occasions I have caught fish covered in sea lice over 30 miles upstream of the estuary during the summer months, and once over 40 miles upstream in March. It would seem, therefore, that if conditions are favourable both regarding water flow and water temperature and the salmon have not been held back by obstructions, they could, if they wished to do so, ascend to the very upper part of the catchment of any river in the UK within three to four days. This, however, is seldom the case until late in the season. It is more usual for both salmon and grilse to ascend in stages of 4 to 5 miles and those which have been impeded or held up are very often more inclined to loiter and ascend a river far more slowly than those that have had a free passage with favourable weather and water conditions throughout.

In the early part of the year and again in the autumn water temperature largely controls the salmon's ascent of the river (I deal with the effect of water temperature in a later chapter of this book) whilst water flow is probably the most important single factor that not only controls the ability of these fish to ascend the river, but also the speed at which they move upstream. Water flow can be critical; it can determine whether or not the salmon can negotiate obstacles such as falls, weirs and fish passes, mainly because many of these can only be ascended within a fairly tight range of water height. Falls can be impassable when a river is either too high or too low, unless an alternative by-pass provides a route in the higher water flows.

Very often fish are incited to move upstream as soon as a rise in water occurs and this is particularly so when they have been held up by low water for an appreciable time. However, their speed of ascent is considerably slowed down as the water level rises to peak flows because the velocities in the main current are usually too high to allow speedy movement. Under these circumstances, fish may move up on the quiet side of the river where the flow is often baffled by projections from the bank which divert the main current away from that side of the river, or they may choose to stop in a quiet haunt and rest until the flow begins to recede. It is usual for the main fish movement upstream to take place on the second day after the flow has peaked and to continue on as the river drops slowly through medium flow ranges, until the fish movement begins to slow down and cease altogether as the river reaches low flow once again. When the river is still high but dropping steadily, fish will ascend throughout the twenth-four hour period, but as it reaches lower levels fish movement is mainly confined to the hours of darkness, or dusk and dawn. Once the river has reached its lowest levels, movement between pools literally ceases because fish become stranded and confined to local movement within their holding pools. A possible exception occurs immediately upstream of the tidal influence where even under low flow conditions some fish may struggle upstream of the tide into pools in the lower reaches of the river, where they generally remain until such time as the river rises before moving on upstream. However, it is possible that these fish may descend back into the estuary if they are held up for a significant period. Any movement which does take place under these conditions is normally confined to either late evening or the hours of darkness.

Both salmon and grilse are gregarious fish and this may well be the reason why they are often seen to move in small groups normally termed runs. There is little doubt that this habit has a bearing on their behaviour as they ascend a river. They are often seen to congregate in certain holding pools rather than take up lies in pools or runs which are not populated, though they may stop to rest briefly in such pools. Fresh fish, entering the river early in the season when they are few and far between, often prefer to rest in a pool which is already occupied by kelts descending the river after spawning, rather than push further upstream into uninhabited areas. Once other fresh fish have joined them they often move on upstream together. When there was a dearth of surviving kelts during the period when the UDN disease was particularly serious in the late sixties and early seventies, it was very noticeable that fresh fish entering the river in the early spring seemed to change their normal pattern of ascent significantly. Instead of pausing in the large holding pools in the bottom sections of the river where kelts would usually have been residing, these fish pushed further and further upstream in search of company, until they were eventually forced by exhaustion to rest in areas of the river that previously would have been devoid of kelts. During this era beats which had long since been famed for their catches of spring fish suddenly became the poor relations, whilst beats much further upstream that in the past only killed an odd early fish, became the forte of the early spring period on many rivers.

In spite of the fact that since the 1868 Salmon Fisheries (Scotland) Act was enacted each and every man-made dam or weir must have a fish pass incorporated on it to enable fish to ascend, both these barriers and natural rock obstacles, such as falls, do at certain times of the year and under certain conditions, impede the free passage of fish as they ascend upstream. This is particularly so in the early part of the year when water temperatures in the river are in the low ranges, and again in the autumn when fish are gravid and therefore not nearly so active as they are when their ovaries are not so fully developed.

Early in the season each and every barrier has a fixed water temperature at which it can be freely negotiated, and this is closely associated with how formidable the barrier is. Normally this is closely allied to the depth of water in the fish pass (in the case of weirs and dams) or of the water which is flowing over the obstacle. When either of these are sparsely watered, fish can be deterred from ascending in water under 42°F. However, when there is a liberal flow in the pass they will usually be able to ascend, except in the lowest temperature ranges, provided the velocity is not too high. Obstacles which have to be jumped instead of ascended by actually swimming through, mostly require water temperatures of at least 45°F before salmon are willing to attempt to jump even the smaller ones; a water temperature of 52°F is required at the most formidable obstacles. I know of no passable falls which require a higher water temperature than that to prevail before they can be ascended.

In many cases, however, one degree Fahrenheit is critical and if a cold wind suddenly rises then that will cause fish to stop jumping; no further activity will be seen until such time as the water temperature rises. Even sparsely watered shallows can be a complete deterrent to salmon ascending a river in frosty, cold weather periods when the water temperature is under 42°F, whereas salmon are perfectly willing to ascend these, even with their backs half out of the water, when water temperatures of 50°F or higher prevail during the summer period. There is little question that this is not merely a matter of choice, but of their physical inability to ascend high velocity flows in cold water temperatures, probably due to the fact that there is insufficient dissolved oxygen available to the fish under these conditions to supply the energy required. It is sometimes interesting to watch the behaviour of fish which have been held up below a falls for some considerable time waiting for the water temperature to rise to the correct level. As the temperature comes within two degrees of the critical level, these fish will come up to the white water immediately under the falls and begin to jump and splash in the pool. Then, when the temperature rises a further degree, they will lunge into the white water, making porpoise-like movements. When the correct temperature is attained they literally queue up underneath the falls, often with their tails cutting the surface of the water, and begin to jump cleanly at the obstacles, some ascending the first time they attempt it whilst others have to make two or more attempts before they succeed.

By the autumn most fish native to the areas of a river system upstream of formidable falls will normally have ascended these obstacles long before they become too gravid to make the ascent. However, in years when there happens to be a period of prolonged drought extending through the months of July, August and September, problems can arise if fish stocks have been held back either in the sea or in reaches of the river downstream of the obstacles. Those fish native to areas upstream of the most formidable obstacles can quite easily have well-developed ovaries by the time the drought has broken and, therefore, be quite incapable of ascending the most severe falls, and even have difficulty in ascending the less formidable ones. This can lead to a drastic change in the distribution of fish stocks within the river systems affected during a drought year. Typical years were 1955 and 1976, when this problem badly affected stock densitites in certain river systems, with the higher catchment areas lying upstream of falls being under-populated, and the lower catchment areas over-populated.

It would seem that the overall pattern of fish ascending rivers differs materially according to the season of the year, and is significantly affected by water temperature and river flow. In the early part of the season, with water temperatures in the range of 34°F to 52°F, fish can, in certain situations, be impeded in their ascent of some rivers by shallows, man-made obstructions and natural rock barriers. thereafter, they do not seem to be in the same hurry as they would have been had they not been hindered, being quite content to remain for several weeks in the same pool before continuing their ascent of the river. Fish that enter the river later in the year, when water temperatures have risen to 53°F or higher, are seldom held up or impeded for any reason other than unfavourable water flow. When water flow is appropriate they usually take full

The Round Pool Falls, which holds fish back until the water temperature rises to 45°F.

The Crows Nest Falls, River Cassley, which can only be ascended once the water temperature reaches 48°F.

The Falls of Shin, a natural barrier to salmon until the water temperature rises to 52°F.

advantage of it and quickly complete their ascent to their final destination. Whether this urge of summer fish to ascend the river quickly is due to a fear of being stranded by drought flows must be a matter of speculation, but since the summer period is considered to be the driest of the year, this would seem to be a reasonable explanation.

These days few of the rivers in the UK remain in their natural state regarding river flow regime. In some cases large parts of rivers' catchment areas have been intensively drained for agricultural, hill grazing or afforestation purposes; in other cases water is abstracted for supply by the water authorities or harnessed for hydro-electric purposes. In many cases this has altered the stable flow regime of a river. Previously the norm was natural seepage drainage where the water, having been absorbed by the ground like a sponge, slowly filters into existing watercourses and eventually into the rivers, causing them to rise slowly after rainfall, reach a peak, then fall equally slowly as rainfall on the catchment eases off. Now water regimes have turned flashy: water runs off the surface of the ground as soon as it falls – instead of being absorbed by the ground it drains directly into an existing watercourse or the main river system, thereby creating a quick rise leading to a much higher peak flow and then a sudden, quick fall in water levels as soon as rainfall on the catchment ceases. This new type of river regime does of course tend to curtail the number of days when water levels are suitable to entice fish out of the sea and ascend the river, significantly extending the number of days when fish are unable to move freely throughout the river system.

When a large acreage of young conifer trees is planted on the catchment, water losses from the canopy interception of precipitation and transpiration can be material. This water loss can often result in fish being impeded when they wish to enter their native tributaries late in the year to spawn. It can, in the worst cases, lead to fish having to ascend to areas of the catchment where they do not belong.

In other cases, rivers that have had their water harnessed either for hydro-electric or water supply purposes are immediately subjected to a much altered water flow regime which can significantly alter water flows within the entire river system over the whole year. In some cases, water is diverted by aqueduct from one catchment into another, in other cases it is diverted by pipe or tunnel from one part of the catchment to an entirely different part. In both cases valuable water, which should have been available to encourage fish stocks to ascend to their secluded parts of the river system, is diverted elsewhere, thereby in many cases creating unnatural water losses within the catchment, and hindering the ascent of indigenous fish stocks. In other cases, dams are built throughout the catchment, either for the purpose of impounding water in reservoirs or in order to divert water. The usual practice is for fish passes to be incorporated on the dam and provided the fish pass is properly designed fish can still ascend to their native areas of the river. However, in cases where these fish passes do not work efficiently or no fish pass is incorporated, fish are debarred from their native areas and forced to occupy sections of river where they do not belong. Fish which, as smolts, have descended sections of a river which has subsequently been dammed, are often hesitant to pass through the fish pass arrangements on the dam on their return to the river as adults. In many cases this deters them from returning to the appropriate sections of the river. Areas of a river upstream of a dam which is without a fish pass or where the fish pass is not working properly, become barren and lost to the productivity of the species unless these areas are artificially propagated with migratory fish stocks.

Sections of river below these dams are immediately subjected to regulated flow regimes, which depend entirely on compensation flow agreements that have been written either into the Water Order which controls water abstraction schemes or the Hydro Electric Construction Scheme which lays down conditions regarding water generating schemes. The basic compensation flow conditions are liable to alter materially between winter and summer periods and, in many case, are supplemented by a block grant of water stored behind the dams, which can be called upon by fishery managers at their own discretion in order to provide freshet flows within the river, downstream of the dam. The freshet flows are designed to aid fish movement in the section of the river between the dam and the sea and to encourage them to ascend the fish pass at the appropriate times of the year.

There are really three different types of flow arrangements downstream of a dam:

1. When the dam is a diversion dam with little storage above it, merely designed to divert the water from the main river into a separate catchment. In this case, very small compensation flows are made available to the river and in many cases burns which would have flowed into the river some distance downstream of the dam, are led back upstream to above the dam by further aqueducts or pipelines. In this case, although a block grant of water is made available for freshet release, it is only available when there actually is water running off the catchment, as there is merely a small head pond and no storage above the dam. This water is critical to enable fish to ascend the sections of river downstream of the dam, between the actual dam and the first untapped tributary, because otherwise the compensation flow between these two points is insufficient to allow fish movement within the section. Therefore, the freshet water is vital to enable access over the last section, which is denuded of water, and allow fish to reach the fish pass.
2. When there is a diversion dam sited below an impounding dam, in order to divert water away from the main river down an aqueduct

flowing parallel to the river to a generating station, it is possible to provide not only a generous compensation flow down the river but also a liberal block grant allocation stored upstream in the impounding reservoir. The latter is to be used for freshet releases if and when they are deemed to be necessary by the fishery management. In some cases, when compensation flows are in the medium flow ranges, fish movement within these rivers is always possible and, therefore, fish are never stranded by river flows falling to levels in which they cannot ascend. In these cases, the natural distribution of fish stocks downstream of the dam can be interfered with.

3. When there is an impounding dam on a river system and the water is actually used for electricity generation as it passes through the dam. In this case, a compensation flow is fixed to control water flows downstream when the water impounded in the reservoir is not being used for generation purposes. However, when the turbines are switched on and electricity is being generated, large volumes of water pass on downstream, thereby increasing to spate volume the compensation flow already existing in the river. In these cases, a block grant freshet allowance is seldom required. Fish movement in rivers downstream of these dams seldom ceases and once again the natural distribution of fish stocks can be interfered with.

All these different alterations to the natural flow regimes of river systems interfere with the natural ascent of returning stocks, in the latter two cases by improving the ascent unnaturally and in the first case, by impeding it.

The fact that certain parts of main tributaries, or of rivers themselves, are reduced to regulated flow, can pose difficulties concerning the actual cleansing capacity of those rivers.

Once any part of a river has had its natural flow regulated by the placing of a dam or barrage across its width, either to store water or to divert it, then the natural flow regime downstream is entirely altered. No longer is it subjected to the high spate flows so essential to scour the bed of the river clean and quietly brush debris, trajected into the main river by its many tributaries, down the sides of the river, where it is quickly dispersed. Instead, as the main river is subjected to a regulated compensation flow at a volume usually comparable to a natural medium low water capacity, any sand, gravel or boulder stones carried downstream by the tributaries when they are in spate, is deposited well out into the main river course. This happens because the main river flow is no longer the major volume or velocity of the water in the system; the unharnessed tributary in spate often exceeds the flow of the regulated main river. At times, this can lead to the main river becoming congested with deposited material to such an extent that the main flow is diverted from its natural course. This change can lead to bank erosion, which may cause a change in the topography of the river, or curtail free access for ascending fish.

As water temperatures rise quickly to 55°F and higher from May onwards, fish movement within the river is no longer inhibited by water flow or obstructions. Even in the low ranges of flows, apart from minimum dry-weather flows, fish movement out of the estuary into the river and over shallow fords between pools still takes place, but with the main activity occurring at dusk or during the hours of darkness. It is interesting to note there is one exception, in that once darkness closes in practically no movement takes place at falls where fish actually have to make a leap in order to ascend; here the greatest activity is from 5 p.m. to dusk. However, falls which can be surmounted by swimming through do not impede fish movement during the hours of darkness. Once daylight dawns, provided there is no cold wind or air frost, fish once again begin to jump falls and do so throughout daylight hours, the main activity tending to take place towards evening.

Any incitement, such as a rise in water, particularly after a long drought when fish have been held back for some considerable time, or a sudden rise in air temperature during the day, can produce an immediate response of intense activity on the falls at any time during daylight hours. A sudden rise in water level will also induce the same response in sparsely watered shallows, if fish have been impeded on their ascent of a river by low flow.

Once water temperatures have risen to levels in excess of 50°F the clarity of the water in many rivers begins to be stained by peat and this can become very marked during spate or high water flows. Rivers flowing off moorland and higher catchments are particularly vulnerable and in some cases the river takes on a colour similar to that of light ale. With this advent, the coating of the early-run fish begins to tinge to a pinky maroon colour before becoming an even darker red or even black as autumn approaches. Even fish straight out of the sea do not carry the same shining silver hue as those in the spring, but a duller silver hue which quickly takes on the pinky tint after only a few weeks. In the autumn some fish straight out of the sea, and even with sea lice still attached, have a pinky tinge and become quite discoloured in a matter of days. At its most intense stage this discoloration is often referred to as the spawning coat, but since it can be fully attained by the early-run fish up to four months prior to the act of spawning, it is more likely to have a further significant role to play in the well being of the species. The most likely explanation is that it helps the fish to camouflage themselves better as the environment they inhabit during the summer and autumn also changes materially. Not only does the water's chemical make up and colour change significantly with the rise in water temperature, but there are also changes in the area of the river where the fish now reside. The depth of water, the composition of the river bed and the banks of the pools in which the fish lie, all change. The further the salmon move

The diversion dam on the River Shin.

A small falls that forms no barrier.

upstream away from the deep, stony pools of the lower river and through the narrow rocky sections of the gorges, the more they encounter and reside in shallower, dark, slow flowing pools, or gravel pools with black peat banks, and a darker river bed, often covered by peat and muddy, weedy beds. Here, with peat stained water flowing over them, the coat they have so recently adopted helps them to blend in far more effectively with their surroundings and safeguards them from their many predators, of which the worst of all is probably mankind.

Some of the early-run fish will have arrived in the close proximity of their spawning grounds by the month of June and will choose a holding pool with suitable characteristics which will afford them a safe refuge regardless of what water or weather conditions may prevail during their long wait before it is time for them to spawn. Often, a canal-like pool of adequate depth with high banks is ideal for this purpose as these pools, although they may have little current movement at low water flow, are as a rule well oxygenated. Their high banks and depth also provide adequate shade from the powerful ultra-violet rays of strong sunlight, while weed growth, which often becomes established in quiet bays of sluggish water, affords both shade and cover. Other favoured haunts in these upper sections of rivers are deep holding pools alongside rock ledges, with streamy necks and long gravelly tails. Those which have birch, alder or rowan trees overhanging the pools are especially favoured as here their inhabitants can be peacefully shaded and screened by this important aspect of bank cover. Even a strategically placed bramble, whin bush or sapling overhanging a deep area in the pool can provide merciful relief against relentless sunlight, and adequate lies for several fish. Those pools which lack bank cover of this sort often have shelving rock ledges, large boulders or banks that are undermined, all of which provide a safe, cool haven for fish in times of drought and intense sunlight. Then, in the cool of the evening, during the night and at dawn, the salmon tend to push up into the streamy neck of the pool to enjoy the well aerated water before dropping back into the deeper water or shaded areas of the pool, as the sun rises high in the sky. In a large tree-lined pool, I have watched fish change their position as many as eleven times in a day in dead low water, as regular as clockwork over a period of seven days, moving to the same lie at almost the identical time every day, as they took full advantage of the most suitable position as the sun moved round in the sky; sometimes they lay deep, sometimes they lay in shallower water when shaded by a bluff or bank cover, then lay tight in under a ledge, sometimes they lay in a backwater facing downstream, and then with only their tails visible sticking out from under the bank or a rocky crevice. On occasions a change of lie could be 50 metres away from the previous one, upstream or downstream, or across to the other side of the pool; at other times it might be a 5 metre movement up, down or across, just to edge forward or backward as the shaded area altered with the movement of the sun. The duration of the occupancy of each of these lies was seldom varied form day to day. Some were only occupied for an hour, whilst others were occupied for three hours or more, and when one fish changed its lie, invariably the others in the group followed shortly after. If either vibration or movement alerted them, at first they would lower themselves perceptibly in the water and, if further alerted, became invisible as they melted into the depth. If, however, the water was too shallow to afford this refuge, then they would move off into deeper water or, if further alarmed, take cover under rocks, banks or ledges.

In higher flows, salmon movements within a pool are not nearly so marked or regular once they have reached their final residence although, admittedly, because of the movement on the surface of the water and its velocity, these pools are not nearly so easy to monitor visually, except from an observation point high above the water. It would seem, though, that under these conditions much more time is spent to one side or other of the main current, or in the draw towards the tail of the pool. There is no doubt, however, that even in these higher flows, shade is still of prime importance. In full sunlight I have seen well-shaded lies under trees or high cliffs fully populated for long periods of the day, whereas on dull cloudy days, under otherwise identical conditions, these lies would be completely vacant throughout the day. Fish are also far less easily disturbed in higher water flows; vibrations seem to alarm them to a greater degree than movement in these circumstances. Even when they are disturbed, it is not easy to see what remedial action they take as they disappear from view, either into the depth or under the riffling water.

On rivers which have a loch situated on the catchment, such as Loch Tay on the Tay, Loch Ness on the upper catchment of the Ness system, and Loch Lomond on the River Leven system, as well as numerous lochs on the smaller north and west coast river systems, both early and late run fish move quickly into the lochs and may remain there for a considerable period before moving on into the rivers which flow into them. It is not uncommon to catch fresh fish in Loch Tay and Loch Ness in January, on the opening day, and some fish may have already been inhabitants of these lochs for several months. Some early run fish often reside in the larger lochs for up to six months or more before finally pushing on into the tributary rivers and burns where they will eventually spawn, whilst others remain there until they are ripe for spawning. Others, however, may pass on through the loch into their native river after only a brief pause, and those reaching the loch later in the season probably pass through more quickly than the early run fish, if the in-flow tributary is large enough to accommodate them and has sufficient water flow to entice them into it. In the case of the smaller west coast loch systems, such as Loch Stack and Loch More on the Laxford, or many of the rivers on Lewis, the in-flow tributaries of the lochs are so small that the majority of fish entering the loch systems remain there until spawning time and only move into the tributary burns specifically to spawn. Those which survive pass quickly out to the sea as kelts. During the period when these fish reside in the lochs they are virtually safe from health fears when long droughts prevail, mainly because of the wide expanse of well oxygenated water which is available to them. At the same time, they can choose the depth at which they wish to lie according to weather conditions on any particular day, either seeking refuge from sunlight in the deeper parts of the loch on bright days, or residing on the shallower banks and bays to be found close to the shoreline, around islands or above high points in the loch bed, when fresher, duller conditions prevail. On some lochs, such as Lomond and Maree, islands out in the loch itself and parts of the shoreline are wooded, and these places can provide well shaded creeks which are favourite haunts, while steep cliff faces or rocky promontories also provide both shade and refuge against numerous predators and varying weather conditons. Many fish will take up residence in close proximity to the burn mouth or the tributary in which they will eventually spawn, and may remain in that section of the loch for many months.

As the upper catchment areas become fully populated, later running fish begin to take up their final residence both lower down the river system and in the larger tributaries which flow into this section of the river, and as these areas fill up so the layering downstream continues until, by the end of the season, the entire stretch of river system suitable to accommodate spawning stock is fully populated. By this time the entire spawning population will be residing in holding pools close to the areas where they will breed. After they have finally completed the long arduous journey between their sea feeding grounds and their spawning areas, there is no doubt that the fish are both exhausted and weakened by lack of nourishment as, in many case, it is a long time since they last took food. Therefore, these fish lie patiently conserving their remaining energy in order to retain sufficient strength to carry out the final vigorous act of preparing their redd in the gravel of the river bed, to plant their eggs in it, and then cover them with a layer of gravel.

SPAWNING

Once the ovaries of the salmon are fully developed and they are ripe to spawn, the hens leave the deep holding pools and begin to explore the spawning area either upstream or downstream of where they have been residing, in some cases for a considerable period of time. Normally, the first sign of spawning activity comes during the last few days of October in the upper catchment areas of the river systems, and by 7 November large numbers of salmon can readily be seen in these areas working the gravel on the spawning fords.

Although others claim to have seen completed redds in September, the earliest I have ever seen a completed redd (in a tributary at the top of the Oykel catchment) is 18 October, but I have often seen fish making exploratory cuts early in October, and these fish usually start cutting their redds in earnest shortly afterwards. However, lower down the catchment and in rivers with little high ground in their catchment, spawning is more likely to be phased from late November through December, and in some cases, well into January. It is possible, on large catchments such as the Tay, to have fish spawning upstream of Loch Tay and in the headwaters of the Tummel and Gary from 15 October to 15 November; downstream of Loch Tay and Loch Tummel in late November to mid-December; and downstream of Dunkeld in late December to 15 January. This is nature's way of making sure that all the spawning fords throughout the catchment are fully populated and utilised by the natural stock of the river. Although spawning takes place over a long and extended period of the autumn and winter months, all the eggs from the various parts of the catchment will actually hatch out almost simultaneously, or within a fortnight of each other at the most. This is because water temperature largely controls the incubation of the eggs in their redds. Once again, this is nature's cleverly devised formula for ensuring that regardless of where the eggs are placed in the catchment, there will be sufficient food bloom in the river to sustain the young fry once they hatch out; if perchance the food bloom is checked by a late cold snap, so also is the hatch of the eggs.

In rivers such as the Hampshire Avon or the Fowey in Cornwall, almost the entire spawning period is confined to December and January, due entirely to the geographical placing of these rivers, whereas in the Kyle of Sutherland rivers, such as the Cassley, Oykel and Carron, it would be rare to find a clean unspawned fish on 1 December because the entire stock of these rivers spawns in the six week period from 18 October to 30 November. The Shin and the Evelix, however, two other rivers in the same group, both have fish spawning well on into December. This may be due to the fact that both these rivers have a large proportion of reservoir capacity on the catchment, leading to the prevalence of higher average water temperatures than are found in the other three spate rivers, which are steeper and flashy in character.

Once the female is fully ripe, she moves out of her holding pool in search of a suitable spawning ford and at this time she is always closely accompanied by the male with which she has paired. Once she finds a suitable spawning ford, she begins to make a few exploratory cuts on the surface of the bed, in all probability in order to find out the texture of the gravel and at the same time to ensure that the gravel on the surface of the bed is workable, and not impacted. As the female works away, her male companion trundles round the pool like a battle cruiser, chasing away any intruders which might impede or distract the hen fish's activities. Having found a suitable area of the river bed to make her redd, the female then begins to work in earnest to dig her trench in the gravel. First she turns completely on her side and contorts her body in such a way that her whole body and tail convulse into a flailing motion, forcing a volume of water onto the surface and then with a flexing motion, sucking it upwards again. This wild, flailing action creates a force and suction effect, which makes the gravel jump out of its position on the bed, whilst current flow moves it away from her working. Having made several of these violently energetic movements, the hen has usually succeeded in making her initial depression in the bed of the river. Once she is satisfied with this depression, she turns back off her side and swims into the cut, where she begins to deepen and perfect it by wriggling her tail and ventral fins in the depression. With much manoeuvring, she eventually succeeds in removing the debris slowly but surely, until she is left with a cut in the bed of the river some six to nine inches in depth.

During this entire operation, which can take a considerable time, her mate continues to charge up and down stream and across river, as he chases other cock fish (often the mates of spawners working on the same spawning ford) who might intrude near to his mate. His performance, often with his mouth wide open, is comparable to that of a rutting stag or a cock pheasant guarding his harem of hens, and equally exhausting, as he seldom stops to rest.

Once the female has finished and perfected her cut, she nestles into it and goes into what is known as the crouch position, whereupon she opens her mouth. Her mate sees this signal and immediately draws alongside the female; then she ejects the eggs whilst he emits the milt to fertilise them. They then go their separate ways, he to continue warding off inquisitive cocks whilst she draws immediately upstream of her first nest and begins another initial cut, to repeat the whole process once again. This second cut provides the gravel to cover the eggs laid by her first ejection, and at the same time prepares another nest for her next extrusion of eggs.

A large female fish may make four or five separate nests before she empties herself, as she ejects approximately 2000 eggs each time. She then has to make another initial cut upstream of her last ejection of eggs in order to glean gravel to cover these eggs. Once the redd is completely finished it looks like a mound on the surface of the river bed, with a fan of fresh gravel lying downstream of it and a saucer shaped depression in the gravel bed immediately upstream of it.

It is difficult to assess the exact number of eggs that are laid by each female as this can vary significantly both from river to river and from female to female, mainly according to her size. Some of the bigger fish carry larger eggs than the smaller females, such as grilse, and this can also make a significant difference. On the whole, however, females under 5 pounds should be expected to average 350 eggs per pound of flesh, small salmon weighing up to 8 pounds should average 600 eggs per pound and larger salmon, from 12 pounds upwards, should average 800 to 1000 eggs per pound.

The actual process of spawning remained a complete mystery for many, many years, mainly because it largely takes place in relatively shallow water. Even if one could get close enough to observe it, detailed observation is almost impossible due to the commotion on the surface, the turbidity of the water caused by the female's cutting and the continual bow waves caused by the cocks chasing each other. Even if visual observation were possible, another major problem is that of getting close enough to the bank without being seen and, therefore, disturbing the fish carrying out the act of spawning; one would need a previously prepared, well-sited hide. Thus many of the old experts relied on visual observation from vantage points, such as bridges, high above the water but unfortunately, due to turbidity and distance from the surface of the water, they were unable to witness clearly the whole event but only part of it. It is not surprising, therefore, that in many of the early written reports on spawning authors clearly mistook the female's initial vigorous cutting convulsions for the actual moment when she extrudes her eggs, believing that as these eggs mixed with the gravel she was dislodging from the river bed, drifted into crevices between the stones and gravel particles, and lodged there. These early authors believed that the eggs were then fertilised by the male sometime during the female's vigorous cutting activity.

It was not until Professor Jones of Liverpool University had built an observation tank on the banks of a spawning tributary that, for the first time, the whole spawning process of salmon was fully witnessed, recorded and filmed. This marvellous piece of accurate research on this highly technical operation is fully described in J. W. Jones' book, *The Salmon*, first published in 1959. Many revelations which came to light during these experiments showed up the inaccuracies that had inevitably resulted from not having been able to witness the entire operation.

Professor Jones' observation tank was constructed at Pont-Barcer on the banks of the River Alwen, a tributary of the Welsh Dee, just upstream of Corwen. Mr King, who was then Fisheries Superintendent of that river, and his bailiffs assisted Professor Jones with the construction work. The observation tank was sited immediately downstream of the Dee Fishery Board's holding tanks, where fish were kept at spawning time until they were ripe, to strip the eggs for the board's hatchery. Within the tank, natural holding pools with large stone lies were simulated and gravel was taken from natural spawning grounds within the river system to simulate a spawning ford within the tank. The depth of water, velocity and water flow within and through the tank were controlled by in-flow and out-flow sluices, and could be regulated as required. A hut with armoured plate glass windows let into the bank was erected on the inshore side of the tank to afford shelter for the observers. Over the years that these experiments took place, the facilities were improved upon considerably from time to time to ensure that the salmon in the tank were spawning in an absolutely natural environment, and at the same time to improve the conditions for the observers during their long tedious hours spent in the observation hut.

At the time these experiments were taking place my father was a riparian owner of a salmon beat on the Welsh Dee, some three miles downstream of Langollen and owned by my family for over a hundred years. As he was a very keen angler he not only knew Mr King extremely well, but also took a great interest in these experiments and everything else to do with the conservation of salmon stocks on the Dee. It was, therefore, shortly after these experiments started that he was first introduced to Professor Jones and, because of my avid interest in salmon and salmon fishing, I accompanied him on his many visits to Pont-Barcer. Through the years, I was privileged to have the chance of spending many hours in the observation hut and gleaned a large amount of knowledge about the salmon's behaviour in the wild and its spawning activities. It was fascinating to watch these fish barely inches away from the plate glass window swimming around seemingly quite unaware of our presence as they carried out their vital business.

Since Professor Jones' experiments on spawning in the forties and fifties, further research in the field has confirmed the results gleaned from his painstaking studies. More recent research by the DAFS Fisheries Research Department undertaken on the Girnock Burn, a tributary of the Aberdeenshire Dee, has led to video filming of salmon spawning.

For many years it has been known that some male parr become sexually mature in fresh water, whereas few if any female parr do the same. As long ago as the middle of the last century experiments were carried out to fertilise an adult female's eggs with the milt from these mature male parr, and from these experiments it became apparent that these little fish were capable of fertilising the eggs of an adult hen fish. However, it remained unclear exactly what role, if any, these little fish played at spawning time or why nature allowed this phenomenon to take place. From observations through the years on spawning fords, it became clear that parr were nearly always in attendance when the adult fish were cutting their redds and actually spawning, but most people believed that these little fish were merely there to scavenge for eggs washed out of the redd. Indeed, there is little doubt that these parr do predate heavily on the loose eggs and benefit greatly from this easy source of nourishment, particularly as it is available in abundance just before the long drawn out winter months set in, when food is scarce and hard to come by. It was not until Professor

Jones carried out his work in his observation facilities at Pont-Barcer that, for the first time, the performance of these male parr during the spawning period could be visually monitored at close range and noted. Not only was he able to confirm the role they were playing in the act of spawning but, as a result of further painstaking research on this very subject, he was also able to show that these male parr were positioned at the bottom of the nest below the female's vent, and did indeed fertilise the eggs of the female fish as they were extruded into the redd, often simultaneously with the male adult lying above him. Professor Jones also carried out further research into the fertility of the gravel parr by dividing a clutch of eggs from a female fish and fertilising one half with the milt of a mature parr and the other half with that of an adult cock salmon. Once these eggs had hatched in a hatchery, he monitored the growth rate of both batches and found that up to the smolt stage there was no material difference in either the quality or size of the two batches of fish. Professor Jones devotes an entire chapter of *The Salmon* to this fascinating subject.

It can only be assumed that the reason why some male parr become mature in fresh water is to provide nature's biological safeguard to ensure that all the eggs of the female salmon are fertilised. Especially when spawning takes place in high water flows, there must be some doubt as to whether the milt from a male lying alongside the female but slightly higher in the water than her ever reaches the eggs in the bottom of the redd; maybe it is merely washed downstream by current velocity. Even if it does reach those eggs in the bottom of the redd, it may be too diluted by water to have the necessary strength to fertilise the entire clutch and that is where the male parr, lying beneath the vent of the female, in the bottom of the redd, plays its vitally important part in the act of spawning. It would seem that, in many cases, the mature parr plays a primary role in ensuring that the species is regenerated.

In many river systems spawning gravel is a relatively scarce commodity. It must have certain requisites, firstly to enable the act of spawning and, secondly, to enable the eggs to remain safe, enclosed in the gravel for several months over the incubation period. The gravel also has to be suitably sited in the river system, at the correct depth, because current velocity at the river bed level plays an important part, not only in making it possible for the female to spawn in that place but also to assist her in the whole operation. It is important that the gravel be clean, open and workable to enable the female to cut a groove from six inches to a foot into the gravel with ease, there to plant her eggs and then cover them over. At the same time the gravel must be of the right texture to enable water to percolate through it at all times to enable the eggs to breathe. If the gravel is impacted with silt the female will be unable to cut into it in the first place, but even if she did manage to do so, the silt would smother the redd and prevent the eggs from breathing, thereby destroying them by suffocation.

Impacted gravel is often caused by bank erosion, drainage operations or road works, and results from particles of clay, loam or sludge being washed into the river system and forced by water velocity into the crevices between the gravel on the river bed. Through time, this sediment sets hard and literally cements the gravel particles into place, leaving what was once clean, open gravel, impacted and hardened on the surface and, therefore, unworkable.

If, on the other hand, gravel is unstable it is easily workable but liable to move during high water flows in the winter. In such circumstances the gravel and the eggs incubating in it will be washed away downstream and the eggs destroyed. Banks of unstable gravel are a common occurrence in river systems where in recent years there have been large afforestation programmes or land drainage operations on the catchment. Heavy, torrential rainfall on the catchment, often occurring during thunderstorms in the summer months, can also lead to unstable gravel in river systems.

The female salmon is dependent almost entirely on water power to remove the debris from her cutting and nest-building workings. It is, therefore, essential that the spawning fords be sited in an area of the river system with suitable depth and sufficient current velocity at river bed level to enable this to happen. Because of the amount of material involved in spawning operations, suitable current flow conditions are only to be found in selected areas of the river system, and of course, these must coincide with the right texture of material on the river bed. This is the reason why, in some watercourses, suitable spawning fords are a scarce commodity. In some cases there may be an abundance of gravel deposits in a relatively flat area where insufficient current flow is available, while in other cases these gravel deposits may lie at too great a depth where there is too little current to keep the gravel free of silt. Only where there is a down gradient between pools or a fast draw at the tail or neck of a gravelly pool, are these ideal spawning facilities usually available. Without the correct current velocity to aid the female fish with the preparation of her redd and actual spawning operations, the gravel moved off the surface of the river bed by the hen fish would simply fall back into place instead of drifting away downstream on the current. This is the main reason why salmonids cannot spawn in still water lochs. However, with the correct current speed, the entire spawning operation is comparatively simple for, as the female works the river bed, any algae, silt or fine particles are forced into suspension in the river flow and therefore washed away down river, clear of the operation. Larger gravel and stones drift quietly away from her workings and lodge on the surface of the bed a short distance downstream. This is the reason why, when the female has laid her first clutch of eggs and moved upstream to start her next nest, the debris from her second cut covers the first batch of eggs that she has already laid.

The ideal spawning depths range from 9 inches to 2 feet 6 inches below the surface of the water, with a surface current velocity of 12 to 18 inches per second. With surface velocities of less than 5 inches per second spawning is rarely undertaken, and seldom completed successfully if it is. Only in the larger rivers where high volumes of water are readily available can spawning be completed successfully in greater depths of water.

In addition to the main river and its major tributaries, spawning takes place in the smaller burns and brooks which feed these watercourses. It is sometimes the case that these minor watercourses afford a much safer environment for salmon to spawn in. This is mainly because the water flow in these burns is often well contained between firm banks and, therefore, the spawning fords are not so liable to dry out with fluctuating water levels as they could on the fringes of a larger watercourse. Nor are these burns so prone to either high peak flows or gravel movement, unless their catchment area has been subjected to intensive land drainage or afforestation and has, therefore, become unstable. Burns as small in width as two to three feet (provided they meet the necessary requisites) can play an important part by accommodating a certain percentage of the overall spawning stock of the river system. Eggs incubating in the gravel bed of these minor watercourses are often in far less danger than those incubating in the main river. Because it is often the case that a large part of the water flow in these burns derives from springs and ground water sources, both the water flow and water temperature remain at a far more constant level than watercourses which rely on surface water for their supply.

The texture of the gravel suitable for salmon to spawn on varies in size considerably, and can vary from a pebble the size of a ten pence piece up to stones the size of your fist or even up to that of a small brick. These larger stones are often important in keeping the redd open and preventing it from consolidating and solidifying, whilst the smaller gravel fits into the crevices in between the larger components and actually covers the eggs. It is interesting to note that when a female is making one of the numerous individual nests, which are really components of the final redd, she usually manoeuvres two large stones into place at the bottom of her nest. Then, when she is ready to deposit her clutch of eggs, she places her vent, tilted downwards, in between these stones and ejects her eggs into the compartment thus created.

Many people query whether a salmon is capable of moving such large material during spawning but in actual fact this is not as difficult as one might assume because even this size of material can be moved with relative ease, due to its buoyancy when it is immersed in water. This is the main reason why current velocity is of the utmost importance. There is no doubt that the female salmon is very selective when choosing the actual place where she will spawn, and takes considerable care in ensuring that she will not waste her precious energy by working on unsuitable gravel. As her tail and fins are the only tools available to her with which to excavate her nests and complete her redd, she seems to have an uncanny knack of testing the composition of the bed of the river and knowing exactly where she can or cannot complete her task. Very often, if one wades quietly around on a spawning ford after the spawning season is over, and explores the untenanted areas one will find that although these places look to be of excellent quality, in actual fact they are not. Sometimes one will find that these patches are unused because only a thin layer of gravel is lying on rock or peat, whilst at other times one will find that the patches are impacted or too silty to work. Very often, one will find a redd angled one way or the other across the river instead of up and downstream, and on further exploration one can see that the reason for this is that the current flow has been deflected at this particular point by two or more large stones or rocks. Therefore, the female has chosen to make her redd at that particular angle in order to obtain aid from a suitable current. If low water flows have prevailed over the spawning period redds can often be found in this type of situation because it is only sites such as these that are capable of generating suitable current speeds for the redd to be cut under these conditions.

When very high river flows occur for long periods during the spawning season, fish are forced to spawn at the edge of the river, often on areas of gravel that are high and dry for much of the year. In consequence, some of the eggs either dry out or are destroyed during the winter months by frost, but others often survive even if the water recedes several feet, due to the percolation of water seeping underneath and through the gravel. In very severe winters, redds laid on shallow edges can often become encased in tables of ice or they can be exposed by rolling slabs of ice when the thaw sets in; in both cases substantial losses can ensue. It is surprising how these ice flows roll and tumble as they are swept down the shallow spawning fords when the thaw begins, literally gouging deep furrows in the river-bed gravel. On occasions, large trees which fall into the river where banks are eroded have a similar damaging effect on spawning grounds as they roll and tumble over, scouring the gravel bed with their branches. However, normal high peak river flows in themselves seldom cause damage to redds dug on stable gravel, unless of course these high flows actually deposit debris on top of the redd – and even then, provided this material is open and does not suffocate the eggs, the eggs can still survive, regardless of the depth of the material which lies on top of them.

On the smaller burns and watercourses, provided no large change of land use has occurred on the catchment or no landslides have taken place, the redds are generally comparatively safe from this type of danger. However, if either of these occurrences has taken place, these smaller watercourses can be incapable of cleansing themselves due to lack of water flow. If this happens, the clean gravel becomes completely immersed in sludge, silt or sand and its spawning potential is lost for ever more.

KELTS

After the female fish have emptied themselves and completed their task of covering up the final batch of eggs, they return to their holding pools to recuperate. The cocks, however, often remain on the spawning fords for some considerable time after the females have vacated them, and still cruise around chasing each other. Whether or not this is because they have not completely emptied themselves of milt and are hoping to find another mate must remain unclear, but sometimes they remain on the fords for a long period, before finally returning to their holding pools.

Once salmon have spawned, they are known as kelts. These spent fish are completely exhausted after their vigorous activity during spawning time, which comes at the end of many months of fasting in fresh water. Some of the early run fish may not have taken any food for well over a year, merely surviving on their own body fat for that appreciable length of time. Even the late run fish barely have time to rest in the river after their lengthy homeward migration across miles of ocean, before they have to face the task of regenerating the species. Not surprisingly, this final burst of energy proves too much for the fishes' systems to stand and a significant percentage of the spawning population die shortly after they have completed their work. Although it is the female that has undertaken the most arduous part of the operation, strange to say, by far the largest percentage of the mortality at this stage is among the male population. It is estimated that nearly 80 per cent of the males die almost immediately after they have shed their milt. After the first spate in December, the banks downstream of the spawning fords are littered with their dead bodies, many badly marked and splattered by different types of fungus, and sometimes wounds. Many people believe that a proportion of these male fish die either of furrunculosis disease, brought on by the extreme stress they are placed under during the final act of spawning, or else of sheer exhaustion, because they seldom rest at spawning time. These awesome looking carcases with huge hooked kypes on their bottom jaw and literally a ruddy tartan in colour, some of a very large size, remain rotting on the banks for some time before they are washed seawards by peak floods in the winter. A few males do survive and wend their weary way back to sea, but this is a tiny proportion of those that actually took part in spawning. It is, however, rare to find a second-spawning cock fish, although not unknown, and one can only assume that most either perish as kelts in the river or once they have reached the sea. Of the female population, about half die immediately after spawning, while the other half survive. Those that die could well be the ones which entered the river early and were, therefore, severely weakened by their long fast and used up their remaining strength during spawning time. Often these thin, emaciated creatures who have fulfilled their duty in life are not nearly so marked by fungus as their male counterparts, and their carcases can be easily recognised by their much darker, maroon/black colour.

However, those kelts that do survive return to the deep holding pools where they lie quietly resting after their strenuous activities. Once they have regained their strength and when river flow rises to a suitable level many will take advantage of the higher water and begin their journey back to sea. For the main, they merely drift quietly downstream tail first, allowing the current to do the work for them, but in still, quiet pools they may swim head first downstream over short distances, in the same manner as smolts migrate out to sea. Some will make a fairly swift descent down into the estuary, whilst many more loiter for a considerable time in the river once they reach the larger, slower deep pools in the lower reaches. Sometimes, a proportion may decide to over-winter in lochs or canal-like pools in the higher catchments before making their downward migration in the spring, especially when a long dry spell occurs immediately after spawning, when the number remaining for a significant time in the head-waters may be greatly increased. Those that choose to remain in the river for some time after spawning begin to lose their tartan coats and become silvery in colour once again, but do not regain condition, remaining thin and emaciated. These are usually referred to as well mended kelts.

Once the angling season begins, from January onwards, kelts take lures freely and many, although returned to the water if caught, die either of exhaustion or because they have been badly hooked. No doubt some well mended kelts are kept by inexperienced anglers in mistake for clean fish.

By April, nearly all the kelts will have descended the river and reached the sea. Those that are strong enough and have not fallen prey to one or other of the many predators, will feed at sea once again and eventually those which survive will return once more to their river of origin to spawn again. These second return fish are generally appreciably heavier than they were on their previous visit to fresh water. They are also easily recognisable because they bear a purple patch, about the size of a one pound coin, on the outside of the gill casing, and often have maggots in their gills.

It is very difficult, in fact almost impossible, to assess the number of kelts that survive to spawn a second time and there is no doubt that this can vary significantly not only from river to river, but also from year to year. Water flow levels that prevail both during and after the spawning season are likely to significantly influence whether kelts survive or perish. If conditions are adverse and changeable, the stress and strain on the spawning stock will surely take its toll, in comparison with a season when conditions are optimum. Similarly, if a drought followed by a period of severe frost catches the fish in the shallow spawning areas, mortality is likely to be greater than when a moderate spate flow following immediately after spawning time aids their descent to the haven of deeper sanctuaries lower downstream, or even out into the estuary.

Experiments carried out over the years confirm that an appreciable number of female fish do return to the river to spawn a second time, a lesser number a third time, and it has been known for one to spawn for a fourth time. These experiments have also shown that the number of males which spawn twice or more is a mere fraction of the number of females.

It would seem that, of the total annual spawning stock of a salmon river, barely 5 per cent are fish that have spawned at least once before, the rest being virgin stock. However, it is apparent from research into the return of kelts carried out by Menzies (1931) in Scotland and Hutton (1920) on the Wye, that there are some rivers which do have a far greater return of second spawners than others. However, whether this is an event that remains fairly constant from year to year or is more a one-off situation, is not entirely clear.

There is no doubt that after the outbreak of UDN disease in the late 1960s and early 1970s, the number of kelts which survived to go back to sea was minimal in comparison with the number surviving prior to the outbreak. Even in the present era, twenty years after the disease was first seen, the number of kelts that survive has not reached pre-disease numbers.

Kelts that do reach the sea may either journey to their feeding grounds far from our shores, or feed more locally not far from land. Those that journey many miles across seas will stay two or more sea winters on their feeding grounds and then return, once again in prime condition. These fish often weigh around 12 pounds if they have spawned previously as grilse, and considerably more if they spawned previously as salmon. Those that remain closer to our shores and re-enter fresh water during the summer or autumn of the year when they descended as kelts, are not nearly in such good condition as those that return to their feeding grounds across the sea. These more locally feeding fish usually only manage to increase their kelt weight by a few pounds and lack both lustre and condition. This is probably due to the fact that the quality and quantity of food available to them in the estuaries and in close proximity to our shores is lacking in comparison to the lush food available further north.

CHAPTER TWO

Temperature

It is an interesting thing to say, and entirely true, that water temperature is the single factor that has a greater bearing on the different stages of a salmon's life cycle than all other factors.

It is a fact that temperature is largely responsible for determining the incubation period of the egg, the period parr spend in fresh water prior to smolting, the timing of the spring outward migration of smolts, certain aspects of the salmon's sea feeding life, and on their return to fresh water temperature often determines the time early runs of salmon take to ascend their rivers. Also, in some extreme cases, it may even prevent late running fish from being able to complete their spawning cycle.

Added to these very important aspects of the different stages in a salmon's life, there is little doubt that both air and water temperatures play an important role in governing the salmons' unpredictable taking habits on their return to fresh water, thereby often having a significant effect on annual exploitation levels by rod fisheries. Also, sea and river temperatures may be an important factor in dictating the availability of fish and levels of exploitation in coastal and estuary net fisheries at certain times of the year.

Due to the extreme importance of temperature levels, especially that of water, this subject merits a chapter of its own.

On their return to fresh water, the early runs of fish occupy the headwater catchment areas, the summer runs the centre catchment areas, and the autumn runs mainly the lower reaches. On certain river systems some overlapping of runs occurs and, in fact, a river fills from top to bottom. Those fish which return as grilse after spending only one winter at sea, ascend to their appropriate areas within the river system.

Therefore, the various runs of fish can be subjected to vastly different climatic conditions during the autumn and winter months, according to where they are positioned in the river system. These conditions can not only vary drastically between the upper and lower reaches of a single river system, but also from river to river according to where it is geographically.

These factors, therefore, have a very large bearing on the temperature of water levels prevailing in a river system, not only over the spawning period, but also throughout the entire period during which the ova are incubating in the redd. For instance, in a normal year temperature levels to be found in the Spey during these periods are generally much lower than those which would be expected to prevail at the same time of year in the Hampshire Avon; whilst temperatures to be found in the Dochert, upstream of Loch Tay, would be several degrees lower than those found in the lower reaches of the Tay.

Due to the possibility of widely different temperatures prevailing in various parts of the catchment, and from river to river over the incubation period of the egg, it would follow that if all the eggs hatched in a given number of days, those which were laid in the colder climes or higher catchment areas might well hatch out before there was sufficient food bloom in the river to sustain the fry. Nature has, however, overcome this problem by making water temperature the control that governs the duration of the incubation period. For instance, if eggs are subjected to a mean water temperature of 45°F they will hatch in approximately 80 days, whilst eggs that are subjected to a mean of 37°F, only 8°F lower, will not hatch out until around 120 days. This control, therefore, deals adequately with the problem of eggs which are laid in parts of the higher catchment where, during severe winter weather conditions, hard frost and snow melt may keep water temperatures in the river well below a mean 40°F for not only a large part of the winter, but often well into the spring. Salmon inhabiting these areas normally spawn in late October or early November, whereas salmon spawning in lower catchments or rivers found in warmer climes may not spawn until December or even early January. Therefore, in both cases this control assures that the eggs will hatch out in the spring when there is plenty of food available for the young fish.

Water temperature also plays an important role in the fresh water feeding life of juvenile salmon, being one of the main factors responsible for determining the duration of the time they spend in fresh water, before migrating to sea.

This is due to the fact that fry and parr only feed readily on the nursery areas when water temperatures are over 42°F, only feeding sporadically below this temperature. Once again, the time when water temperatures fall below this level varies vastly in different parts of the catchment, and also from river to river as well as from year to year, according to the severity of the winter period. In seasons when there is appreciable snowfall on the hills and mountains, some of the tributaries and headwaters lying in the upper catchment area take an appreciable time, often late into the spring or even early summer, before warming to over 42°F, and temperatures in these same areas can fall below this level again early in the autumn. This can severely restrict the duration of the annual feeding period for fry and parr residing in the sectors of the rivers concerned. On the other hand, in some of the south coast rivers and low lying catchment areas of many rivers throughout the country, or on the islands off the coast, water temperatures may only fall to these levels for a few weeks per annum and even, on some rare occasions, not at all. Therefore, fry and parr inhabiting these areas have little or no lull in their fresh water feeding life during the winter months, and thus grow far more quickly than their counterparts inhabiting the colder climes.

There is little doubt that the time when parr become smolts and migrate to sea is mainly governed by size not age, for this very reason. In this country, wild parr which smolt at one year are not numerous but this does sometimes happen in the south and elsewhere, more commonly, during mild winter cycles. Parr which smolt at two to three years of age can be called the norm, with more smolting at two years in mild weather cycles and more at three years during colder weather periods. Cases of parr not smolting until four or five years old is not uncommon in high catchment or poverty stricken areas, particularly so during cycles when severe winter conditions prevail.

Water temperature levels throughout the summer months also play an important part in keeping the environment of the nursery areas in a healthy state. If perchance, the temperatures rise to an unacceptable level dissolved oxygen in the water will be reduced to a degree that can, on occasions, lead to fish kills amongst the fry and parr. These conditions occur more frequently now, especially during prolonged hot weather periods, where tributaries and river flows have been seriously depleted either by water abstraction, large forestry plantations or land drainage schemes. The worst problem can be caused by irrigation schemes affecting small but important feeding tributaries flowing through arable plains, or when water is diverted from one catchment to another for hydro-electric purposes. Tributaries that are drained of a significant part of their flow, or drawn down to an extremely low flow, are very susceptible to unusually high water temperatures which may result in fish losses.

Spring fed tributaries often benefit from their source of supply because spring water has a constant temperature of around 42°F. This part of the supply, therefore, acts as a warming agent during the winter months and a cooling agent during the summer, as well as being the main source of supply during times of drought. It is important that any change of land use is carefully planned so as not to interfere with this valuable source of water.

As the water temperature warms up after the long winter period, the increased temperatures help to promote and encourage food bloom in the river system, which is essential to the welfare of feeding fry and parr. At the same time, the warmer air temperatures help to hatch out the many terrestrial insects, which form an important part of the food supply available for the feeding fry and parr. In the more poverty stricken catchment areas where low pH values are to be found, it would be true to say that terrestrial insects, in many cases, form the backbone of the food available to fry and parr residing there.

Turning now to the migration of parr from fresh water to the sea: in some parts of the higher catchment areas it has recently come to light that there may be a marked pre-smolt parr migration downstream in the early autumn from late August through September and October, and occasionally into November. This migration usually takes place as water temperatures begin to drop when the nights grow longer, and ceases once the temperature falls to the low forties Fahrenheit. This is probably only a tactical manoeuvre to enable the parr to be better positioned lower down the catchment at the end of the winter. Then, in the early spring, having first taken on their silver coating and turned into smolts, the fish can take advantage of the more assured water flow and slightly more favourable water temperatures to make an early start on their long seaward journey than would have been possible if they had remained in the headwaters. Other pre-smolt parr may not carry out this manoeuvre, remaining in their habitat until the spring then, having smolted, start on their outward migration. These, once again, rely heavily on warmer water temperatures in the early spring which signal to them that the time has at last arrived to start their next stage in life.

Temperatures around 42°F to 45°F seem to be the trigger that starts them off. This is not usually attained until mid-March, but varies from river to river as well as parts of the catchment, and many smolt shoals do not begin their migration until April, May, or even into June. Whether the early migrants are smolts destined for the far distant feeding grounds and which will return as salmon; the later migrant smolts destined for feeding grounds closer to our shores or even smolts which will return as grilse, must remain hypothetical, but this would seem to be the logical conclusion.

Once the smolts reach the river estuary and head on to the oceans detailed knowledge of their movements virtually ceases. Many years ago an eminent salmon fisheries consultant advised the government against researching into their movements at sea on the grounds that if and when their feeding grounds were established, exploitation would be bound to follow. These words of wisdom were heeded, and it was not until many years later, in the early 1960s that the feeding grounds off the Greenland shores were discovered, and as we all know to our cost these were inevitably and quickly exploited.

SALMON IN THE SEA

Even today, although we know very little about the sea life of the salmon, there is little doubt that during their wanderings in the oceans these fish will encounter both warmer and colder currents, where temperature ranges will differ significantly. It is possible, therefore, that their behaviour and movements, within and while they pass through these different zones, may well be determined by the sea temperatures which prevail. Whether or not cold sea temperatures have effects and restrictions on their movement similar to cold river temperatures, must remain one of the many facts at present unknown.

If sea temperatures do have an important bearing on the speed at which smolts are able to swim at sea, it is possible that this factor could be partially responsible for determining which destination they make for once they migrate from fresh water into sea water. Indeed, the month that smolts actually migrate to sea may be of far more importance in determining their future destiny than we have previously been led to believe. The very fact that in usual circumstances the earliest smolts descend the rivers in March, whilst the latest migrants do not descend until early June must, one would imagine, determine the distance they can travel before arriving at their feeding grounds. In other words, the later migrants may literally have missed the bus, and have left themselves insufficient time to reach the grounds furthest from our shores. It is both possible and probably that some smolts use the Gulf Stream and other warmer current flows to take them on part of their journey to some of the far distant feeding areas, because if sea temperature is an important factor their progress in these warmer currents could be substantially faster than in colder currents. If we are correct in this assumption, then sea temperatures may well be an important factor in determining the time when they cease feeding and begin to wend their way across the oceans on the start of their homeward migration to their rivers of origin. It is also extremely likely that sea temperatures will in many cases partially control the time taken to complete the homeward journey.

From data gleaned when reading the life of salmon from their scales, it is apparent that their growth rate is retarded during the winter months spent at sea in much the same way as it was during their young feeding life spent as parr in fresh water; whilst during the summer months the rings on their scales expand dramatically, showing a much more rapid rate of growth. Once again, it would seem obvious that sea temperatures must be primarily responsible for not only governing their feeding habits but also the availability of their food during the winter and summer months.

There is also little doubt that the movement of salmon shoals within their feeding area will be very much dependant on that of the shoals of fish and crustacea such as sprats, capelin, krill and sand eels, to mention but a few of the species known to comprise some of their favourite foods. When these species move, either along the coastline or offshore, so the salmon will follow. Some of these local migrations are almost certainly due to change in sea temperature.

Whether or not the mean sea water temperature prevailing during the period spent at sea has a material bearing on the duration of time actually spent at sea, or when the salmon actually cease feeding and begin their homeward journey, must still remain among the many unanswered questions about salmon.

SALMON ON THEIR RETURN TO FRESH WATER

Once salmon return to the mouth of their river of origin and begin the last stage of their homeward migration by ascending that river to the proximity of their spawning grounds, water temperature again plays an important role at certain times of the year, as it is primarily responsible for controlling the speed at which they can ascend the river. This is particularly so in the low water temperature ranges between 34°F and 45°F, but can also affect their ability to ascend the most formidable obstacles, such as falls, up to 52°F.

It is the early run fish that come into the rivers in late October, November or December and will not spawn until the following autumn, or the spring fish that enter the rivers from January to April, which are most affected by low temperatures during their ascent of the river. If these fish are faced with low water temperatures from 34°F to 40°F, their progress upstream in normal water flows is usually fairly slow. If they are faced with low flows at the same time, they often congregate in holding pools below weirs and falls and remain there for some considerable time until there is either an appreciable rise in water levels or water temperature. Even a long shallow incline of broken water or a shallow ford can deter their progress early in the season at low water temperatures, and they will only be encouraged to continue their upstream ascent once these shallows are covered by an appreciable water flow.

In the present era, with very mild winters prevailing, the recent weather pattern has been for October and November to be mild, with snowfall and frost mainly confined to December, January and February. Therefore, the earliest run fish entering the rivers in the late autumn have been able to ascend well up the catchment before water temperatures have fallen sufficiently to impede their progress for a short period during late December to mid-March, and during some of the milder winters in the 1980s they have often only been checked for a matter of days, just sufficient to hold the fish for a brief period in the lower reaches. However, when the winters were appreciably harder during the 1920 to

1960 period, winter weather generally took a hard grip in the late autumn and continued well into the spring. This, as a rule, held water temperatures well under 40°F and many of the early runs of fish were duly held back in the lower reaches of most rivers, or below the first formidable obstacle on the river system for an appreciable period, sometimes running well into April before water temperatures rose sufficiently to enable them to continue their ascent.

This is largely the reason why on the opening day of the rod season, on some of the longer rivers such as the Dee, Spey, Tay and Tweed, fish are distributed widely throughout the catchment and are often caught on beats much further upstream than they would have been during the colder winters of the past. Previously, when hard winters prevailed on the Aberdeenshire Dee, beats below Banchory often caught ten fish or more on the opening day, whilst upstream a fresh fish on the opening day was more an exception than the rule. Now, fish caught on the opening day on beats all the way up as far as Braemar are a common occurrence, and the large catches on beats below Banchory usually a thing of the past. On the Spey, catches on all beats up to Grantown are common on 11 February (the opening day) whilst in the past, Brae, Orton and Delfur all used to expect double figure catches.

The same story is to be found on the Tweed and Tay, but on these rivers formidable weirs or caulds were in place at a number of sites during the 1930 to 1960 era. Many of these have been breached and eased in recent years by either the Tweed Commissioners or the District Fishery Boards, in order to allow fish to ascend these obstacles more easily. Therefore, it is really a combination of higher water temperatures and better access that is responsible for allowing fish on these rivers to penetrate further upstream earlier in the season. Famed pools such as the Pitlochry Pool below Stanley Weir on the Tay, and the Junction Pool on the Tweed at Kelso, seldom now record the large catches which once made them so famous for spring fishing.

On the shorter spring rivers to be found mainly in the north of Scotland, more formidable natural obstacles such as falls, completely debar the free ascent of fish until water temperatures rise appreciably to between 40°F and 52°F, according to the varying sizes and formidability of the obstructions. However, if these falls are passable to fish, and they are not debarred, even the most formidable can be negotiated at 52°F. Most falls which are negotiable at 40°F to 45°F, are fast deep rushes of white water of very high velocity which, in most cases, can be swum through and do not require to be jumped by the fish. Those that require higher water temperatures, from 46°F to 52°F before they can be ascended, are nearly all rock barriers over which the water cascades and require salmon to leap or jump them. Sometimes these are stage falls, where fish jump into a pot or deep hole halfway up the fall, and them jump from that pot over the upper lip of the fall; other times a single vertical leap is needed to ascend the falls.

On rivers such as the Shin and Orrin, formidable falls a short distance upstream from the mouth, delay fish until the water temperature rises to 52°F. On rivers such as the Oykel and Carron, lower falls delay fish for shorter periods low down these rivers before they reach more formidable falls further upstream. The Cassley has three falls of varying degrees of formidability above consecutive pools. On this river, the lower falls are passable at 45°F, the middle falls at 48°F and the top falls at 52°F. In over sixty years of catches being recorded, fish have never been seen above these three obstacles before such water temperature levels have been attained.

When Calderwood was superintendent of Salmon Fisheries in Scotland in the early part of this century, many attempts were made to ease falls throughout Scotland in order to allow salmon to ascend above these obstructions earlier in the year. Most of this work failed, simply because it was not necessarily the size of the barrier that was impeding the passage of fish, but because of the temperature of the water flowing over the obstacles.

Once water temperatures in the rivers have risen to above 52°F, fish can move through a river system at their will and some of the progress made upstream in such temperatures is really astonishing, with 20 to 30 mile journeys in a day quite common. It is interesting to note, however, that once a fish's ascent has been checked, this fish is normally never in such a hurry to move on upstream as it was previously. It is quite common to find a fish that has entered a river early in the spring, overtaken by fish which do not enter the river until many months later.

I remember once losing my fly in a fish at the mouth of a river on 3 February, and catching the same fish with my fly still in its mouth, only a quarter of a mile upstream on 27 May. On the same day, a friend of mine fishing 20 miles up the same river, caught five fish, three of them covered in sea lice.

It is also interesting to note that when water temperatures are below 45°F and the river flow low, little fish movement occurs; but once the water temperature rises above this figure fish can, and often do, move upstream at dusk or during the hours of darkness – even in low flows. Once the water temperatures rise to over 50°F, at dusk fish can be seen pushing their way through the shallow fords with their backs out of the water, even in the lowest flows.

At the present time, scientists are monitoring the movement of fish in estuaries and within the river systems by use of acoustic and radio tags. Some very interesting results have been obtained from these experiments. However, one must question whether, when some of the more erratic movements are recorded, these are not due to some form of discomfort caused to the fish by the fitting of these tags, thereby interrupting their natural movement and behaviour. Basically, however, most of the information gleaned from this work helps to confirm the conclusions already formulated after years of studying the behaviour of salmon once they return to fresh water.

SALMON SPAWNING

Whether temperature of water actually plays any significant part in determining when the various runs of salmon spawn, is not only unclear but almost impossible to prove with any degree of certainty. What seems likely, however, is that due to the extremely strenuous physical energy required to complete the act of spawning, and knowing how low water temperatures affect the ability of the salmon to carry out strenuous activities, it is probable that fish cannot complete this act successfully once the water falls below a certain temperature. J. W. Jones, in his book *The Salmon* (1959) confirms this, stating 'Below 1°C cutting is languid, beds are not finished and the orgasm does not take place.'

It is, therefore, possible that in winters when intense cold periods set in early, fish spawning either in December or January may well be unable to spawn successfully. This could well be one of the main reasons why the Tweed and other rivers famed for their autumn runs see this particular run of fish fluctuating from time to time. One such fluctuation at the beginning of this century, when very hard early winters were prevailing, saw a marked decline of autumn fish in the Tweed system and, coinciding with this decline a significant increase of spring run fish. During later years, with mild winters now the norm, the pendulum has swung back and at the present time the autumn run in the Tweed is extremely strong and the spring runs, on the whole, showing a decline. However, with the marked escalation, over the past twenty five years, of the legal English north east coast drift fishery situated just south of this river, one cannot compare like with like. This fishery opens in time to exploit the tail end of the spring run and closes before the main autumn run has begun. Therefore, it is both possible and probable that it would have some effect on the balance of salmon runs native to east coast rivers in that area. It is difficult now to make the same scientific comparisons as one could in the past with such an intense interceptory fishery so close to the mouth of some of the main east coast salmon rivers.

SALMON TAKING HABITS

No discussion on temperature and its effect on the behaviour of salmon would be complete without mention of how this factor is so important in controlling exploitation levels by the rod fisheries, once salmon return to fresh water. We already know that during their feeding period both in the river as parr, and from the smolt stage to maturity at sea, cold water temperatures do have an important bearing on growth rate during the winter months. How much this is actually determined by the effect of temperatures below 42°F on their actual physical system, and how much by the availability of their food chain, must remain a question largely unanswered. In all probability, with food difficult to come by at these temperatures, nature allows the fish to remain more or less dormant in order to conserve their strength rather than expend precious energy in search of a scarce commodity.

What is of extreme interest to us all is why, when it has been accepted for generations that salmon do not need food on their return to fresh water, do they ever take an angler's lure? I will deal with this point in more detail later but there is no doubt that they will take a lure, albeit unpredictably, and this is the point we must consider here.

In the UK the open season for rod angling varies widely from river to river throughout the length and breadth of the country, and it is true to say that angling is permissible on some rivers during every month of the year. Rivers in the north of Scotland are the first to open on 11 January, whilst rivers in Cornwall do not close until December. Of course, the length and duration of the angling season also varies tremendously, some rivers remaining open for eight months and others ten months – mainly according to the numbers of seasonal runs which frequent each river. Therefore, anglers are faced with widely different ranges of temperatures according to the months of the year they partake in the sport. These can vary from 34°F in early and late months of the season to 65°F or even higher, at the height of summer. What is most surprising is that the fish often take more freely during the lower range of water temperatures, 32°F to 40°F, whilst at the higher ranges they are seemingly far more lethargic and difficult to catch. Most experienced anglers will freely admit that no matter whether spinning or fly fishing, if fish are present in the beat which they are fishing, low water temperatures favour free taking more than any other factor, with certain provisos which I will come to in a moment. This is strange when we are generally led to believe that both during their fresh water and sea feeding lives, salmon lack desire for food once water temperatures drop below 42°F.

One important proviso regarding salmon taking an angler's lure, which I referred to earlier is also to do with temperature, but this time it is air temperature. For some reason which is difficult to explain, salmon take more freely when the air temperature is higher than the water, and rarely take well, if at all, when the water temperature is higher than the air. Therefore, when water temperatures are at their lowest, between 33°F and 38°F, as a result of continuous snow melt on the high catchment or during frosty periods, throughout daylight hours the air temperature could be considerably higher, often 5°F to 15°F warmer than the water, giving ideal conditions for free taking. These conditions are most likely to be found in early spring and, on occasions, in late autumn. Only when frost is actually falling, or a cutting frosty wind is blowing, are conditions likely to be adverse during these periods of the year. Therefore, it is not surprising that a high percentage of the total rod catch in the UK used to be caught from January to mid-May and again between mid-September and 30 November. With a marked decline in the spring runs in recent years fewer fish are available to be caught, and catches have dropped in the early part of the year; but more fish than ever are being caught in the latter part of the season.

Once the snow fields have melted on the mountainous catchment areas, water temperatures begin to rise rapidly in the rivers. This almost inevitably causes the temperature gap between air and water to be radically reduced except on hot sunny days, which are seldom favourable to angling. A combination of long periods of low flow and unfavourable air/water temperature ratios in normal summer weather conditions, often reduces the number of fish caught between mid-May and mid-September. Only during wet, dull summers, such as 1988, when optimum water and weather conditions prevail for some considerable time, are temperature levels likely to favour free taking over a large part of the summer, but these seasons are generally the exception to the rule. Summer water temperatures usually range between 55°F and 67°F, largely according to water flow, and therefore, it only requires a biting east or north-east wind to blow for a short time before the air temperature falls close to or even below the water temperature. On other occasions, it might be a cold mist or dull weather conditions which pose the problem. Many anglers fishing during the summer period often wonder why salmon are dour and stiff to rise in seemingly good conditions and more often than not it is an adverse air/water temperature ratio that is responsible for the lack of response from their quarry.

NETS AND WATER TEMPERATURE

It is extremely likely that, from time to time, water temperatures in the sea and those in the river may cause fish to pause briefly in the estuary or off the coast, before ascending their rivers of origin. This brief pause could well prove fatal if they happen to stop in a netting zone.

Certainly it has always been a bone of contention between the rod fraternity and netsmen that netting is allowed during periods of low water flow, on the grounds that too many fish are taken during these flows. It is interesting to note, however, that in drought years such as 1976, when dry weather lasted over a continuous period of three to four months, many net fisheries around the coast, and within estuaries, recorded some of their lowest catches for years. It would seem that the fish at sea were reluctant to come forward to the coastline and estuaries under these conditions and instead, congregated in shoals several miles offshore. Only when the rains came and the drought broke did fish come teeming into the rivers in their thousands.

Whether or not it was the extremely high water temperature levels prevailing in these drought stricken rivers which directly or indirectly, through reducing dissolved oxygen levels in the rivers, deterred fish from coming in, can probably never be proved, but it is possible that this factor could have been partially responsible for the unusual behaviour of the fish.

CHAPTER THREE

A Salmon River

In order to provide a suitable habitat for salmon stocks, a river must have certain essential qualities before it can meet the needs of this fascinating migratory fish. Atlantic salmon are born in freshwater, spend their juvenile life in the river, and then migrate to sea to grow on to the adult stage, before once again returning to freshwater in order to breed as mature fish.

The salmon river must possess characteristics both wide and varied which can be listed as follows.

1. Be easily accessible.
2. Have an adequate flow of clean, good quality water at all times.
3. Have a liberal supply of clean, open gravel deposits, preferably distributed throughout the entire catchment, where salmon can lay their eggs and where these eggs may incubate safely.
4. Be a good habitat capable of keeping the adult fish safe and healthy during the period between its return to freshwater, and when it spawns.
5. Have sufficient shallow nursery areas capable of supporting and protecting the juvenile fish during their early feeding life in freshwater.

Provided a river system has these necessary requirements, there is no reason why it cannot accommodate and support this species of anadromous fish. However, the actual size of the stock which it is capable of accommodating usually hinges on two important factors. Firstly, the amount of suitable spawning gravel which is available within the river system to cater for the needs of the spawning stock, and secondly, the number of fry and parr that the limited food supply of the various sections of a river system are capable of supporting to smolt stage. This varies tremendously from one river to another, according to the geographic and topographic nature of each river, its fertility, and finally its size and length. A salmon river is really an underwater farm, its productivity comparable to that of a garden or farm, and each and every one has its own capability as to what it can accommodate, seed and rear. This is controlled almost entirely by the river's fertility and size.

It is best to study each of these points carefully, in order to fully understand their importance to salmon conservation.

ACCESS

Under natural conditions, most rivers are accessible to salmon, though it must be admitted some are easier to ascend than others. As fish come in from the sea, their actual entrance to the river system is assisted greatly by the tidal influence at the mouth, or in the estuary leading to the mouth. Twice daily on the top of the flow tide any sand bars or restrictions are covered by a considerable depth of water and, therefore, with the possible exception of extreme drought flow, fish have no problem with obstructions, and have a safe means of entry. The tidal influence also has the benefit of stilling the velocity of flow at this point, and even on rivers which have a fairly torrential descent as they discharge their water into the sea any problem of ascent is much alleviated by welling back these rapid discharges.

Fish often use the flow tide to reach the river mouth, and then enter the river either at top of tide or on the ebb which follows. Often they come up the estuary tail first on the flow tide, in exactly the same manner as smolts and kelts descend the river, allowing themselves to drift backwards as they face the race of the incoming tide. Once this stills, they turn and are drawn into the river by the influence of its superior flow.

Having actually entered the river system, their passage upstream is largely dictated by water flow, natural obstructions such as rock barriers or falls and, in some cases, man-made obstructions, such as weirs and dams. The latter problem is covered elsewhere in this book. There are many rivers that are entirely free of natural barriers for a considerable distance upstream, and the salmon's progress is then entirely controlled by the rise and fall of the rivers. In this case, salmon will be free to move at their own will at any time during the twenty-four hour period during high and medium water flows, and then more restricted during low to medium flow ranges, and often stranded in the main holding pools at low and extreme drought flows. Although they can move up river even on high peak floods and as the river rises to these levels (rivers normally become very turbid at these flows) their tendency is to move once the river settles and begins to drop after the peak when turbidity levels are much reduced and the water is clearer. In low to medium flows their ascent is often controlled by water temperature as well as flow. In these heights of water they tend to move mainly at dusk and during the hours of darkness, resting for most of the day after their nocturnal journey. As the water temperature rises to over 52°F it is surprising how little water they require to negotiate sparsely watered sections. They can often be seen at dusk on a mild night ascending these shallows with their lateral line literally out of the water and their backs dry. Whereas at lower water temperatures they would have required a considerable depth of water to be flowing over these same shallows even to contemplate ascending them.

In Scotland, large rivers such as the Spey and Dee, which flow down kindly valleys of low gradient, have practically no natural obstacle to impede their passage until they reach the headwaters. The Tweed, Tay, Welsh Dee and Wye, with similar characteristics also have practically no natural impediment, but in these rivers the free ascent of salmon is at times impeded by man-made weirs.

Rivers where the ascent of salmon is impeded by natural obstructions can really be split into two definite categories. Firstly, individual rivers that either drain a catchment on steep ground, where the overall depth of the catchment is extremely narrow, and secondly, where major tributaries of some of the larger river systems drain the steep upper catchment areas of these rivers. The first are often to be found sited on the mainland north of the Caledonian Canal, or on the west coast of Scotland, Wales and, to a lesser extent, the West Country. In all these situations the catchment draining east or south is usually significantly greater than that flowing west. Due to this fact, the flow in most of those rivers has to descend far more steeply to the sea than is the case in the longer, larger river systems flowing east and south, where the distance between the steep mountainous area in the upper catchment to the sea is considerably greater and therefore, more gradual. In the case of the shorter river or upper tributary, the steep mountainous terrain is drained by cascading watercourses emptying themselves into the river flowing quietly down the valley below, and then onwards downstream through a series of rocky gorges when it falls appreciably in height, before discharging its water into the main river, a long estuary, firth or sea loch. In some cases, the fall can be 300 to 400 feet in twelve to twenty miles, whilst in other cases much greater.

The natural rock barriers and falls lie within the rocky gorges, some of which are far more formidable than others; although most are still ascendable by salmon provided the right water flow and water temperature prevails. Both these factors control the salmons' ascent of the rivers. In the former case high water flow over falls make them impassable unless there is a way of bypassing the main obstacle; whereas salmon can usually ascend over a narrow deviation of medium or low flow. Water temperatures are of even more importance and strictly control fish movement over the obstacles, according to how formidable they are. However, once the water temperature in the river has risen to 52°F any natural barrier that is surmountable, can be ascended.

In some cases, however, rivers do flow over sheer rock faces of either critical angle or height, thereby completely debarring the passage of fish further upstream. This type of obstruction is more often found on tributaries high up a large river system, but there are a few cases in Scotland where some large rivers are affected. For instance, the Clyde, the Kirkaig in west Sutherland, and the rivers Brahn and Erricht in Perthshire, to name but a few. In all these cases, large expanses of the river's catchment with a very high potential for rearing salmon are completely debarred to the species and the productivity of these salmon rivers is severely curtailed.

In some cases during the last century, formidable obstructions which either impeded the free passage of salmon or debarred their ascent, have been eased on many rivers in order to allow the fish upstream. In most cases these works have been a remarkable success. The falls have been reduced in height by raising water levels in the pool below the falls, bypassed by constructing an alternative route around them down which part of the river flow is diverted, or the rock face itself has been altered by blasting with explosive. In the latter case, there have been as many failures as successes, as rock shatter created by the blast often defeats the purpose. Therefore, the other two methods, if they are practical, are preferred.

The passage of both smolts and kelts downstream is yet a further vital part of the life cycle of this species. Under natural flow regimes this migration is not interfered with in any way. The fish usually descend tail first, allowing themselves to drift downstream quietly propelled by the current of the river. On occasions when they come to still water, such as a loch or canal-like section of river, they will turn round and swim head first to speed up their rate of descent. When they come to falls or cascades of fast flowing water they still drop tail first when conditions are favourable, normally in medium flow ranges and seldom in very high flows or low flows when rocks are exposed that could cause damage. After having descended the rougher sections they rest for a short period when they reach quieter, deeper water such as the haven of a holding pool. Here they pause briefly to draw breath after the buffeting they have just endured. For the most part, both these components of salmon stocks utilise the higher water flow, but seldom move until the peak of flood flow has settled and the river is quietly falling and when turbidity levels are much reduced. The smolts also feed voraciously, both when they are held up by lower flows or when they are actually moving downstream, and there is no doubt that kelts will pick up a tasty morsel if it comes their way. The worst hazards on their journey are either man-made dams or water diversions. Predators are a constant threat to the smolt shoals, particularly in confined, shallow areas, where their silvery sheen makes them very conspicuous. Probably the worst natural condition these fish can encounter during their downstream migration is low water flow over a long period. If they are forced to move in these flows, those which have to descend over rocky, rugged sections can be prone to damage from being thrown on or scraped against jagged rocks, or sometimes stranded in crevices, as they descend falls or torrential cascades. Any damage or loss to their silver coating as a result of this can cause mortalities on their arrival in the sea. Predation levels are also likely to be heavier in these flows, mainly because these migrating shoals can be more easily spotted from the air, have to spend longer periods in lochs or deep pools where they are readily preyed upon by fish and birds alike, take longer on their journey and are congested into much more confined areas.

WATERFLOW AND WATER QUALITY

Provided salmon are able to ascend and inhabit a river system, a stable flow of good quality water is obviously the next most essential factor concerning the safety of this species and the conservation of stocks. Under natural river regimes this is nearly always assured, the exception being when rivers or certain tributaries of these rivers, flow off a mountainous terrain where there is a significant outcrop or seam of poisonous substances, such as lead or other heavy metals, lying close to the surface. Where this situation arises that river cannot accommodate salmonids, although this is a fairly rare occurrence: in this country there are certain small rivers or tributaries in Wales and the West Country, which are affected in this way.

Salmonids are also very dependant on the pH values of all the watercourses they inhabit, firstly because this chemical factor has a very important bearing on what species and varieties of their food chain can be promoted. It would generally be true to say that the higher the pH value, the more nutritious the fish fauna in that tributary. However, when the pH falls below 4.6 these streams are unacceptable and cannot support a salmonid population.

Many rivers and lochs in Scandinavia have lost their salmonid stocks purely because of the fall-out of industrial pollution suspended in the atmosphere; this is known as acid rain. Its source has been traced to neighbouring industrial nations. There is very little doubt that it is also affecting rivers in south west and north east Scotland, as well as other parts of the country. It would seem that trees with dense canopies such as spruce may well aggravate this problem, with the fall-out building up during dry weather in the canopy and then being washed down the trunk or through the branches by rainfall, in a far more concentrated form. With the annual increase in the acreage of land being developed for forestry purposes, much of which is planted with conifer trees, and the rapid growth rate of existing plantations, this problem is likely to get much worse, and could affect the pH values of many watercourses at present suitable for rearing salmonids. Therefore, the productivity of

The Gardeners Run and Gardener Pool, River Carron.

Upper and Lower Craigs Pools, on the River Carron.

these watercourses could become severely retarded or, in some cases, parts of a river system might no longer be capable of supporting salmonids.

Normally, in most rivers in this country, under natural conditions with no form of industrial or other types of pollution being present, water quality was of a reasonably high standard with the most productive burns, tributaries or rivers enjoying a pH value of 6.5 or over, but in some catchments pH values of 5.5 to 6.5 were more the norm and the growth rate of fry and parr was significantly slower. Other tributaries, mainly to be found in the upper catchment areas, had even lower pH values, from 4.6 to 5.5, and in these the growth rate to smolt stage was even more retarded. The natural pH values of some watercourses have been altered as a result of water being diverted from one catchment to another, and have been abstracted or subjected to various forms of pollution. However, I deal with these aspects later.

Water flow is of vital importance not only to the health and ecology of the river system itself but also to the welfare of the fish that inhabit it. Under natural conditions a fairly stable flow pattern prevails supported both by rainfall and ground water resources such as springs. Some rainfall penetrated through gravels and replenished ground water sources, whilst the rest seeped quietly out of the ground into the natural watercourses. This meant that after rainfall, burns, tributaries and the main river system rose quietly to a peak flow, then fell equally slowly as the rainfall subsided. At times of drought, if there were lochs on the catchment these regulated the flow of the river as water levels in these lochs gradually reduced. If there were no lochs on the catchment, then these rivers were termed as spate rivers which rose and fell quietly, but once the surface of the ground had dried out their low flow levels were generally supported by ground water from springs. This type of water ideally suited the needs of the salmon, both as regards access and the needs of both juvenile and adult stocks within the river system and was more than adequate to cater for their health and safety. This type of water had yet another advantage, as by rising slowly and falling quietly, no undue pressure was placed by high peak flows on the river's banks and beds. The river was, therefore, trained within its banks: this was also the case with regard to the burns and larger tributaries, consequently bank erosion problems were not common. Incidents did happen from time to time, mainly when quick snow melt on the hills coincided with heavy rainfall, or after torrential thunder storms. On occasions, landslides also happened in the higher steep catchment, but these were not as common as those which occur today. Due to this, turbidity and silt levels were on the whole considerably lower. Hatchery supplies were taken either from spring feed or burns, and due to the stable flow in the latter case, silt levels were not too serious and these hatchery intakes seldom required more than filtration over gravel and sand trays.

In the last four decades, however, water flow regimes have changed significantly and it is now more an exception than the general rule to find a river with a completely stable flow and without some sort of interference. This radical change is due firstly, to mankind's effort to improve land use practices on all parts of the catchment and to improve hill grazings and the means of access to these isolated areas. Secondly, it is due to mankind's attempts to utilise water for supply, to generate electricity, and also to irrigate crops.

It is sufficient to say at this stage that land, hill and forestry drainage have been largely responsible for running water quickly off the surface of the ground, instead of allowing it to seep through. This in itself has led to a stable regime being turned into a regime whereby the watercourses tend to rise and fill quickly, with higher peaks and extended periods of low water flow. This new pattern of water flow is now aptly termed a flashy regime. Also, with the depletion and diversion of waterflow on many catchment areas, neither of which cater for the needs of salmon as well as the previous regime, conservation of salmon stocks can in some cases be threatened.

Quite apart from this considerable alteration in the flow pattern allied in some cases to a drastic reduction in volume of flow, there are also side effects which can have wide repercussions regarding water quality. Firstly water temperature, as it alone controls so many aspects of the life cycle of *Salmo salar*. However, these flashy water flows and the severe reduction of volume, both tend to raise the water temperature. This can result, particularly on well drained areas, in the failure of springs because they are often no longer replenished by water seeping into the substrata. As this source has a constant water temperature of 42°F it acts as a cooling agent in the summer and a warming agent in the winter. If springs do fail on parts of the catchment, it is likely that the low water flow running off this catchment will also be reduced with the result that higher water temperatures are likely under these conditions. Diversions of water outwith, or even within a catchment, can also materially affect water temperature levels at certain times of year. In the worst cases the levels may rise to the extent that they affect the amount of dissolved oxygen in the water and, in consequence, lead to fish losses.

Secondly, open contour drains, preparation of land by ploughing for forestry planting, road building and high peak floods leading to bank erosion, are all sources of an influx of sand, silt and gravel. This material much increases turbidity and in the worst cases can affect the health of newly hatched fry and other juveniles in the river, by causing irritation to their gill mechanism.

It can also cause severe problems if it finds it way into water sources being used to supply hatcheries and even the most comprehensive filtration methods sometimes fail to deal with it satisfactorily. It has reduced the quality of many sources of supply which previously had the right potential for hatchery purposes but had not been utilised.

SPAWNING AREAS

Spawning gravel is certainly the most important single commodity a salmon river must possess because without it salmon are unable to lay their eggs successfully and thereby, regenerate the species. Many people do not realise how important it is for this substance to have the right qualities to enable fish to prepare their redd, lay their eggs at the correct depth and then cover them with gravel, and also to keep these eggs safe in a healthy environment during the time they are incubating. This period can vary considerably, and it is usually three to five months before the eggs hatch and all the alevins have emerged throughout the entire length of a river system. It must be sited in a part of the river system where there is sufficient current flow at river bed level to assist the female fish in preparing her nest, where she will eventually lay her eggs, then help her to cover up these eggs and finally perfect her redd. This is absolutely essential because if there is no appreciable current passing over the point where the female is working on the river bed, the debris disturbed by the fish would merely fall back into place. Due to the great necessity of current flow, the depth at which the gravel lies underwater and the gradient of the river in the spawning area are often vital factors. Water depths flowing over the gravel of 9 inches to 3 feet, are generally ideal for the purpose, but can be deeper in certain places on rivers with high velocity. A flat still pool or section of the river, seldom has the right qualities, which are usually to be found either in fords above or below a main pool where there is a good gradient, or in the section of the tail of a pool where there is a faster draw. There are, therefore, many places in a river where there might be large deposits of gravel which are quite unsuitable for spawning because they are badly placed.

The texture of the gravel is also of prime importance and can range from a piece the size of a ten pence piece to that of a man's clenched fist. Larger pieces of gravel and stone are very useful in making sure that the gravel in the redd remains open, allowing water to percolate through it at all times, whilst the smaller pieces fill the crevices and keep the eggs in place. A redd consisting entirely of small material can flatten more easily thereby allowing silt to settle on top of it. It must be stable and well-anchored so that the eggs are firmly encased and cannot be washed away. Unstable gravel, normally found after torrential rain, landslips, or bank erosion, is quite unsuitable because inevitably it will be moved on downstream in the winter spates and with it any eggs that are incubating. Sometimes these new deposits are easily cut by the female when she is spawning, but on other occasions it is too lively to cut properly and can be compared with trying to dig a hole in quicksand, it fills in as soon as an indent is made.

Other gravel with excellent spawning potential often becomes impacted when fine particles of silt, sand, soil and clay are forced in between the crevices on the surface of the river bed and harden, literally cementing the gravel particles together. This is a common occurrence when bank erosion, landslips and large drainage schemes or forestry planting take place in the vicinity of the spawning fords and can completely destroy large spawning fords, merely because the female cannot break the crust with the means at her disposal. However, if this occurs and comes to the notice of fishery managers, sometimes it can easily be rectified by raking the surface of the gravel and loosening it, or if larger deposits are affected, by harrowing the surface with a tooth harrow drawn by a tractor, during the summer months when rivers are low. In the worst cases, however, clean gravel can become completely immersed by silt and sand, and when this does occur little can be done in the way of remedial action.

Spawning areas are not confined to the main river systems, but are also to be found in the many side burns and major tributaries flowing into the rivers. Sometimes, if these burns have a stable regime and are neither too steep nor too torrential, provided they have the right qualities, they can be of prime importance and equally productive. Even burns of only a few feet in width can play a vital part in this intricate network, and eggs planted in small watercourses are probably in a safer habitat than some of those deposited in parts of the main system.

The amount of spawning gravel which is available varies tremendously from river to river, and also from one part of the catchment to another. In some cases, in the headwaters of major rivers or in the upper catchment of short steep rivers, the side burns are too steep for fish to ascend or are barred by sheer falls, and in these cases spawning facilities are confined to the main course of the river. Often this flows down the floor of a gravelly valley, meandering its way quietly in an erratic manner as it winds and twists with many ox-bows on its path. Seldom in these situations will it follow a straight course, very often this winding descent provides ideal spawning grounds on every corner and kink. With quiet, gentle sections intermingled with faster shallower fords, these areas provide excellent spawning facilities and good holding pools.

Other rivers flowing through more gentle terrain often have a wealth of spawning grounds, both in the main river and on almost as many of the network of burns flowing into it. Some rivers flowing through the arable coastal plain have spawning facilities through the entire length of their systems, whilst the more rugged, shorter rivers found on the west coast, may have no spawning potential in the lower boulder strewn section, and only limited areas high up the river system. On the islands off the west coast of Scotland, it is usual to have very short rivers flowing out of a series of lochs of varying size, all of which are interconnected by short sections of river and fed by numerous side burns. This type of situation is ideal, with the lochs providing a safe haven for the adult fish prior to spawning, and the many side burns and connecting channels providing excellent facilities at spawning time. Many west coast mainland rivers have similar characteristics.

There is no doubt whatsoever that the productivity of any river is almost entirely allied to the amount of good stable gravel, suitable for spawning purposes. In some countries this specific point is thought to be of so much importance that attempts have been made to create man-made spawning channels in order to increase salmon stocks in rivers where spawning facilities are scarce. This is achieved either by incorporating them in the natural river course by encouraging the river to meander more slowly through a gravelly strath instead of allowing it to follow a straighter more torrential course, or by cutting an alternative channel parallel to the main course, then styling it to natural requirements and diverting part of the river flow through this section. In some cases, suitable gravel has to be imported from elsewhere if this is not readily available on site. The flow through these artificial sections can then be regulated by sluice control, if need be, as can the size of the adult stock which is allowed to accommodate these areas. Remarkable success in overall stock enhancement has accrued from this type of action, but it can be an extremely costly operation.

HABITAT

Salmon stocks, on their return to freshwater, may have to spend a considerable time in the river system before their ovaries are fully developed and they are ripe and ready to spawn. In the case of winter and spring runs this may be as long a duration as eight to twelve months, with summer and autumn run fish spending a shorter time in the river. It is, therefore, essential that there is a plentiful supply of good holding pools distributed throughout the entire length of the river system in which salmon can spread out in any height of water, wherever they wish within the river and its main tributaries, in a healthy state and, hopefully, in reasonable safety. These main holding pools must have several essential characteristics such as depth, bed and bank cover and, at the same time, be well oxygenated. This is because fish may have to remain in the pools for a considerable length of time, either once they have reached the proximity of their spawning grounds where they eagerly wait until the time is right for them to spawn, or if they are stranded in pools elsewhere in the river during times of drought. Depth, and bed and bank cover are all essential for helping to protect and conceal them from predators, whilst trees, scrub, undermined banks, crevices under rocks and the dark depths of the pool all provide, at certain times of the day, safe refuge from the relentless rays of sunshine, especially at low water flow. Streamy necks or tumbling waterfalls at the head of the pool keep the water circulating and with it the dissolved oxygen levels throughout the pool, and these are favoured areas of the pool particularly in the early morning and in the evening. Provided depth is also available in these streamy sections of the pool, fish may choose to occupy these areas for most of the day, whilst others may prefer the slower deeper areas often lying alongside a rock ledge, under a cliff face, behind a large boulder, or even lying at a greater depth, in the last case where the water is often cooler. In these slower moving areas of the pool, they can often lie inert expending little energy. Loch systems and canal-like stretches of water to be found in many river systems, are also well populated and are ideal safe havens in extreme low water conditions, with depth, overhanging banks or weed beds providing the necessary protection from both predators and sun rays. These deep layered slower sections of the rivers and lochs are also usually well oxygenated, with plenty of room for fish stocks to spread out and lie at virtually any depth they wish. Quite apart from the main holding pools, there are many smaller pools, runs and pots, all deep enough and capable of accommodating lesser numbers of fish. These help to spread out the fish more evenly throughout the system and often prevent the whole population of a section of the river from being crowded into too few larger pools, where they are more prone to disease and the risk of poaching. There are also many shallower areas of the river which, in low water conditions, are untenantable, but in high and medium water flows have the right qualities and depth to provide useful resting places for tired fish. Their duration of stay in this category of pool varies tremendously from a brief pause to a matter of days, provided the river does not drop too fast, whereupon fish would be forced to vacate them. In the faster flowing pools, rock ledges, boulders and large rocks on the river bed are necessary to baffle the current velocity and thereby, create quiet places, both upstream and behind the obstructions, and in which fish can lie without having to expend excess energy. Pools which lack this important requisite are often completely neglected in all but low flows. The obstructions also afford cover and camouflage for their residents. A promontory or bluff projecting from the bank also provides useful shelter both upstream and behind it in higher water flows; these prove to be favoured haunts at certain levels of river flow.

It is also of prime importance to have an adequate number of holding pools intermingled with the shallower spawning fords in the upper reaches of the river system, so that fish native to these areas do not have long distances to travel when the time comes to utilise the spawning grounds. Instead, they can lie in the pools in peace and comfort and then move only a short distance to the fords when the time comes to spawn.

Spawning areas that are not served by holding pools are often entirely or partially neglected by spawning fish, as they are too far away from the resident spawning population.

In recent years, with mankind's change of land use on the upper catchment areas of many rivers, holding pools within these shallow areas tend to become silted up with sand, sludge and gravel and, therefore, their holding capacity has been severely retarded. In consequence, spawning areas may well become under-populated if there is insufficient holding accommodation close to the fords for native stock to occupy.

In low water temperatures salmon stocks favour the deeper, slow moving areas of the pool where they can gain shelter behind rock ledges or large stones and thereby are protected from the relentless velocity of water flow. On the whole, however, they seldom lie at a depth of more than 8 feet, unless they have been disturbed or go deeper in order to escape the full rays of the sunshine. Very often they can be seen lying approximately mid-level, between the bed of the pool and the surface in the very deep sections of a pool, and only cling to the bottom in pools that are relatively shallow.

In warmer temperatures of 55°F and over, for the most part they lie at a shallower depth and are quite content to inhabit pools of around 3 to 4 feet in depth. Only in very hot weather, during the heat of the day, do they seek refuge at greater depths or when they are disturbed. At these temperatures they prefer to lie for parts of the day in streamy water and fast runs, which were rarely inhabited when temperature levels of 32°F to 40°F prevailed, unless of course these faster areas also had sufficient depth and good bed cover, below the fast ruffled surface.

As these adult fish do not have to feed in fresh water in order to sustain them daily, a salmon river does not need to provide this requirement, once the spawning stock returns to freshwater.

FEEDING AREAS

Once again these are sited in strategic parts of a river system, normally close alongside the spawning fords; mostly in the shallow areas of the river, where there is plenty of bed cover such as small pebbles and stones. These afford excellent cover where fry and feeding parr can seek refuge when disturbed by predators, or shade against intensive sunlight during dry weather periods. The fry often favour the finer gravel fords, whilst the older parr prefer stonier, riffling sections of the river and usually each individual has its own territory, which is zealously defended. Both fry and small parr which venture, either of their own free will or in error, into the deeper holding pools stand little chance of survival, as larger resident trout or other cannibal fish will soon devour them. In these shallower areas with plenty of hiding places readily available, they are relatively safe from diving birds such as cormorants, mergansers and goosanders, because these have no depth or room to dive and manoeuvre. Large predator fish are not keen to venture into these areas, unless they do so under cover of darkness. Herons, however, with their long necks and reach can still take their toll.

Bank cover is another important factor, with decidious and heavy undergrowth lining the bank being a distinct advantage. This affords shade, sanctuary under the roots and undermined banks, and at the same time produces a bountiful supply of food in the form of terrestrial insects. In the wider areas, sunlight, free to beat down on to the surface of the water, is essential to promote algal growth which in turn, increases the productivity of these areas. Under natural conditions, with untampered water resources free to flow off the catchment, and little disturbance to banks or the landscape alongside, an ideal stable regime prevails. This enables the young fry and parr to feed at their own free will in a healthy environment, barely disturbed or endangered by any problems – apart from fish and bird predators.

Mankind has altered the stability and safety of many of these nursery areas by striving to improve the productivity of the land surrounding our rivers, and at the same time utilising the water resources which drain into them. Any substantial change in water flow, especially in times of drought, can lead to unending problems such as forcing feeding fish to vacate their shallow havens and move into deeper water where many dangers lurk ready to decimate them. Any drop in pH values which results can severely retard the productivity of the area and thereby reduce the size of the population it is able to support. Any appreciable rise in water temperature levels can reduce the level of dissolved oxygen in the water and, in extreme cases, this can lead, because of stress, to fish kills due to suffocation or disease. All these complications frequently arise when water is abstracted or diverted from a catchment, or as a result of irrigation or intensive drainage on a catchment. Even river regulations can cause problems by denuding a river of too much water or keeping nursery areas flooded to too great a degree, in either case opening the door to unacceptable levels of predation.

Impounding dams to create new reservoirs or enlarge existing ones, floods out large areas of priceless feeding grounds upstream of the dam and these are lost for evermore; a loss in productivity that no salmon river can possibly afford without a consequential reduction in salmon stocks.

Land drainage, afforestation, road building and peat workings can all lead to severe deterioration of the health of the feeding areas when in close proximity. Compaction of the gravel fords often prevents the young salmonids from taking refuge in the crevices of gravel and stones, whilst in other cases clean gravel is replaced by sludge, silt, and sand, a completely characterless bed, lacking any form of cover or safe haven. Bank erosion can also result in loss of bank cover and the silting of feeding areas downstream, and once this occurs it can be a weeping sore for years to come, unless it is rectified.

Grazing of stock, especially cattle and horses, planting of conifers too close to the banks of burns and rivers, and the use of brush and vegetation weed killers on the edge of river banks, are all liable to induce bank erosion, resulting in loss of stability. Heavy stock not only crop the vegetation, but because of their weight they often crumble or pock mark the bank, which induces erosion. Dense conifer plantations kill out ground vegetation and its binding root growth, due to the shading of the ground beneath the trees; whilst selective vegetation and brush weedkillers destroy the roots of bank vegetation. In all cases, it is the loss of the tree and vegetative root growth binding the bank strata which weakens the banks, and leads to erosion taking place. At the same time, any loss of tree or plant growth on the river banks severely retards this valuable source of terrestrial food and also reduces shade and bank cover, all of which are important requisites of any nursery area, a loss which no feeding area can afford without repercussions. Forestry, such as thick conifers planted too close to the bank of burns or larger watercourses, soon close their canopy and shade the surface of the water from sunlight. Sunlight is essential to promote algal growth, which in turn both breeds and feeds fish fauna, particularly waterborne invertebrates; so the result is that the productivity of feeding grounds lying within these forests, is retarded accordingly.

The application of chemicals in the form of fertilisers to land on the river catchment may also severely alter the natural chemical metabolism of the river water, and this change is not always beneficial. Weed growth can be promoted by these nutrients to the extent that at times useful nursery areas become completely overgrown and lost. The spraying of weed killers and chemicals to control agricultural pests may also result in fish kills especially in the smaller watercourses, if these substances happen to find their way into the river. This also applies to industrial pollution, and although in the modern era purification authorities have gone a long way towards controlling this source of danger, accidents still can and do happen on occasions. When they do, the effect can be seen for several years afterwards, by a decline in the number of fish returning. Not only are there losses to the fish population due to these incidents, but a similar loss to fish fauna occurs. Any loss or retarding of the nursery areas within a river system as a result of these problems, merely reduces pro rata the number of fry and parr the river is capable of supporting to smolt age.

The way nature has devised the layering of salmon stocks throughout the length and breadth of a river system so that each and every spawning and feeding area is utilised, is one of the main reasons why salmon stocks are so resilient.

In the hydro-electric era of the late forties to the early sixties, drowning out or debarring fish from access to their spawning nursery areas often unbalanced the productivity of a river system to such an extent that the result was similar to severing a limb from one's body. Any failure of a nursery area, regardless of where that particular area lies within the river, means that an intricate part of the network is weakened. This can lead to an imbalance in the different runs of that river, and is often the reason why runs of fish, and the periods of the year when fish run, may vary so much from one river to another.

NURSERY AREAS

The most productive nursery and feeding areas in a river are those on which salmon have a predominance over other indigenous freshwater fish. In other words, the less competition this species has on the main nursery areas, the better the results. This is mainly due to the fact that trout and many other species are predators of salmon fry and parr and if these were predominant losses during the fry/parr stages would be unacceptably high. It also follows that there would be more mouths to feed and, therefore, the young salmon would be competing with others, including larger competitors, for the limited food supply to be found in most rivers. Cannibalism would, therefore, inevitably play an important part in this struggle for survival. Unfortunately, as the number of people who wish to fish increases vastly year by year, the pressure on freshwater fisheries also increases. A recent estimate of the number of anglers in the UK alone was put at four million. In many rivers in the UK, especially in England, Wales and, to a lesser extent in southern Scotland, in order to cater for the increasing number of fishermen, brown and rainbow trout fisheries were established not only in freshwater reservoirs but also in the river systems. As early as the 1960s it became common practice for angling clubs and water authorities to release large numbers of takeable trout into certain sections of some of the famous salmon rivers, as well as stocking many stillwater lakes, lochs and reservoirs, many of which drained into these rivers. These were given the apt name of 'put and take' fisheries. However, inevitably many of these sizeable brown trout put into the river systems were too wily to be caught and along with others which escaped into the river from the 'put and take' stillwater fisheries, they greatly boosted the wild breeding population of this species in the river systems.

In the late 1960s and early 1970s, salmon stocks throughout the UK were decimated by a virulent disease named UDN. Many mortalities occurred and in some of the worst affected rivers, a large percentage of their salmon stocks were literally wiped out. Salmon stocks, or a component of these stocks, declined for several years in many parts of the country and indeed, in some cases have never really recovered. Because of this dearth of salmon, more angling associations and owners of river fisheries, especially in the south, resorted to stocking their waters with trout, in order to give their clients something to fish for. Unfortunately, instead of redressing a difficult situation and thereby benefiting it, it is likely that these 'put and take' fisheries have, if anything, delayed the recovery of salmon stocks. Mainly because, in many famous river systems south of the border, trout and other freshwater species have taken predominance on the most viable nursery areas of some of these rivers. This is due to the fact that by sheer misfortune, the drastic decline in salmon stocks happened to coincide with an increase in the trout population, due to an appreciable increase in the breeding stock of the trout.

I once heard an eminent salmon fishery scientist comparing restocking with takeable trout in a salmon river as being just as detrimental as expecting to get more eggs from a hen run by putting a wild fox in it, and I wholeheartedly agree. There is very little doubt that the balance between indigenous species of freshwater fish and the stocks of this anadromous species on the nursery areas is an all important factor in salmon conservation.

There are many, many areas in this country where trout stocks could be promoted without interfering in any way with salmon stocks. Therefore, we in this generation must be very careful that we are not responsible for mankind, no matter how good his intentions, once again disturbing a delicate balance of nature in this manner to the lasting detriment of one of our most valuable natural resources, the salmon.

CHARACTER

Salmon rivers that are inhabited by *Salmo salar* differ widely in their characteristics, according to how they are placed geographically and also their topographic nature. In the UK, because it is an island, salmon rivers do not have the same depth of catchment to drain that either North American or European rivers have. Therefore, their length is in most cases very much shorter than their counterparts abroad. Even in the UK itself, due almost entirely to the siting of the mountainous terrain within the island, there is a wide variation both in the depth and width of the catchment that is drained by individual rivers or river systems. For the most part, it would be true to say that with few exceptions the southern and eastern flowing rivers drain into the sea from a significantly greater area of the country than those which flow both west and north. Salmon rivers such as the Wye, Tay and Tweed are among the longest rivers in the country. However, throughout their length these rivers have several major tributaries flowing into the main course, which significantly increases the volume of water passing down. In some cases, the tributaries are as large or even larger than many individual rivers draining the narrower part of the country lying to the north of the Caledonian Canal or shorter catchments flowing west. Other major rivers, however, such as the Welsh Dee, Spey and Aberdeenshire Dee have far fewer major tributaries but, instead, countless small side burns swell their flow. North of the Caledonian Canal, the area where the mainland is at its narrowest, in many cases the rivers flowing east are four to five times longer than those flowing west, and even those flowing north into the Pentland Firth, are considerably larger than most of these flowing west. On the islands lying off the west coast of Scotland, the rivers, including their loch systems, are even smaller in length than their counterparts on the mainland flowing west, and tiny in comparison to even the smallest of the east coast rivers. Each and every one of these rivers, regardless of length or where they lie in the UK, unless they are too steep to allow salmon stocks to ascend, play an important and integral part in supporting this valuable natural resource. In some cases the productivity of even the smallest river far exceeds that of one of its much larger neighbours. In other cases, the productivity of a river hinges on one small area of its catchment where its spawning and feeding potential lie, whereas its neighbour may well be blessed with spawning and feeding facilities distributed throughout its entire length. Therefore, the stocking density of a salmon river bears absolutely no relationship to the length and breadth of the catchment, but instead is entirely dependent on the ecology of each and every individual watercourse and the network of watercourses of which the salmon river is composed. Obviously, the more that ecology suits the needs of salmon, the more productive that unit or network of units is as a producer and maintainer of salmon stocks.

We know that there are four definite individual runs of salmon; the winter run (now termed, unfortunately, by modern scientists as early spring fish) entering fresh water from October to December of the year prior to spawning during autumn the following year; the spring run entering the river from January to early May; the summer run including grilse coming in from late April to August; and finally, the autumn run ascending the rivers from late August to early December – also including grilse. The latter three runs will also spawn in the autumn: the spring run doing so in late October to early November, at the same time as the winter run; the summer run in late November to early December; and the autumn run in late December and into January. As all these runs of fish overlap

The Gruinard Run, with the Lodge in the background.

A rugged Highland burn.

each other it is both possible and probably that in the larger river systems of the UK, there will be few days throughout the entire season when salmon do not enter that river system.

For many years it was believed that these runs of fish were not separate components of the overall salmon stocks of a river, and there was no reason to believe that spring fish actually bred spring fish, etc. There now seems to be some evidence that these runs may well be individual units which do reproduce progeny with similar characteristics, although there is also little doubt that environmental factors may have a bearing on this matter and be of equal importance. One thing which does seem to have been proved fairly conclusively recently, is that smolts of the older age groups are more likely to return to fresh water as multi-sea winter fish.

It is a well known fact that the winter and spring runs which enter the river either in the autumn of the previous year, or during the early part of the current year, occupy the upper catchment of the river they return to. Therefore, they propagate in that section of the river system.

Winter runs are becoming increasingly scarce and in all probability the high seas fisheries are responsible for this. The three to four sea-winter fish naturally spend more time at sea and are inevitably longer in the danger zone where they can be exploited. Rivers such as the Welsh Dee and Wye have only a fraction of the winter run they used to enjoy and in Scotland, the Aberdeenshire Dee, Esks and Tay are amongst the few rivers that are still fortunate enough to have some of these fish. Although in the present era the spring runs are also showing marked declines, they are common to many east coast rivers and some on the west and south coasts of England and Wales. There are also a few rivers in the south west of Scotland that enjoy a spring run, but it is a rare commodity north of the Clyde on this coast.

Provided the upper catchment of these rivers flow off high mountainous terrain, this section of the river system can be expected to enjoy a colder climate throughout the twelve month period of the year than sections of the river lying further downstream or in the headwaters of rivers draining lower altitude catchments. At the same time, pH values of the watercourses in these sections of the upper catchment can often be lower than those to be found further downstream. Due to these two important factors, the progeny of the early run fish are likely to have a substantially slower growth rate than juveniles born in the more kindly sectors of the catchment elsewhere. The age at which the feeding parr will migrate as smolts from these areas is likely to be considerably higher than those born in other parts of the river; consequently they are more likely to return to the river as multi-sea winter fish when they mature.

The summer run, including grilse, either seem to return to the mid-sections and certain tributaries of the larger river systems, or the shorter individual rivers throughout the country. This latter category drain lower altitude catchments on the east coast; short steep rivers on the west coast, or the smaller rivers with significant loch systems either to be found in the islands off the west coast or on the western part of the mainland. (This type of river seldom enjoys a run of early fish.) It would be true to say that each and every salmon river accommodates this run of fish, regardless of its length and size. The progeny of the summer run often born at lower altitudes and subjected to less rigorous winter conditions, may well enjoy both a longer annual feeding period and be supported by a more nutrient rich food supply promoted by better quality water of higher pH value. This may well lead to some of the parr smolting at an appreciably earlier age and this can lead to stronger grilse runs pertaining. Some summer salmon, however, can grow to an appreciable size.

The autumn run, which is by no means common to all rivers, either occupies the lower sections of a river system, or penetrates to a specific section of a river system. It is interesting to note that when the Aberdeenshire Dee enjoyed an autumn run it normally occupied the section downstream of Banchory. For many years that run seemed to have faded completely but in the last few years there is some evidence that it may be reviving. In the case of the Tweed, the autumn run seems to be going from strength to strength and occupies a large section of the main river and many of its tributaries. It is interesting that it also occupies the main river upstream of Innerleithen where early run fish are seldom, if ever, seen. This is mainly because most of the early fish moving into the upper river, seem to turn left and run up the Ettrick Water. From August to November, however, the Innerleithen to Peebles section becomes fully populated, mainly by this autumn run. This is a very interesting feature of this great salmon river. In the case of the Tay, Ness and Esks, the autumn run populates large sections of the lower river. It would appear from the wide variation in size of the fish that comprise these autumn runs, that their progeny spend an inconsistent period as juveniles in fresh water, some smolting at an early age and others remaining in their freshwater nursery areas for a significantly longer period. Some of the grilse component of these runs are considerably larger than the average summer grilse, weighing between 10 and 16 pounds, whereas salmon of 15 to 35 pounds are not uncommon, mixed in with the normal 8 to 12 pound class. The overall weight of these autumn fish is, on average, probably greater than at any other period of the year. Rivers that have formidable natural rock barriers, such as falls low down the river system, seldom accommodate this run of fish, because with well developed ovaries these salmon are too gravid to ascend such obstacles.

The reason why fish enter certain rivers throughout the entire year, whereas in other rivers their timing of entry is curtailed to a more specific season, seems to be a combination of circumstances and factors rather than one single motive. In the case of the longer river systems with major side tributaries, where either the main river and/or some of its tributaries drain high mountainous terrain, there is no reason why that river cannot accommodate all four runs of salmon, because somewhere on the length and breadth of this river there is likely to be suitable ecology, environment, and accessibility to meet the needs of each individual run. However, it is rare to find a river which does accommodate all four runs and even if it does, it is generally the case that some runs are stronger than others. On the smaller, short rivers, it is unlikely that their spawning and feeding facilities are capable of accommodating, seeding and rearing more than one or, at the most, two seasonal runs of salmon. It is also probable that either its environment or accessibility will not suit the needs of certain of these seasonal components. Even if a short river did have the necessary high catchment to suit the needs of winter and spring runs, because these fish spawn earlier than the other runs, it may well be a fact that the summer and autumn runs which spawn later destroy the eggs laid by the earlier runs in the process. Therefore, predominance of one run over another on the spawning fords may well be one of the factors that has an important bearing on why certain rivers accommodate only one specific run, whilst others enjoy two or more.

If these seasonal runs did not differ genetically and each run did not breed like, i.e. spring fish breed spring fish, it would be reasonable to expect that each river, no matter how large or how small, would have some fresh fish entering the river system over the entire twelve month period. This, however, just does not happen in practice.

This is a fascinating subject, and one we will probably never be able to prove scientifically. It is, however, a most important aspect of salmon conservation. At this stage it would seem that the balance of seasonal runs depends on a combination of factors, such as the size of the river system, and that of its spawning and feeding facilities; genetic strains; environmental impact; accessibility; and predominance on the spawning grounds.

With the so called 'greenhouse effect' being in the forefront of most people's minds, particularly regarding what effect this may have on weather patterns in the future, could the natural environment be materially affected? Obviously, any significant changes to the weather pattern could alter the temperature of the water, both fresh water and sea, and if this did happen it could have wide repercussions on the timing of the migratory habits of salmon, as well as altering the environment they live in, which is so vital to their conservation.

CHAPTER FOUR

Changing Land and Water Use and its Effect on the Health of a River's Ecology

This is such an important influence on salmon fisheries, salmon reproduction and conservation of the species that it warrants a chapter on its own. I deal first with land use and then with water use. It seems best to divide the catchment into three different sections – upper, mid and lower – and then to list the types of change of land and water use as well as the problems which can arise from the changes.

It must be remembered that the very essence of salmon breeding and rearing, hinges on stability of the water, river bank and river bed. If rivers begin to take on a more flashy characteristic, such as higher peak flows that rise quickly and fall as quickly, then problems in stability are inevitable. This often causes a torrent, leading to bank erosion and with it, large influxes of gravel, silt and sand moving around within the river system. Alternatively, if large quantities of water are diverted, abstracted, or impounded and then controlled within that river, then the river immediately loses its natural characteristics and with it its cleansing capability. In other words, its ability to keep its main course clear of debris from its side burns and tributaries.

LAND USE

UPPER CATCHMENT

Grazing

Sheep, and to a lesser extent cattle, are a constant source of erosion, especially in hot weather, as they rub and dust themselves in sandy and other easily erodable banks often found on the sides of cuttings or hillocks. Cattle and horses, mainly due to their weight, pock mark and crumble the sides of watercourses with their hooves and this in turn can lead to erosion.

Muirburn or heather burning on a large scale, or getting out of control, generates excess heat and this at times destroys the roots of heather and other vegetation so essential for binding together and protecting the surface of the ground. This is another common cause of erosion.

Land drainage to run off the surface water more quickly before it seeps into the ground can be a problem. On the upland areas this normally takes the form of an open ploughed drain, following the contour of the land and eventually discharging into a minor or major existing watercourse. Provided the sole of the contour plough remains within the peat seam, then apart from the initial influx of peat sludge immediately after the drains have been cut, erosion levels remain low. However, if the sole of the plough breaks through the peat and exposes the soil, sand or gravel crust beneath, then these moveable substances are quickly eroded by the high water velocities within the drain. Inevitably, they are washed down the course of the drain and discharged into the river system. Often, the point at which the drain enters the watercourse is a further source of erosion. The banks of the watercourse are also subject to erosion if larger peak flows than usual result from a number of these contour drains discharging into the same stream.

Forestry

Ploughing furrows for planting exposes large areas of erodable substances to the elements, both in the actual furrow and on the upturned sod. Once the ploughing has been completed and for a considerable time afterwards, during times of heavy rainfall particles of soil, sand, silt and gravel are washed off the surface and large quantities of this material find their way into watercourses, via the forestry drainage channels. This newly prepared land is a source of erosion for a considerable time; in fact until the exposed area has been bound together by the growth of new vegetation and the trees which have been planted. It usually follows that the steeper the ground which is prepared for planting, the more material there is likely to be washed off it.

The planting of conifers too close to the banks of watercourses can seriously affect the productivity of these feeding areas, leading to a retarding of invertebrates and fish fauna in those which lie within forests where the dense tree canopy prevents sunlight from promoting both algal growth and ground vegetation. This can have serious repercussions on the value of these streams.

The close canopy of trees means the shade and thick cover kills vegetation under the forest and with it the root growth so essential to bind and give strength to the banks of watercourses. In time, this weakens the banks and often leads to erosion taking place – both to the detriment of the forest and the stability of the stream.

Flow regime in afforested areas is further accentuated by water loss from the tree canopy interception of precipitation, and transpiration. It has been shown quite conclusively that the trees intercept substantially more water than open moorland and this has adverse effects in long periods of dry weather and irregular rainfall. It is unlikely that the nursery streams can afford the water losses which the afforested areas incur. This can also cause problems to and impede salmon stocks attempting to ascend these burns for spawning purposes.

The spraying of forests against the Pine Beauty Moth and other insects must be carefully controlled as these sprays are often toxic to fish as well as the food they so heavily rely on to survive. This particularly applies to streams flowing within a forest which is infected.

Road Building: Roads for Agriculture and Sporting Activities

Road systems to open up access to agriculture and amenities in the more inaccessible upper catchment areas, are now much in demand. In many cases these are badly constructed and, therefore, often lack the necessary drainage. Such roads are constructed on harder sections of the hill land and for that reason usually follow the course of a burn. Both during and after construction, these roads and the open scars left on the hillside on the upper side of them, can be a constant source of erosion during heavy rainfall. Most of the derbis from these works eventually finds its way into existing natural drainage channels.

Road Building: Forestry Roads

Forestry roads in the forest can also be a source of erosion, as once again the construction of these means breaking the surface of the land, and exposing large quantities of easily erodable material to weathering by the elements. These roads, however, are usually built to a higher standard than those for sporting or agriculture. After the initial construction phase is over, they seldom cause further problems unless there happens to be a landslip on the steeper slopes.

Road Building: Trunk or Main Roads

These often cross the upper catchment areas and are part of the country's arterial road system. Some of these main roads are of considerable width, and during the construction period when the foundations are laid, large quantities of bare earth are open to the weather. Silt and sand in large quantities run off the open scars on the hillside as thousands of tons of materials are both removed and imported, and the local quarries exploited. Much of this material, during times of heavy rainfall, is washed into local watercourses and from thence into the river systems, leading to a marked increase in silt levels and, therefore, turbidity. Once the foundations have ben laid, culverts passing water from the hillside under the roads have to be constructed, not only to carry each individual water artery no matter how large or small, but also drainage from the road itself. In order to prevent scour at each of these points, either a flat concrete plinth is formed and set in the bed of the watercourse for the water to run smoothly over, or in the case of smaller sources, the water is conducted through various sizes of concrete or corrugated pipes. In most cases, the velocity through the culverts is extremely high, often making access to fish completely impossible or partially curtailing their free ascent to the lower range of water levels.

MID-CATCHMENT

As one moves further downstream naturally many aspects affecting the river's ecology change significantly. Not only does the river now drain a larger catchment leading to a substantial increase in the volume of flow, but the geographical nature of the ground now added to its catchment can differ materially to that of the headwater catchment and at the same time there can often be a marked increase in human population as well as industrial practices. The latter can lead to increased pollution, although at the same time the greater volume of water in the river is better able to dilute it. With the advent of increased powers and stricter controls being given to purification authorities, on the whole discharges of both domestic and industrial effluent are far better monitored, and no longer pose the threat to fish stocks and the health of rivers which they had previously. Although from time to time major incidents do occur which lead to losses of fish stocks: the offenders now face far stiffer penalties if they are prosecuted and found guilty. It is more common in the present era for fish kills to occur as a result of minor incidents such as effluent from silage pits, agricultural sprays or road accidents involving chemical tankers, fuel carriers, etc. Most of these incidents usually affect the smaller watercourses draining into the main river, rather than the river itself.

In this sector of the catchment lies much better quality arable land, therefore agricultural activities are increased in their intensity. Larger acreages of land are put to the plough for growing cash crops, the improvement of grazings, and providing fodder crops for cattle and sheep. Weather conditions in these catchment areas can at times be unpredictable. Therefore, many farmers prefer to make silage rather than hay, as they are more certain of harvesting it in prime condition. Silage pits are often hastily constructed, many have inadequate drainage facilities so that any spillage of this toxic effluent into watercourses can have fatal consequences to both fish and fish fauna in them. Since purification boards came into being the standard of silage pit drainage has been much improved and is more stringently controlled. But as such pits are so numerous in these agricultural areas it is difficult to keep check on them all. Therefore, incidents still occur – although in the last decade these have been far more the exception than the rule.

Agricultural sprays of many kinds are also toxic to fish and are used more frequently in arable valleys than they would be on the more rugged terrain of the upper catchment. Pollution incidents from this source occur through carelessness, such as using a spray tin to fetch water from a burn to fill the sprayer, or washing the sprayer in a burn after use, sheer want of forethought – but often an expensive error.

Watercourses and tributaries flowing through arable areas are generally very productive with high pH values, full of nutrients from deciduous tree-lined banks and the run-off of artificial fertilisers and lime through a network of underground tile drains. They are also well shaded with a plentiful supply of both bed and bank cover. Therefore, they have most of the right qualities and are ideal feeding and nursery areas, with even the smallest being of prime importance to salmon breeding. Cattle and sheep still cause problems to the banks of these rivers, many of which are used to water livestock. Banks crumble easily due to the weight of these animals as they wander down to drink, or graze on the well watered vegetation at the water's edge. This, unfortunately, creates a constant source of erosion unless the banks are adequately fenced. In the smaller tributaries, large scale bank erosion can lead to silting of the actual bed of the watercourse. In some cases, clean open gravel so essential for spawning and feeding may either become immersed in mud or impacted by fine particles and, therefore, made unworkable. In either case, this priceless commodity loses its essential qualities for salmon rearing, both for spawning and feeding. In the main river, the volume of water flowing down will be able to keep its course clean of this debris, unless this flow is regulated by impoundment works upstream, in which case debris borne into the main river cannot be scoured out by the reduced flow and often engulfs a section of the river bed in the close vicinity of the burn mouth. This in turn, can in time cause the river to alter course at this point and thereby create further bank erosion.

With over-production of certain agricultural products in the EEC countries, marginal arable land owners have been encouraged to diversify their use of land. Many acres of this type of land have, therefore, been planted with trees. In cases where conifer plantations have replaced agricultural activities, this has been a poor substitute and watercourses flowing through these areas of high productivity concerning salmon rearing, have had their potential severely retarded for the same reasons given earlier concerning forestry on the upper catchment.

On occasions, gravel is taken out of small tributaries or the main river, in order to mend or make farm or forestry roads or tracks. In actual fact, any disturbance to salmon spawning areas at certain times of the year is an offence, but many people do not realise this. Often, spawning areas where ova are incubating under the gravel are dug up for these purposes: this leads to the loss of any ova that are disturbed, and may destroy the stability of that spawning ground for some considerable time to come.

LOWER CATCHMENT

Once this section of the catchment is reached, the volume of flow in the river has risen to an appreciable level and, especially during times of flood, is a major force to be reckoned with. In most cases this final section flows through the arable coastal plain. It is usual, therefore, that the banks through this section are of a much softer composition than those of its upper reaches, in many cases consisting of earthen banks underlaid with a gravel sub-section, and rocky outcrops few and far between. In some cases these banks are fortified by the root growth of decidious trees while in other cases over the centuries these banks have been armoured with stone revetments or flood embankment works which train the river and keep it within its natural course. Unfortunately, however, with modern man-made drainage practices, it is usual for higher peak flows to prevail. There is also a tendency over the years for the course of the river to become silted with debris washed into it from the surrounding landscape via the various smaller watercourses and tributaries throughout its catchment. Both these factors add greater pressure at flood flow to the embankments and if there is any weakness or previous erosion, this can be quickly aggravated and, at times, exploited. This often leads to either the river changing course, widening at that point, or even islands of gravel becoming deposited in the main course thereby partially blocking the discharge and causing it to meander. Once a major problem has arisen, the river bed and its banks at that point become unstable and, therefore, are liable to considerable change for years to come because of gravel, silt, sand and sludge within that area and downstream leading to constant change in its natural regime.

Because of the substantial cost of any bank revetment works in many cases no remedial works are carried out, and instead it is just left to nature to take its own course and allow the position to be restabilised through time. Only in exceptional cases where population or agricultural land are under threat does money become available in the form of local grant or from central Government to rectify such problems, the later generally under a flood disaster scheme.

The effect of these events on salmon conservation within the main river makes the breeding and rearing of young salmonids fairly unpredictable in this lower part of the catchment. In stable areas where the river has been fragmented, there can be a very high potential both for spawning and rearing, particularly in the smaller more kindly back channels away from the main flow, and on the perimeters of evenly watered riffles which are not cambered to one side or the other. In the latter case, even if the gravel on the fringes dries out there is usually sufficient water percolating under the surface of the gravel at the depth the ova are incubating in the redd to keep them safe and healthy. However, if the river cambers to one side or the other markedly, eggs laid on the side away from the water due to this camber can be dried out completely in low flow and possibly destroyed.

Any fry that do hatch out in this environment are reasonably assured of a plentiful supply of lush high quality food and, therefore, a reasonably quick growth rate. Therefore, a higher survival rate can be expected during the fry stage here than in the more poverty stricken river course often found in the higher catchment. There are, however, two sides to every coin, and on the debit side in this section of the river there is a substantially higher risk of these young salmonids being devoured either by other fish or bird predators. This is mainly because, with the greater volume of flow, these avid feeders have far more manoeuvrability and freedom of movement as they search for food than they would have in the more sparsely watered river or tributary areas further upstream. Seldom are these sections of the river too shallow to debar passage for diving brids such as cormorants, mergansers and goosanders, or large pike, trout and perch. Therefore, these predators can prowl and plunder at their own free will, not only on the native fry and parr population but also on smolt shoals passing through as they migrate.

In the unstable sections and the centre of the main river course, continual movement of gravel, silt and sand and high flow velocities, mean the regime is too torrential and changeable to enable successful spawning or, if it does take place, for good expectation of the ova to incubate successfully. Therefore, it is reasonable to expect that appreciable losses of ova do occur in sections where the river bed is unstable, as the loose gravel in which redds can easily be planted is often washed downstream and out to sea during the winter floods before the eggs incubating in it have had time to hatch; or they are suffocated by silt and sludge being deposited on the redd in which they are incubating.

The side tributaries and smaller watercourses flowing through these arable areas are often very important spawning and feeding areas, provided they flow on a down-gradient and are not too canal-like. These are usually high in pH value boosted by the run off of lime phosphates and nitrates from the arable fields, and therefore, can have particularly high productivity. They can, however, suffer from water loss as a direct result of irrigation schemes, or either become silted as a result of bank erosion or made unstable by drainage operations if these are carried out within the main course. Water loss can also prevent fish movement within these tributaries, and if this coincides with the spawning period, can debar access to the spawning stock. Weed and algae bloom may be promoted by an excess of both nitrates and phosphates which can, in the worst cases, lead to eutrophication and, in consequence, fish losses. Silage effluent, waste diary products, sheep dip and certain sprays can all lead to fish losses when pollution incidents from these sources occur. Pollution from industry and the population has now been almost entirely controlled by the purification authorities and serious pollution incidents are now a rare occurrence. Phosphates from sewage works can promote weed growth, and cause other problems. The increased flow in the rivers over this lower section is in itself a very important factor concerning this problem, as in most water flows it is capable of diluting and dispersing all but the worst discharges that are likely to take place.

No problems are likely to take place concerning access or descent of migratory fish stocks over this section, except in times of extreme drought. Even then, the adult stock can remain in relative safety within the estuary, or move further offshore when these conditions prevail. Smolts descending will have sufficient flow at all times to find their way seawards even at times of low flow. However, extreme drought periods rarely, if ever, coincide with the March–June migration period.

SUMMARY OF LAND-USE CHANGES

Throughout the entire catchment area many of mankind's attempts to try and improve the land use on the catchment of river systems has, unfortunately, not been compatible with good husbandry concerning the breeding and rearing of salmon. This is mainly because stability of water flow, river bed and bank is the very essence of successful regeneration of this species. I have already dealt with the problems derived from interference with the natural flow and, therefore, will now deal with only the worst aspects of land use.

It really comes down to the basic fact that the earth under natural conditions is bound together and protected from the elements by root growth of ground cover, or living vegetation of some type or other. If this living vegetation is removed or damaged by any means, then the earth or pan underneath is exposed and this, with the exception of rock, is a highly erodable substance. Through time, in nearly every case, the elements will loosen the earth and when subjected to water force it is washed away. Almost inevitably it will eventually find its way into a watercourse of some sort or other whether it be a drain, burn or brook, and thence into the river. Naturally, any exposed areas on slopes or steeper mountainous areas will erode much more readily than those on flatter terrain unless there is an actual flow through those areas. Under natural conditions, landslides, high peak flows after thunder storms, torrential rain or quick snow melt and erosion from stock, were the commonest forms of an influx of sand, silt and gravel into river systems. Now, as a result of man's activities, those I have highlighted and many others are constant sources of this problem. Once the ground cover has been disturbed, unless it is quickly replaced these areas can be a constant source of debris for years to come. In some of the worst cases, what started as a small scar or drain of only a metre wide and one foot deep can easily turn into a ravine in a matter of a few years and this will only stop eroding either once bed rock is reached or remedial action taken.

Gravel and light texture materials from these sources are constantly on the move in many river systems, either creating a torrential unstable regime or alternatively silting up sections of all sizes of watercourse. Due to the importance of clean, stable gravel deposits, it is not surprising that many important spawning and feeding areas within these river systems are either completely destroyed or else retarded in productivity due to these means, with the consequential loss of ova, young fish and habitats for future salmon stocks.

Therefore, the actual potential production of salmon stocks within that river must decline pro rate in respect of the overall loss or damage to these essential facilities. Fish losses due to pollution, eutrophication or other means are relatively serious but remedial action can be taken by restocking from hatchery reared stock. However, if breeding and feeding grounds are lost, this is a permanent loss and has dire consequences to the potential productivity of the system.

WATER USE

POLLUTION

As the population of the country steadily increased and more new industries were established, it was the usual practice to site these developments close to the banks of a river and towns to house the work force soon followed. The main advantage of being close to the river was because it not only provided a ready source of water both for domestic supply and to produce power, but at the same time it provided an ideal means of disposing of effluent and other waste products cheaply and effectively.

Unfortunately, in the throes of the Industrial Revolution no one paused to think or concern themselves as to what consequences would result from these discharges to either the health of the river or that of fish stocks indigenous to the river.

Dams were often built totally or partially across the width of the river in order to divert water into lades leading to water wheels to create power for working machinery, or to meet other industrial requirements. Sometimes this water was returned to the river in its natural state, whilst at other times it was badly polluted or returned at a different temperature. Water was also required for domestic use and many other different purposes in industry and development. Therefore, rivers in the industrial belt were no longer looked on as a feature of beauty providing a valuable natural food resource, but instead just as a work horse or open sewer. Unfortunately, many of these waste products and effluents, comprising chemicals, heavy metals, dyes, etc., were extremely toxic to many species of fish, fish fauna and plant life indigenous to these rivers, and losses naturally occurred. Fish movement within the river systems was severely curtailed by the construction of weirs and dams, and also by diversions and abstractions. In particular it was the migratory species such as the salmon that were most affected.

In the upper catchment areas large towns were more an exception than the general rule, but these were built for the purpose of housing the work force for local industries, such as woollen mills, quarries, mines and, in some cases, distilleries. Further downstream, more diversified industries were founded and with them a vast increase in population, to be housed. It would be fair to say that the further downstream one got, the greater the problem became as a larger volume and variety of effluent was released into the rivers.

In many cases, navigable estuaries and sea ports were a favourite place to found intensive industries and in these areas pollution discharged and passed down river was increased by the tidal influence. With the tidal cycle backing up these estuaries twice daily, the effluent built up and often grew in strength because it was not allowed to flow away freely but was brought back up by the flow tide. In the worst cases, in major salmon rivers such as the Mersey, the Clyde, the Tyne and the Thames, migratory fish stocks were made virtually extinct for this very reason. Fish stocks either descending or ascending the river were poisoned or suffocated by the strength of the effluent, as they passed through these lethal zones.

In the 1860s in Scotland the Government at last realised the importance of salmon stocks and that these were under threat. Legislation was brought in which partially dealt with the problem of access. This was done by imposing strict legislation whereby each and every new or existing dam must have a fish pass incorporated in it.

It was not until many years later that there was a major attempt to clean up the river systems by stopping existing pollution and preventing further discharges of effluent into the rivers. At first this job was put into the hands of local authorities, then after the last war strong legislation was passed through Parliament. In Scotland, the Rivers (Prevention of

Polution) (Scotland) Act, 1951 was introduced. The powers of this Act were further strengthened by the Rivers (Prevention of Pollution) (Scotland) Act, 1964 and a decade later the 1951 and 1964 Acts were repealed and the Control of Pollution Act, 1974 replaced them. This Act has now been replaced by Schedule 23 of the Water Act, 1989. During this time, similar powers were granted to water authorities in England and Wales.

There is no doubt that the strengthening of the powers of purification authorities since the war has improved conditions in many rivers, but this did not come in time to prevent many rivers losing their valuable salmon stocks and others seeing their stocks seriously depleted. It is, however, very gratifying to note that since 1951 great strides forward have been made by purification authorities and pollution discharges are no longer the threat they were in the past. Rivers which have not been inhabited by salmon for very many years are now being cleaned up to such an extent that they can support this valuable species of fish once more. Rivers such as the Tyne, the Clyde and even the Thames, are now beginning to see a revival of these species and I have no doubt that many other rivers where salmon have been extinct for a hundred years or more will, before long, once more be frequented by *Salmo salar*.

WATER POWER AND ELECTRICITY GENERATION

Water has been used as a means of power for several generations, in the earlier days mainly to drive water wheels. However, once electricity became a known source of power, water was the obvious natural resource to generate and produce it. In the 1930s, the first major schemes of hydroelectric power were constructed and sited on major river systems. In order to achieve the most effect and generate the greatest amount of energy, impounding reservoirs were sited as high up a river's catchment as possible, to create the necessary head of water to drive the turbines. Following a slight pause during the second world war, by the 1960s many rivers and loch systems, mainly in Scotland but also throughout the UK, had been developed for this source of power. Valleys were flooded by the construction of large dams, loch systems were enlarged, and water was diverted by aqueduct from one catchment to another or from one area of a catchment to another. The main source of supply was, therefore, augmented by these diverted flows. Electricity was either generated by turbines sited in the main dam, or diverted from the main reservoir by a tunnel leading to the power station. Sometimes generated water is returned to its river of origin, whilst at other times it is diverted into a neighbouring river.

Where valleys were flooded out or loch levels raised, both spawning and feeding grounds lying within these newly flooded areas were immediately swamped and destroyed, being lost for ever. Diverted flows of water depleted the affected rivers of a significant part of their natural flow, and in most cases, completely changed their ecology; with water flow, water temperature and pH values all being subjected to change. Regulation of water flows to a lower and more constant level downstream of impounding dams not only changes that river's ecology but also the distribution of fish stocks within it.

Competition

In the flooded area upstream of the impounding dam the food within the reservoir, particularly in those areas which have been newly flooded, is significantly enhanced for the first few years after ithe initial immersion of fresh land, and is full of high protein fauna. As a direct result, therefore, freshwater species especially *Salmo trutta*, grow rapidly in size and multiply in number. As a result they require not only a much larger share of the available food supply, but also more spawning facilities. This often leads to them gaining predominance over all other freshwater fish on the nursery areas upstream of the dam, to the detriment of the *Salmo salar* population which migrate to and from these areas. As trout are amongst the many fish which predate on young salmon, this is another factor that can materially affect the strength of salmon stocks. This is mainly because once the food bloom checks and begins to deteriorate in the succeeding years after the initial flooding, many of the larger trout turn cannibal and instead of foraging for invertebrates take the easy way out and predate on other fish stocks.

Access into and out of the dam area

Once a dam is built, free access for migratory fish is impeded. Therefore, fish pass arrangements are required to allow them to ascend to their spawning grounds upstream of the dammed area. Unfortunately, however, the same old saying 'you can lead a horse to water, but that does not mean it will drink', often applies with regard to migratory fish ascending a river. You can provide what are thought to be the necessary facilities to enable them to ascend, but often due to some small discrepancy in the design, fish will shun these or not readily pass through, often choosing instead to remain in the section of the river below the dam. Even if they do ascend into the reservoir and eventually spawn upstream of the dam, there is no guarantee that those of their progeny that survive will find their way out of the flooded area as smolts on their downward migration. Problems that can occur in reservoirs for smolts trying to find the exit are due to lack of current flow through the reservoir, often leading to them being forced to follow landfall. This often entails a journey round the full circumference of the reservoir, with the added fear of being caught in shallow waters and predated on by cannibal trout: in some cases a hazardous journey of some 45 miles instead of 1 to 2 miles in relative safety, had they the current flow to guide them. In other cases, they may come to the entrance of the tunnel where water is diverted to the power station before reaching the exit, and spend precious time trying to force their way down this entrance through the screens which are placed there to prevent them from doing so. Or, if they are unlucky, they get pinned to these screens by suction and/or the force of water velocity, or else get drawn into the tunnel and passed through the turbines. Few, if any, stand a real chance of survival. Predatory trout and diving birds, such as cormorants and mergansers, are also a constant source of danger as the silvery smolts mill around the tunnel entrance mystified by their inability to continue on their outward bound journey. Those that do eventually reach the proper exit then go through the fish pass, compensation water sluice or the dam overspill virtually unharmed, and continue their migration downstream.

Due to the loss of spawning facilities and in some cases, impeded access, the distribution of spawning stocks on their return to fresh water is significantly altered. Those fish native to the spawning grounds which have been drowned out and therefore rendered useless together with fish which have been impeded from ascending to their native areas, have got to find alternative places in which to lay their eggs. Therefore, they have to turn to other areas to do so, but these sites are likely to be fully populated by their own native stock. The incomers are surplus to the area's capacity and, therefore, the spawning fords may become over-crowded. If this happens, over-cutting of spawning gravel in which eggs are already incubating may well take place, to the detriment of these eggs. Unfortunately, if over-cutting does occur it is usually at the expense of early run fish because they spawn first, with summer and autumn runs spawning approximately a fortnight later than each other.

WATER SUPPLY SCHEMES

In the case of the larger schemes where water is impounded and led by aqueduct from the reservoir to the point of supply, exactly the same problems apply as I have described in the previous paragraphs on hydro-electric power.

Another method of abstracting water is to take it directly from a watercourse or river, by diverting it into an intake set either in the river bank or on the bed of the river. It is then led by gravity or pumped by machinery to a treatment works close by, and thence distributed.

Problems can arise from young fish being drawn to or sucked into this intake. In the case of bank intakes, these can be a problem when high up a river catchment and close to a feeding area or during the smolt migration. Even with adequate screening the problem still arises with small fish being pinned to the screen by water velocity or suction, or drawn into the intake when the screen chokes with leaves, weed, grass and other heavier debris. Choking of screens by floating debris is a constant source of trouble, especially when small fish are present. To overcome this problem, in recent years intakes actually set in the bed of the river have become a popular method. Chambers are dug below river bed level and these are covered with screens of various sizes which are covered with clean gravel. The water is then drawn down through the gravel layer into the chambers by suction pump, and then piped to the treatment works. If perchance, the clean gravel screens choke with silt, they are cleaned by blowing water back through the chambers and up through the screens. This virtually safeguards fish stocks from any form of damage, and at the same time overcomes the problem of floating debris. There is no doubt that as far as salmon stocks are concerned, direct water abstraction through screen intakes set in the bed of a river goes a very long way towards alleviating damage from this source and is infinitely preferable to impounding schemes, which are fraught with different problems. This applies to water abstraction schemes for both domestic and industrial use.

OTHER ABSTRACTIONS

Apart from large public water supply schemes, there are also many small private schemes for various purposes, such as domestic supply, agricultural use, fish farms, private hydro-electric supply, etc. Although the volume of water abstracted by these schemes is relatively small, it can at times constitute a significant part of the low water flow of that tributary. Problems can, therefore arise concerning access and the fact that fish may be drawn to the intake and diverted away from their natural environment. During the smolt migration, any decrease of flow in the main watercourse may well entice fish into the intake. It is extremely difficult to screen this type of intake adequately, with fear of impeding the constant flow of water down the diversion channel and, in consequence, significant losses of fish can occur. At present the law covering screening of this type of abstraction is completely inadequate and must be considered as a grey area in the conservation of migratory species. With the use of old mill lades now being diversified for various other purposes, it is imperative that this loophole in fishery legislation is more clearly defined and better controlled, in order to reduce the unnecessary wastage of this valuable and vital component of salmon stocks.

Ground Water Supplies

A further source of water being exploited in the modern era, is ground water supply from the gravel sub-strata. In many cases this is tapped in river valleys some distance from the main river for many different purposes. The advantage of this source of supply is that it is of a more constant water temperature and is generally of high quality requiring little, if any, filtration. Even so, although it cannot be considered to be a direct abstraction from the river or watercourse close to it, it is in actual fact the river that is indirectly the source of supply and the river which will replenish the underground reservoirs if and when water is removed. As regards direct interference with fishery conservation it must be admitted there is none, apart from the fact that it further depletes the overall flow of that source. In times of drought, large scale abstraction of ground water from a river valley may amount to an appreciable overall loss in dry weather flow.

Pump Abstraction

In recent years, water engineers have been turning more and more to abstracting water from the main river much further downstream; in some cases, at a point just upstream of the tidal influence. Usually this water is either pumped out through intakes set in the river bed or through side intakes set into the bank of the river protected by band screens. Not only does this reduce the capital cost by not having to construct impounding dams or long aqueducts to lead the water close to the point of supply, it at the same time reduces damage to the most important aspects of salmon conservation. On the other hand, pumping and running costs can be appreciably higher. As far as salmon stocks are concerned, the lower down the river the abstraction point is sited, the less damage usually occurs because the water is left to flow down the course of the river in its natural state without any regulation, until it has virtually reached the estuary or sea. Therefore, damage to spawning and feeding areas is almost non-existent. Access is rarely impaired and the effect on angling is very small as it affects such a short stretch of the entire river system. Provided proper and comprehensive screening is devised at the intake, little if any damage can occur to either smolts or kelts descending or adults ascending. This also safeguards young salmonids if there are any close by. Therefore, salmon stocks overall are definitely better protected by this type of abstraction than any other method sited elsewhere on the catchment.

Irrigation

Another demand for water abstraction comes from crop irrigation. This is mainly practised in fertile arable plains close to the coast where crops are often short of water during the vital growing period. These irrigation plants are often placed on tributaries rather than the major river systems, and in times of low water flow such schemes can reduce the important feeder tributaries to unacceptably low levels, which can lead to serious fish losses and/or can impede fish movement within such watercourses. In either case, this can severely deplete salmon stocks in these usually important watercourses many of which have high pH values and, in consequence, are very productive.

RIVER DIVERSIONS

In the hydro-electric era, mainly of the 1940 to 1960 period, it was common practice to divert the headwater of one river into the neighbouring catchment of another. This was done in order to increase the volume of water in the catchment where the generating scheme was to be found thereby increasing the generating capacity of the scheme. This was achieved by constructing a small diversion dam on the river to be diverted and then tunnelling through the hillside at a point just upstream of the dam, to a point on the neighbouring catchment. The water then flowed from the head-pond created by the dam through the tunnel into the hydro exploited catchment next door.

It was also sometimes necessary to generate electricity at the site of the diversion dam in order to supply power to work the mechanism at the site. This was normally achieved by taking burns from below the diversion dam into an aqueduct, which led the water from the burns upstream to work the generators sited close to the entrance of the tunnel.

This type of work was naturally a costly operation and, therefore, when the diversions were constructed it was only worthwhile if an appreciable flow of water was diverted from the denuded river. Therefore, during times of high water and in spate flow, a very large percentage of the water flowing into watercourses above the point of abstraction was diverted down the tunnel, leaving only a very small flow to continue down the natural course of the river. This water was not only diverted during times of rainfall, but during the whole period in the spring and summer when snow was melting on the high catchment above the diversion. In these cases, there was usually no reservoir capacity above the diversion dam, that being the main reason why the compensation flows allocated to the river were much smaller than where an impounding reservoir was sited on a river. Because of the lack of reservoir capacity, freshet allowances, to be used at the discretion of fishery managers, could only be called upon during times of rainfall or snow melt on the catchment.

These water diversions were, therefore, much more damaging to salmon conservation in the denuded catchments than any water abstraction scheme for supply, or in the catchment which was actually being utilised, for the main generation.

The main problems concerning salmon stocks were

1. The diversion dam itself impeded free access, and usually required the installation of a fish pass.
2. The section of the river between the fish pass entrance and the point downstream where the first large tributary joined the river was drastically depleted when water was being diverted. If some of the burns downstream were taken back by aqueduct to above the diversion dam, this could extend the depleted section significantly – in some cases to several miles. Therefore, the only time this section could be ascended by salmon was either during dam overspill or when freshets were released down the river.
3. The loss of the river's natural spate flow from the diverted catchment, resulted in the river loosing its cleansing capacity below the point of diversion. The entire ecology of the river downstream was, therefore, liable to change.
4. Due to the loss of a substantial volume of the river's run-off from its high catchment area, the natural chemical metabolism of the river was altered. pH values in the river, particularly in cases where this run-off flowed from mountains containing minerals such as limestone were lowered appreciably, leaving the more acid run-off from the moorland catchment further downstream to be undiluted by the higher quality run-off from the upper catchment.
5. Water temperatures in the river downstream of the diversion were also liable to significantly higher levels due to the loss of the high catchment run-off, particularly during times of snow melt.
6. Any impeding of the fishes ascent of the dam or section of the river immediately below the dam inevitably resulted in spawning facilities upstream becoming under-populated. This often led to the feeding areas upstream of the dam being artificially propagated with fry at great expense.
7. During the smolt and pre-smolt parr migrations these fish were often drawn to the greater outflow from the head pond. This was usually the tunnel entrance, and these fish were, therefore, either held up in the head pond, or worse still, due to inadequate screening, diverted into the neighbouring catchment.

There are many cases where this type of water diversion has severely crippled salmon stocks in a river that was denuded of this valuable water. Undoubtedly, the worst case of all is that of the headwaters of the

Perthshire Garry, north of Calvine, alongside the main A.9 road. This productive tributary of the Tummel was virtually dried out by water diversions for approximately 8 miles of its length. Due to this, a fish stop to prevent salmon from entering this section of the river had to be placed across the full width of the river at the point of its confluence with the River Errochty, in order to prevent the fish becoming stranded.

This led to the salmon stocks native to this upper section of the Garry having to redistribute themselves either in the Errochty or in the Garry downstream of the fish stop: areas that may themselves have been fully populated. The Garry fish, therefore, would have been surplus stock on the spawning fords. Worse still, the productivity of any spawning and feeding facilities that existed upstream of the fish stop in the River Garry, was completely destroyed. No river system, no matter how large, can afford to lose such an extent of its breeding grounds without seriously reducing the overall productivity of the species.

CHAPTER FIVE

Fish Passes

For many years, in fact since 1868, in Scotland it has been an offence to impede the free ascent of salmon up a river system. Under Schedule G of the 1868 Salmon Fisheries (Scotland) Act, it was stipulated that a fish pass must be incorporated on every new or existing mill dam. Therefore, fish passes are by no means a new invention, and many have been in operation for a considerable number of years. In the same era, both the Government and owners of salmon fisheries were becoming more and more conscious of the value of salmon and, therefore, of the need not only to conserve the species but also to develop the salmon fisheries. During the latter half of the 1800s when labour was cheap, more river improvement works were undertaken than during any other period. High on the list of the improvement works undertaken at that time, were the easing of natural obstacles such as falls, or alternatively creating a bypass around these obstructions in order to allow salmon to populate areas upstream of them.

In those days the most favoured method of passing fish over a man-made obstruction such as a weir or dam, or around an impassable natural rock barrier, was to create a fish ladder or a pooled pass to make it easier for fish to ascend them. In either case, the idea was to lead fish over the weir or around the obstacle in gradual steps with short, vertical falls in between each step which were easy to ascend. The number of pools or steps that were required to achieve this objective depended entirely on the steepness and height of the incline which had to be overcome. In some cases, a series of wide steps of shallow depth, on the principle of a ladder, was quite sufficient, not only to dissipate the velocity of the water passing over the obstacle but also to ease the angle of incline enabling fish to pass over the dam or weir without the need to rest on their ascent. In other cases, either due to the steepness of the obstruction or the length of the incline, a proper pooled fish pass had to be created. Each pool of the pass required a dam sited at the tail of it, with a lowered notch set either to the side or in the centre of the dam, through which the water flowed from one pool into the next downstream. The fish could then swim or alternatively jump through these apertures as they ascended the pass. In these cases each pool had to be of sufficient length, width and depth not only to dissipate the velocity of the water flowing through the pool, but also to enable fish to lie at ease and rest if they needed to, before continuing their ascent.

In the past, these constructions were nearly always stone built and therefore being flexible lasted for a considerable period. Some of those built in the early part of the last century are still in perfect working order today. In the modern era, most of the ladders or pooled passes are now made of concrete and on occasions their smooth surface can cause problems in high water velocities, unless this is dissipated.

The siting and design of fish passes on weirs or small dams is vital to their success, as it is important that they are adequately served by water in all heights of river flow, particularly at low water flow. It is also vital that the entrance to the fish pass or ladder has sufficient flow through it to entice fish into the pass and that it discharges into a point in the river downstream where fish will be present. A holding pool downstream of the obstruction in the close proximity fo the entrance to the pass is essential, and few fish passes without this vital commodity work efficiently throughout the full range of river flow. Sometimes fish passes without clearly defined pools to still the water velocity, need to be baffled to enable fish to negotiate the fast flow, especially if this is over a smooth surface such as concrete.

The width of the pass is also an important factor, because if it is too wide it can be too sparsely watered and if too narrow it can become torrential. In Schedule G of the 1868 Act it was stipulated that the width of the pass should be correlated to the length of the weir or dam in question. This regulation was in itself one of the reasons why some fish passes failed to work properly, as inevitably, some passes were made too wide. In some cases, the fish passes are sited in the centre of the river, whilst others are sited at one side of the river or the other. There should be no hard and fast rule on this point as long as they are sited in the position that suits the configuration of the river upstream and downstream of the obstruction.

When insurmountable falls were bypassed by installing a pooled fish pass around the obstruction, it was necessary to form a weir across the river upstream of the falls, in order to divert water into the bypass channel once it had been constructed. In most cases it was necessary to have a sluice control on the intake to this channel, in order to regulate the flow of water passing down the fish pass. One of the best examples of this type of bypass, built of stone during the last century, is still working today on the River Carnie, a tributary of the River Fleet in Sutherland, which flows into the sea on the east coast between Golspie and Dornoch. This channel has between thirty and forty individual pools on its entire length, and follows a gully on the right bank of the river before bending back to join the river some distance upstream of the main sheer falls.

Since the turn of the century, however, much larger impounding dams have been constructed for both water supply and hydro-electric purposes all over the world. Many of these, unfortunately, have been sited on rivers inhabited by *Salmo salar*. Therefore, problems of allowing this species to ascend into and upstream of these reservoirs have been greatly increased. For many years engineers favoured the pooled fish pass principle to overcome this difficulty, as they quite rightly believed that this was the most natural method of leading fish up to and enabling them to ascend these obstructions. However, problems did arise in overcoming water level variation in the reservoirs behind these dams. Therefore, several sluiced apertures through the wall of the dam had to be provided through which water could flow to serve the fish pass and at the same time enable fish to make entry into the reservoir at any water level. Naturally, the higher the dam, the more costly and the more problematical this type of fish pass became both to devise and construct, as the siting of both the downstream entrance and upstream exit was often critical to either their success or failure. The engineers began to devise new types of fish passes in order to overcome these problems. Most of the development work on the new models was carried out in Scandinavia where high dams had been in vogue far earlier in the century than in most cases in this country. As a result of this work two completely new designs of fish pass were put into use. Firstly, the Denyl Pass: this type was designed to pass fish up and over a dam at a fairly steep angle. It was in the form of a narrow shute, with retaining walls on either side, heavily baffled with either wooden batterns or bars made of concrete placed in slots between the two concrete walls in the shape of a cross. A notch in these baffles where they met in the centre made an aperture through which fish could pass as they made their ascent. This pass was remarkably successful on steep, short inclines which debarred the free passage of fish. If perchance it was a high structure which had to be overcome, a holding pool, or pools, was generally incorporated in the system, so that fish could run up one section then rest in a holding pool before making their ascent of the next section, and so on. Although this type of pass is commonly used on high dams in Scandinavia, as far as I can ascertain, it has not been used on hydro-electric or water supply schemes in this country. It has, however, been used on steep weirs and similar situations with success.

Second is the Borland-type fish pass, again designed by a Scandinavian. This is a completely different mode of fish pass, worked on an entirely new principle, comparable with a lift except there is no moving machinery involved – apart from sluice controls. It is a vertical shaft set into the dam face with apertures opening from the shaft into the reservoir at, or just below, water level. A sluice gate at ground level connects the shaft to the river flow. Water passes out of the reservoir and down the shaft and if the pass is set on the ascending cycle, the water passes out of

Intake to the fish pass on the River Carnie in Sutherland.

Pools on the second stage of the Carnie fish pass.

The weir on the river Carnie which diverts water down the fish pass.

The sheer falls, by-passed by the Carnie fish pass.

the ground sluice into the river. This is in order to draw salmon into the shaft or fish pass. Once they are in the pool at the bottom of the shaft the ground sluice is closed and the shaft flooded to reservoir level so that the fish can then swim out of the shaft into the reservoir. Similarly, when set on the descending cycle, smolts or kelts can swim out of the reservoir into the flooded shaft, the reservoir sluice is then shut and the ground sluice opened gradually to enable the shaft to empty and the fish to swim into the river. When this cycle has been completed, the pass is then switched over to the ascending cycle and the process repeated. It is usual for each cycle to take four hours to complete; both cycles therefore can be worked three times daily. In principle it is very simple and probably causes less stress to the fish, but having said that, it is unnatural and inevitably some fish behave uncharacteristically when they are faced with this procedure. For instance, when the shaft is flooded on the ascending cycle, once the water level in the reservoir is reached, some fish will not move out of the shaft, whilst others will. Again, some of these, having entered the reservoir, merely turn round and swim back into the shaft, rather akin to children playing in a lift. Often this type of problem can be cured by flooding the shaft to two to three feet below water level in the reservoir, so that they have to jump out of the shaft over small artificial falls into the reservoir. There are still some, however, that refuse to go out and merely go back down when the cycle changes. Another weakness with this principle is that the flow through the fish pass is usually inferior to that being released from the reservoir down the river, as compensation or freshet flow, therefore, in many cases the fish are drawn to the greater flow and waste much time and energy fruitlessly trying to ascend the dam by that means. Sometimes the fish give up and fall back downstream, whilst at other times they eventually try the inferior flow and find the shaft. Whether or not they use it properly having found it, is another question.

This type of pass was adopted by the Hydro Board in this country and was installed on many of their hydro schemes in the 1950 to 1965 era. Some of these work adequately, but others, either badly sited or lacking a holding pool immediately downstream, are unfortunately not working as well as they should.

In more recent years, few if any high dams with fish pass arrangements incorporated in them have been built in the UK. However, some small barrages and weirs have been built, mainly for water supply schemes. Although most of these are not high obstructions, in most cases they do require fish pass arrangements. In some cases the pooled pass system is still preferred, but there have also been innovations such as a moveable top pool. This is hydraulically operated and can be raised or lowered according to the height of water in the reservoir upstream of the barrage. The water flows into the metal tank and thence through an aperture wide

The entrance to a Borland fish pass on the right.

The diversion dam at Lairg, with Borland fish pass in the foreground.

enough to enable fish to ascend through it into the pool below, and thence down the rest of the pass. The pool below the adjustable tank has sluice controls at the tail of it so that if the tank is raised, the water level in the pool below is increased thereby reducing the distance fish have to jump from the pool into the tank, and then from the tank into the reservoir. This ingenious mechanical pass has worked satisfactorily.

FALLS

Easing of falls to allow fish to negotiate either difficult or impassable natural rock barriers is an interesting subject. Sometimes it can be done relatively easily, whilst at other times it is virtually impossible. When fish cannot swim through the cascades, there is no other method of ascent than jumping the obstuction. Therefore, the point of take-off is the most vital aspect. If the current flow is streaming away from the fish's tail, he does not have the same purchase to gather power for his jump when he coils his tail and thrusts. However, if there is a wave wall or backwater coming upstream at the point of take-off, there is a much greater degree of resistance when he makes his thrust, which enables the fish to jump a greater height and distance: in exactly the same manner as a sprinter gleans from starting blocks. In some cases it is possible to make a significant improvement to a fish's ability to negotiate falls merely be creating this type of situation. This can be done by placing a large boulder or other obstruction some little distance downstream from where the fish will take off, in order to turn the water at that point back towards the falls and thus create the necessary resistance to increase the purchase for the fish to exploit as it jumps.

Sometimes it is a thin curtain of water spilling over the rock face and falling on to the actual place where fish have to take off from in order to leap the falls that impedes their ascent, because this completely curtails their vision and they are unwilling to jump when they cannot see what is behind the veil of water. Not only are they unable to see the height of the obstruction in front of them, but they cannot see the direction in which the main flow of water is passing over the falls. Often this is caused by water being diverted from the main flow down minor channels and fissures in the rock formation some distance upstream of where the main flow of water cascades over the rock face. It is sometimes possible to divert this water by blocking the entrance to the side channels and concentrating the entire flow into the main course. On occasions it is one little runnel that is responsible for causing the problem while at other times it is two or three, but as fish can only jump falls that cannot be bypassed at certain water flows, the remedial action only needs to be effective over the range of flow that fish can ascend. In many cases a few sand bags placed at strategic points on the runnels solves the problem. One typical example of this is on the Glencalvie falls on the River Carron, which flows into the Kyle of Sutherland. On this falls a curtain of water comes in from the right hand side and drops into the mouth of the shute which fish have to jump and pass through. Whilst this is allowed to happen no fish will ascend, but as soon as this side flow is cut off fish will readily ascend this difficult barrier without trouble.

Another method of easing the salmon's ascent over falls is to raise the level of water in the main pool, or in some cases the part of the main pool which fish have to jump out of to ascend. This means heightening or restricting the actual bar of the pool, or bar of the upper section of the pool, in order to well back and raise the water level in the pool immediately downstream of the obstruction, and thereby reduce the height fish have to jump to be able to ascend. Again, this influence needs only to be effective over the range of flow that fish could negotiate the falls. Therefore, in higher flows the water does not need to be contained. On occasions, particularly on the smaller watercourse, this can be relatively easy to achieve; on other sites, however, it is a major engineering exercise. Of course, all must depend on the advantage that would be gained by populating the area upstream of the obstacle.

Finally is the matter of easing falls by blasting rock with explosives or by other means. This type of remedial work is fraught with problems, but can be successful on certain occasions. At times it is not the actual rock face which poses the problem but instead how the water is dispersed as it flows over the falls. It is possible, by concentrating the flow to one side or other of the falls, for them to become ascendable over a certain range of water flow. This means that these works need to be carried out some distance upstream of the obstruction. there are situations when this can be achieved by lowering one or two rock ledges which are deflecting and dispersing the flow as it approaches the crest of the falls, and thereby allowing the current to flow over the falls in a more concentrated form. Normally this type of operation can be carried out without fear of aggravating the situation.

However, when it actually comes down to easing the face of the fall itself and re-styling it, the operation becomes far more difficult and fraught with complications. It is not always an inevitable failure, and there have definitely been some successful cases, but there have also been many failures. It must, at the best, be termed a risky business and it is wise only to carry out these works as a last resort when the falls in question is completely impassable in its present state, in which case no harm is done. If it is carried out with the idea of improving access over a falls which can already be ascended, there is always a chance that matters could be made worse.

The main problem of course is fissures and cracks (many of which are invisible) remaining in the rock face after the works are completed. These can, through time, be exploited by water force or as a result of hard frost and weathering in the winter and cause further rock fall sometime in the future. Much, therefore, depends on the type of rock of which the barrier is comprised. There is also the threat that the actual operation is not successful with either too little or too much rock being removed, thereby marring the intent.

CHAPTER SIX

Hatcheries

Since the turn of the century, many private estates and some district fishery boards have run their own hatcheries for propagating salmon stocks, whilst other estates have commissioned commercial hatcheries to hatch out salmon ova and provide fry for planting out in their rivers. Nowadays, there are few river authorities in England and Wales, and district fishery boards in Scotland, which do not run their own hatchery facilities, and in the case of areas where no properly constituted fishery board exists, some river owners run their own hatcheries.

Certainly in Scotland, most of the hatcheries are only capable of incubating eggs to the eyed ova or fry stage and few, if any, have the facilities for rearing on fish to the parr or smolt stage. Some of these hatcheries rely on spring water as their main source of supply, and this can be augmented by water taken directly from hill burns; whilst others are supplied entirely by burn or river water. In the latter case, this source of water is usually passed through a filtration system in order to remove any silt, sand or other foreign bodies before it enters the hatchery. Ground water sources are also favoured for hatchery purposes, and like spring water these require very little, if any, filtration. Another advantage is that both these sources keep a far more constant water temperature throughout the hatching period than burn water supply, which can vary considerably according to climatic conditions prevailing throughout the winter and spring months.

In order to stock the hatcheries, adult fish are netted in the rivers once the rod fishing season has closed, and then held in holding pens until they are ripe for stripping. When the hens are ripe they are stripped, the eggs being run off into a pail. Milt is then stripped from the cock into the same pail, and mixed with the eggs to fertilise them. The eggs are then transported to the hatchery and spread out evenly in trays with water percolating over them. They are left undisturbed in the trays whilst they incubate, as at this stage they are very fragile.

They are inspected frequently during this period and any dead eggs are carefully removed with tweezers. If any sign of fungus appears on the eggs

The lay-out inside a salmon hatchery.

Young salmon fry in a hatchery tank.

Working on eggs in the Ardgay salmon hatchery.

A plastic tank for holding brood fish.

Holding tanks at a hatchery.

they are washed with malacite green to check this fungal growth. In other cases, if silt deposits begin to build up in the trays, then the eggs require washing in order to remove this. Once the eye of the little fish can be clearly seen through the shell of the egg they are far more robust and can be handled without fear of harm. Eyed ova for sale or planting out at this stage are then removed from the hatchery. The remainder of the eyed ova are then reared on to the fry stage in the hatchery before being planted out.

If they are to be carried on to either the parr or smolt stage, they are removed from the hatchery troughs, and reared on in tanks or ponds.

With the sudden escalation of salmon farming on the west coast of Scotland during the late 1970s and throughout the 1980s, the number of commercial hatcheries for rearing salmon increased tremendously. Most fish farmers who reared salmon in sea cages on the west coast sea lochs began to propagate their own stocks and establish hatcheries and tank farms to incubate their own eggs and rear on their fry to smolt stage. There has been, however, throughout this period a constant demand from these salmon farmers for wild eggs in order to establish discrete stocks from many famous rivers throughout the country.

The main aim is to hatch out the fry and get them on to their first feeding period early, so that they can be reared on to smolt stage in the first year: they are then put in sea cages as one year smolts. In order to achieve this, they have to be constantly graded throughout the parr stage; those that are slow to develop are surplus to the farmer's needs. This has resulted in fed fry and autumn parr being made readily available for re-stocking river systems at a very low price for anyone wishing to take advantage of this surplus. Nowadays, it is extremely likely that there will be a large surplus of eggs from this source.

Although most wild-salmon fishery managers do not approve of stocking rivers with the progeny of farmed stock, there is no doubt that if disaster did strike wild stocks in the form of some disease or pollution incident, there is a ready source of supply available for re-stocking purposes, not only eggs but all ages of fry, parr and smolt.

CHAPTER SEVEN

Artificial Propagation

For several centuries now, experiments have been carried out regarding artificial propagation of salmon stocks, by hatching out salmon eggs in hatcheries and then planting out the progeny at different ages of their freshwater feeding life, or at the eyed-ova stage. Whether, up to the turn of the last century artificial propagation was necessary in the first place, or even led to an increase in salmon stocks must remain in some doubt, as in those days the natural environment of most of our salmon rivers remained, on the whole, almost completely unblemished. These rivers were more than capable of self-propagation from the native stock of the river, and could almost undoubtedly produce as many fry and parr as the river system was capable of supporting to smolt stage. Only if these reared fish were planted out into areas of the catchment or river systems that were previously uninhabited by salmon would there likely be any real advantage and in most cases it is doubtful whether in those days sufficient reared fish were available to found a worthwhile stock, even in such areas.

However, things have changed since the early part of the last century, mainly due to mankind's avid desire not only to improve his standard of living but also make the fullest use of natural resources. Land and water were naturally two of the first he turned to: water, both as a source of energy and a means of removing waste effluent; and land, to improve its fertility and productivity and also, to make drastic changes in its use.

Where these activities affected salmon producing rivers there were wide repercussions both concerning water quality and quantity; siltation levels, and access, to name two of the related problems which affected the regeneration, health and migration of salmon.

Artificial propagation of salmon has, therefore, come more into vogue since the turn of this century. In recent years, due to added pressures in these fields and also due to exploitation of salmon stocks by high seas netting, increase in the seal population and other predators, together with the more sophisticated methods of commercialised poaching, the need for artificial propagation is often required to bolster stocks. It would be fair to say that without the aid of hatchery stock to help strengthen natural regeneration, some river systems, or certain parts of their catchment,

A smolt trap on the Gruidie Burn in Sutherland, with catch box on the left by the steps.

A smolt trap showing catch channel below fibre glass slides.

would be unlikely to produce the stock of fry, parr and smolts which is required to found an adequate stock of salmon returning to the rivers.

Haphazard restocking can, however, be just as detrimental as beneficial, because if an already fully populated area is propagated with fry, then almost certainly there will be too many mouths to feed on the limited food supply available in that particular section, leading to overcrowding on the nursery areas. Therefore, it is the under-populated areas which should be concentrated on when planting operations are planned. These can be identified by taking redd counts after the spawning season is over, to determine the number of fish that have spawned in the area. If redd counts are taken annually and records kept, underpopulated fords can easily be identified. Sampling feeding areas by electro shocking experiments on the nursery areas of the main river or its tributary burns, is another modern method of ascertaining fry and parr densities on these sectors. It is then possible, after analysing the results, to identify the under-populated areas.

In some cases, there may be an obvious reason for areas being under-populated, such as fish pass failure on hydro or water supply schemes, pollution incidents, poison poaching attacks, or landslips leading to erosion, to mention a few of the more common causes for stocks declining. These areas can then be earmarked as being in need of artificial propagation, in order to help stem this decline.

In recent years, experiments have been carried out to utilise sections of the catchment upstream of impassable rock barriers, areas that had never previously been populated by the species, by planting these feeding areas with young salmon. In some cases, the feeding grounds were first prepared prior to planting by removing other freshwater fish, such as small trout or eels from the burns, by either electro fishing or other means. This was in order to reduce the number of fish which would compete with the planted stock for the limited food supply available there. In other cases, large numbers were planted in order that, hopefully, some would survive in the face of competition from the other indigenous species native to the tributaries, and in the end the salmon would gain predominance. Monitoring exercises carried out after these plantings both by electro-fishing and trapping, in the Kyle of Sutherland area, have proved that these operations have been successful.

On one of the tributary burns, the Grudie, on the River Shin catchment, which has always been, and still is, debarred to salmon because of an impassable fall, the nursery areas were prepared for planting in 1972, and first planted in 1973. All descending smolts during the spring migration (March to July) were trapped and counted each year. Only in 1979 was the trap worked throughout the period March to December.

The table below shows the number of fry or ova planted and the number of smolts trapped and counted annually in the spring.

	No. and type of fry planted		*Smolts trapped*	
1972	Prepared for planting, but no fish planted			
1973	50,000	fed fry		
1974	200,000	unfed fry		
1975	250,000	unfed fry	4,040	
1976	226,400	unfed fry	1,756	
1977	208,000	unfed fry	4,500	
1978	215,000	unfed fry	4,010	
1979	248,000	unfed fry	5,598	In 1979 the autumn migration was also trapped and approx. a third of this figure were pre-smolt parr
1980	250,000	unfed fry	3,718	
1981	500,000	eyed ova	3,295	
1982	527,000	eyed ova	3,063	
1983	150,000	unfed fry	3,026	
	200,000	eyed ova	1,540	
1984	250,000	unfed fry	1,136	
1985	250,000	unfed fry	3,185	
1986	250,000	unfed fry	3,027	
1987	345,000	unfed fry	3,326	
1988	250,000	unfed fry	3,917	
1989	250,000			

Samples of smolt scales were taken to find out their age class in four of these years.

	Sample size	*1 year*	*2 years*	*3 years*	*4 years*
1980	36	6	30	–	–
1981	37	1	8	24	4
1982	40	1	13	24	2
1983	153	11	23	111	8

By opening up these unpopulated areas to the salmon, not only is the precious feeding potential of these tributaries utilised more efficiently, but the overall productivity of salmon stocks in the river increase pro rata.

There are two main questions regarding restocking. Firstly, at what stage should the progeny be introduced to the river system from the hatchery in order to gain the best results, and secondly, what stock should be used.

Before trying to answer the first question, it is best to explain the different choices available.

1. To rear the eggs in a hatchery until the ova reaches the eyed stage. They can then be moved from the hatchery to gravelly sections of

Full view of smolt trap.

Young salmon fry in a plastic bag ready to be planted out.

the river or its tributaries, and placed in artificial redds under the surface of open, unsilted gravel or placed in plastic boxes with vents to allow the water to percolate through the boxes. Then the box, known as a 'Vibert' after the Frenchman who invented it, is covered with gravel. One of the best ways to make an artificial redd is to use an old zinc washing pail without a bottom and place this in the bed of a shallow gravel ford, thereby stemming the flow of water over the gravel and partially drying out the section where the eggs are to be planted. A groove some six inches deep can be made in the gravel bed, and then several thousand eggs can be planted in the groove without any problem, covered over, and once the pail is removed they are inundated by water, safe under their layer of gravel.

2. When the alevins have absorbed or partially absorbed their yolk sac, they are then known as fry and are ready to be planted out as what are termed unfed fry. The modern method of transporting them to the section of the river where they are to be released, is to fill a strong plastic bag of approximately 18 inches by 15 inches about a third full of water and give this a whiff of oxygen out of a bottle of SO_2. Then syphon about 2,000 fry by hose-pipe from their trough in the hatchery into the bag. The bag is partially closed, and the nozzle of the oxygen cylinder is placed once again into the water for a few seconds, and oxygen is released. The neck of the bag is then tightly closed, doubled over and sealed with two strong rubber rings. It is then placed in a canvas bag, and fitted into a sectional wooden box for transportation, by car, Landrover or Argo machine, depending on how accessible the chosen planting area is. Fry will survive up to eight hours in these bags or even longer, so they can be planted many miles away from the hatchery without any fear for their safety. Each bag can then be spread out evenly, over a fifty yard section of the feeding area, and the planter can move on whatever distance is necessary to the next site where one or maybe two more bags are released. Even the most outlandish parts of the catchment can be propagated by this means.

This method is infinitely preferable to the older one, whereby several hundred thousand fry were placed in a large five gallon urn, and released in waters in the close proximity of the hatchery. Very often the entire urn full of fry was released, or in real terms 'dumped' in the one spot, and allowed to spread out over the feeding area with the aid of current flow. This naturally, at times, led to severe overcrowding. However, in those days the lack of four-wheel drive vehicles or hill machines confined stocking operations to areas within a few hundred metres of a road or track that was easily accessible to transport. The urn was carried down to the nursery area by hand.

3. Once the alevins had turned into fry in the hatchery, they were fed

Fry in plastic bags placed in their carriers for transportation.

on – either for a few weeks to allow the food bloom in the river to develop fully so that there was a plentiful supply available for them, or for longer periods. In the past, this was a common practice because, as many hatcheries were supplied by spring water, fry often hatched out in the hatchery before the food bloom in the colder upper catchment areas had developed and, therefore, the feeding areas would not have been able to support them. Fry were then spread out in larger, wooden troughs and fed on either minced liver or ground hard boiled eggs. Nowadays batches of fry are, on occasions, taken through their first feeding period in troughs in the hatchery and then moved into large circular tanks either in a tank farm within the hatchery complex – outside, or within a building, and reared on to the required size. These little fish are fed by automatic feeders on some of the many specialised dry fish-foods now readily available on the market. They are then planted out on the nursery areas of the river system. Transportation is carried out in the same manner as for unfed fry, or they are taken in a tank on a lorry to an accessable feeding area and then merely netted out of the tank into the watercourse.

4. Fry are reared on for much longer periods in tank farms or rearing ponds, and are then transported to their feeding areas when they are two inches or more in length. In the past, these would have been termed fingerlings, but now they are more commonly referred to as 0+, 1+ or 2+ parr, according to their age group. In the past, few hatcheries reared salmon on to these stages prior to release, but it was common practice to rear trout for restocking purposes on to much larger varying sizes, for 'put and take' fisheries.
5. Fry are reared on to the actual smolt stage in tanks or ponds before release to their wild environment in the river systems. In the past this type of restocking (apart from experimental purposes) was practically unheard of and even today it is not common practice in this country, unless these are purchased from commercial fish farms. It is, however, more widely practised in certain other countries, such as Iceland. Smolts are released in various parts of the river system and some experimental releases have taken place as low down a river system as just upstream of the tidal influence in that river. It is considered to be an advantage if these smolts have been reared in a hatchery (from the fry stage) which is supplied by water fed from the catchment of the actual river in which they are to be released. This is in order that the chemical metabolism of that river is imprinted on their systems.

There are many schools of thought on which of these five alternative means of restocking rivers produce the best results, but really in the long run it is almost inevitably economics which determines the method

Henry Morrice loading fry into bags in the hatchery.

Pens to hold brood fish until they are ripe to strip.

The Gruidie smolt trap, with catch box on the right.

finally adopted. There is no doubt that in the not too distant future, scientific evidence will be available to give us guidance on this matter. This is mainly because of the recent invention of the micro-tag which can be implanted in the nose of small fish without either harming or encumbering them. Samples of these tagged fish can be easily monitored, during all phases of their freshwater feeding life; migration as smolts; if captured at sea; and on their return to the river.

There is no doubt that at present the most favoured method concerning wild salmon stocks, is to plant unfed fry with eyed-ova and fed fry the next in line. Planting of parr is not usually favoured mainly due to the expense of feeding the fish to that age, and the cost of equipping the hatchery complex to make this possible. The same applied to carrying fish on to the smolt stage before release.

I do not think there is anyone in the industry who does not acknowledge that the losses incurred in planting eyed-ova, fry and fed fry, compared with the small proportion which actually survive and go to sea as smolts, is extremely wasteful. At least those that do survive to migrate are strong healthy fish, reared naturally instead of being force fed, and are well used to the natural environment of their native river and its chemical metabolism: one can then expect a reasonable return to ensue. No one can possibly deny that those reared on in a hatchery complex to parr or smolt stage are stronger and the wastage in their early life radically reduced. This is largely because losses from predation and starvation in their early life are much reduced and barely exist. Any intensive rearing of livestock must carry with it an increased risk of disease over those reared in the wild.

The problem with rearing on hatchery stock to the parr stage is that it is unclear at present whether this interferes with their physique, their smolting times, their behaviour at sea, when they mature, and their homing instincts, all of which it is reasonable to suppose must play a vital role in establishing which component of the annual river stock they comprise, on their return to freshwater. Provided they continue to feed once they are released to the wild, it would be logical to suppose that these reared fish would smolt earlier than they would have done had they been subjected to natural conditions from the alevin stage, but do they feed on? Or, are they subjected to a severe check in growth rate when no longer artificially fed, or do they even die of starvation? Or, are they more likely to mature early and return as grilse? Or, will they return as multi sea-winter fish? These are just some of the imponderables that are at present unclear, and will not be established until more scientific evidence is available. It seems to be a fact that the older wild parr are when they smolt, then the more likely they are to return as multi sea-winter fish. That is why parr from the higher catchment and less productive nursery areas are usually of older age groups than those lower down the river system, bred and reared where feeding periods are generally longer and the food supply more plentiful. It is, therefore, highly probable that this may in itself be an important factor, largely or partially determining the strength of the different winter, spring, summer and autumn runs when they return to freshwater. Therefore, the natural staggering of the different runs of fish is another aspect which could well be interfered with, if large numbers of fry were reared on, or even planted out at an early age. It is also possible that certain types of artificial propagation of river systems are at least partially responsible for the increase in the numbers of grilse. Therefore, the sooner more money is spent on research projects to try and find the real answers to many of these difficult questions, the more likely we are to be properly guided on the problems with which we are now faced, and the sooner malpractices can be corrected – if they exist.

The next million-dollar question is, what origin of fish stocks should be used, if re-stocking programmes are to be mounted, and deemed necessary? There is little doubt that if it is feasible, stocks indigenous to that river are preferable. But having accepted that fact, if the stocks are depleted to a serious extent, is it wise to rob Peter to pay Paul, in other words take brood stock from the under-populated river to restock that river, or should the depleted stock be left strictly alone to spawn naturally and stock from other rivers brought in to augment that of the under-populated river?

There are really only four choices open when stock failure occurs.

1. Hope that there is sufficient stock left to regenerate salmon stocks and stem the decline naturally without taking any remedial action.
2. Breed from the native depleted stock.
3. Bring in fish from neighbouring rivers or a river with similar characteristics.
4. Bring in ova or fry from any wild source.

There are really two schools of thought concerning this important matter. The first firmly believe that you must only restock from indigenous stock native to their own river, basing their argument firmly on the theory that the stock of each river has its own individual genetic strain best suited to that particular environment and, therefore, if you mix these stocks you may dilute the genetic build up of the native stock, thereby polluting vital characteristics of that stock.

The other school believe that if a river's stock is depleted to such an extent that it is in need of augmenting, then it is better to introduce stock from other rivers rather than let the depleted stock decline even further. Provided the stock is taken from a river with similar characteristics and one that has similar seasonal runs of salmon, they believe that by introducing stocks it is possible to strengthen runs, pointing out that it is extremely likely that salmon stocks can suffer from in-breeding the same as any other species of living creatures. Also arguing, that in the larger

Fishing a smolt out of the catch box at the Gruidie smolt trap.

The smolt trap on the Gruidie Burn, Sutherland.

Good wild smolts caught in the Gruidie trap.

river systems such as the Tweed, Tay and Wye, it is possible that some of their major tributaries, together with different parts of the catchment of the main river, may well have several different separate genetic strains native to those areas. These strains, intermingling on their ascent of the rivers, may well pair up and then cross-breed with a mate having different genetic characteristics under natural conditions in the river, and this has probably been happening for centuries. In consequence even if rivers are propagated with indigenous stock native to that river, there is still a real possibility that different genetic strains will be mixed on a larger scale.

It is really quite impossible to hazard a guess as to who is right and who is wrong regarding the fact that separate genetic strains are all important to a particular environment. Although scientific research is at present being undertaken to try and establish guidance on this very complex issue, because of the reasonably long life cycle of the species, it may be an appreciable time yet before we know the real answer.

CHAPTER EIGHT

Tagging

For very many years, scientists and fishery managers have been carrying out experiments both to try and track the movements of salmon and positively prove that salmon do return to their native rivers after migrating to sea as smolts. In order to achieve this aim they have attached various types of markings to different parts of the body of parr, smolts or even adult fish, in order that they can be identified at a later date.

The earliest experiment was recorded by Isaac Walton in 1653, when he claimed that it had already been established that salmon did have the homing instinct to return to their river of origin by 'tying a riband or some tape or thread in the tail of smolts and catching them again when they came back to the same place usually six months after'. However, many years later the world's first serious attempt to tag fish was undertaken by P. D. H. Malloch, near Perth on the River Tay, during the first few years of this century.

Since then, especially after the Second World War, large numbers of smolts both wild and hatchery reared, have been marked and released in many countries where *Salmo salar* is an indigenous species. Many different forms of markings have been used from fin clipping to various types of metal and plastic tags attached by silver wire threaded through the skin on the fish's back or through the muscle at the base of a fin. More recently, scientists have invented a very small tag which is placed in the nose of the fish: this is now recognised as one of the most efficient ways of tagging small fish. These tags can be inserted at a much earlier stage of the parr's life without harming the little fish. It is, however, a more costly exercise and requires special equipment to identify fish tagged by this means on their return to freshwater.

For very many years these small fish were tagged at the smolt stage and, particularly in the early years of the experiments, significant losses occurred shortly after the fish were tagged, mainly because they were damaged during the handling and actual tagging operation. Many of these losses were due to damage to their guanine coating, which at this stage is still wet and, therefore, was very easily rubbed off the smolt's skin when they wriggled and squirmed as they were being held tightly whilst the tag was inserted. It was, therefore, very difficult to assess the percentage return to the adult stage because of these losses, although the fact that they did return to their native river was positively established. In the present day the whole operation is carried out far more scientifically. The smolts are trapped on their outward migration in a well constructed trap set on certain feeder tributaries, the smolts are then hand-netted and placed in a bath containing a mild form of anaesthetic. Once they are unconscious, they are lifted out of the bath, tagged, and then placed in another bath of fresh water to recover. Then, having regained consciousness, they are released downstream of the trap, virtually unharmed having seldom, if ever, been in contact with the human hand. Losses are much reduced as the fish are neither subjected to stress nor is their silver livery damaged in any way.

In the United Kingdom, one of the rivers where salmon stocks are monitored most carefully, is the north Esk, where the Department of Agriculture and Fisheries Fresh Water Research Department, have a field centre. The trap is set up on the Kinnaber lade, a by-pass channel which used to divert water from the main river, just north of Montrose. A significant number of both salmon and seatrout smolts descending are tagged, a proportion of which are measured and scaled, so that their age class and growth rate can be recorded. Similarly, a proportion of salmon, grilse and seatrout ascending are trapped and have scales taken, so that their age class can be recorded, and if they happen to have been tagged previously as they migrated as smolts, much interesting information regarding their growth-rate and time spent at sea is assimilated and analysed. For very many years, the officer in charge of this station was W. Shearer, one of the most knowledgeable scientists in this field.

On the same river, just upstream of Morphy Dyke, the Department of Agriculture and Fisheries have constructed one of the most comprehensive fish counters so far in operation in the UK across the entire width of the river. This fish counter monitors and records salmon stocks ascending the river throughout each twenty-four hour period during the year. This is an integral and essential part of the intensive research programme which is carried out on this important salmon river to quantify outward smolt migrations in comparison with returning adults.

Fish counters are also in operation in England on rivers such as the Test and the Itchen. It is hoped to extend the use of fish counters as a means of monitoring and counting runs of fish ascending many more rivers in the UK. These are, however, very expensive to construct, run and maintain, especially on the larger river systems, but the information that can be assimilated as a result of counting fish in and out of rivers is invaluable for salmon fishery management purposes.

Another field research station in Scotland is sited on a tributary of the Aberdeenshire Dee, the Girnock Burn. All fish ascending into or descending from the section of the burn upstream of the trap are recorded. This has enabled scientists to assess the productivity of this burn for a considerable period of time. It is interesting to note that regardless of the number of adult fish which propagate this spawning area annually, the numbers of smolts and parr descending seldom varies keeping to a reasonably constant figure. This is obviously the density that this nursery is capable of sustaining and supporting. Whether or not, when there is a surplus of adult spawners, this in itself alters the usual balance of the various seasonal components of the overall salmon stock must remain unclear.

From data gleaned from these trapping experiments on the Girnock Burn it seems clear that in years when there have been a dearth of adults spawning the numbers of smolts and parr descending do not show any marked decline in subsequent years. It would seem, therefore, that when there is a failure of any particular age class due to some reason or other, this species has the ability to recruit stock from other age groups to make up for this deficiency. This is probably due to the fact that if one age group fails, there is more food available for the younger age groups to exploit; therefore a proportion of these will reach smolt stage earlier than they would otherwise have done if their feeding area had been fully populated with regular age groups.

In England and Wales there are no similar field research stations on rivers to monitor fish stocks on the same scale as those I have mentioned in Scotland, but in Southern Ireland there are several intensive research stations monitoring both ascending and descending salmon and seatrout stocks. In some cases, all fish ascending and descending are trapped, counted and the information assimilated.

Other tagging experiments of both wild and hatchery reared smolts have enabled scientists to estimate the percentage of both varieties that can be expected to return as adults. This has shown an expectancy of between 8 per cent and 10 per cent in the case of wild and a much lower figure, 1 per cent to 3 per cent in the case of reared smolts. There does not seem to be any definite information as to whether the homing instinct of the wild smolt is appreciably more accurate than that of the reared smolt. However, it must be admitted that those actually tagged in these experiments may not have been large enough samples to determine this last point accurately.

With commercial net and long-line fisheries being opened on some of the salmon's feeding grounds at sea, and interceptory drift net fisheries being exercised to exploit salmon stocks on their homeward migration between their feeding grounds at sea and their rivers of origin, it was deemed essential to trace where fish caught in these fisheries originated from or were destined for. It was decided, therefore, to carry out scientific tagging experiments to determine this essential information. Teams of fishery scientists from many nations carried out these experiments off the west coast of Greenland in the early 1960s, in the long line fishery in the Norwegian sea in the mid-1960s, in the long line fishery off the Faroes in the 1970s and in the north east coast of England drift net fishery in the late 1970s and early 1980s. In all cases, the scientists went aboard vessels fishing in these areas, tagged fish caught in the fishery and then released them back into the sea. Many of the fish tagged in the Greenland drift net fishery and the two long line fisheries were recaptured in rivers in North America, Scandinavia, several countries in Europe and in the sea off their coasts; whereas those caught in the north-east coast drift net fishery were recaptured in the estuaries or rivers on the east coast of either England or Scotland, as far north as those flowing into the Moray Firth. Most recaptures came from the Tweed, Forth, Tay and Esk, and it was estimated that nearly 95 per cent of the catch taken in the sea fishery were destined for rivers north of the border, in Scotland. Not only was this information regarding the origin and destination of these fish extremely enlightening scientifically, but it also increased our knowledge of the movement of fish at sea as well as for the first time identifying some of their sea feeding grounds.

These experiments, however, had an added bonus because in all cases it was possible to estimate, albeit in most cases roughly, how long it took the fish to journey to their various destinations in different European countries or North America from the feeding grounds in the northern hemisphere, and their journeying time from the Yorkshire and Northumbrian drift net fishery to their rivers of origin in the north. In cases where their date of release and date of recapture were reasonably close, it was possible to assess the speed at which they swam on the journey from the fisheries to their rivers of origin, which in some cases amounted to a distance of several thousand miles.

Even more recently, a new tagging venture has been mounted by both MAFF and DAF scientists to monitor the movement of adult salmon as they return to their native rivers. In this case acoustic and radio tags are used, the former in estuaries where the water is brackish and the latter in fresh water. The radio tag is inserted down the fish's throat and its movements are then traced and monitored by signals emitted by the radio tag, which are picked up by a receiver carried either in a light aircraft flying overhead, or by a vehicle close to the banks of the river. These experiments have divulged useful information about the movements of fish, and have now largely confirmed the pattern that had already been surmised by anglers and ghillies who have had years of experience on the river bank.

Many of these fish would move a short distance upstream and then lie for an appreciable time in a holding pool, before moving further on upstream or maybe even dropping downstream a pool or two when flow conditions improved or deteriorated. Others, however, would move an appreciable distance upstream in a short time and then stop again in a holding pool or below an obstacle. This pattern of movement confirms that if a fish is once held up, he is not in so much hurry to move on afterwards. Some tagged fish were caught by anglers, whilst others merely went missing either through failure of the radio tag or some mishap to the fish. On occasions a tagged fish would act in an erratic manner, really quite out of character, but in these cases it must be questioned whether the actual tag was causing the fish some discomfort accounting for its peculiar behaviour. Unfortunately, it is impossible to prove conclusively whether an odd fish does behave in this manner naturally or whether these actions were induced by the fitting of a tag.

Salmon's movements in an estuary are normally allied to water flows in the river. If these are good, the salmon usually ascends fairly quickly; if not, he may spend a while laying doggo in the estuary only moving occasionally as the tide flows and ebbs. Or he may move further out to sea and return later when water conditions improve in the river. In some cases the salmon are never traced again, maybe having fallen foul of a net or a predator: in others they might have been in the wrong estuary and have merely moved on in search of their native river.

CHAPTER NINE

Predators

FRESHWATER

Once the eggs have been laid in their redd and covered by gravel, they nestle comfortably there, safe and sound unless the redd itself suffers damage, and in consequence, some of the eggs are exposed. There is no doubt that when this does happen, and also during the act of spawning, many loose eggs float clear of the redd or are not sufficiently covered by gravel. These eggs will be quickly snapped up and devoured by various fish such as trout, salmon parr, perch, chub and eels, or by different forms of birds ranging from the dipper and kingfisher to various duck species. It is extremely probable that few, if any, of these eggs would have survived so this can really be described as unavoidable natural wastage rather than actual loss by predation.

Similarly, redds placed on unstable gravel, or those which are ploughed up either by later spawning stock or by trees and ice flows floating downstream during the winter spates, will release many more eggs that will be devoured in the same manner. It is also alleged that swans and certain duck species probe into and disturb redds with their beaks and thereby create damage. Although this may happen from time to time, I have never heard it actually confirmed and would have thought even if it were so, it would be more likely to be the exception than the rule.

Once the eggs have hatched out as alevins in their redd in the gravel, some six to nine inches under the surface of the river bed, they are much impeded in their movement by the yolk-sac attached to the underside of their body. It is at this stage of their life that salmonids meet their first real danger from predators in the form of eels and stone fly larvae, lurking in the top layer of their gravel redd and due to their severe encumbrance they have neither room to manoeuvre nor escape, in their cramped habitat between crevices of gravel. The larvae prick the yolk-sac and feed on its contents, thereby starving the alevin of its vital sustenance, while the eel merely devours the tiny creature whole at will.

Once the yolk-sac is absorbed, the alevins become known as fry and these little, properly formed, fish emerge from their redds in their thousands over a period of several days. Now far more manoeuvreable as the impediment of the yolk-sac is at last removed, these tiny fish find themselves in a completely different environment. At first they are bemused both by their new surroundings and by being subjected to daylight for the first time, and they are inclined to huddle together in large shoals glued to the bed of the river, inert. In this formation the tightly clustered shoals are very vulnerable to decimation by bird and fish predators. Diving birds, such as cormorants and shags literally pounce on these shoals and hoover them up with flat shovel-like beaks, mergansers and goosanders are also diving predators whilst herons, gulls, terns and even the little dipper, pick the fry off easily in the shallows. Fish predators of many species such as trout, perch, older parr, etc. have a field day and gorge themselves on these innocent creatures. Once these voracious feeders have located a spawning area where redds are numerous, they are apt to return time and time again to wreak destruction as the fry emerge from the gravel, for they can quickly satisfy their hunger on this easy source of prey. Losses from predators are, therefore, extremely high both at this early stage of their life and for many weeks later, until the fry become accustomed to their new environment, and disperse into smaller groups. These shoals of tiny fish are at this stage both innocent of the facts of life and certainly not yet educated as to where danger lies. They are, therefore, no match for these predators.

As the summer wears on so they grow both in size and strength as they learn quickly how to forage for food and fend for themselves. By this time, they have usually become loners and take up their own patch of feeding territory which they guard zealously. Some pay the penalty for getting too bold – straying into deeper pools and being quickly devoured, whilst the unwary ones are picked off by herons as they wander too close to the bank in smaller watercourses. Some are outwitted by diving birds before they can reach shelter. Losses at this stage, however, are on the whole much reduced compared to when they first hatched.

During their second and third years of river life, these parr are quite sizeable themselves and predation from fish is usually much reduced. However, those that reside in a river system frequented by large pike are always in danger during their early life in freshwater, up to the time they migrate as smolts. Bird predators pose a constant threat from which they are never free until they migrate away from our shores to journey to their feeding grounds at sea.

At this stage, probably the worst predator of all is the trout angler or coarse fisherman, who every year catches and often destroys large numbers of these precious parr and smolts, often at the penultimate period of their feeding life. Much of this destruction is anything but wanton, merely caused through these voracious feeders mistaking the angler's cunningly presented flies, maggots and worms for tasty morsels of their food chain, as the anglers innocently search for their bigger brethren. Many of the fish are gently handled, quickly unhooked and returned to the water, but unfortunately, there is always a proportion which are too badly hooked to survive, and do not do so. Other anglers, mainly the young and inexperienced, do not recognise what they have caught and proudly keep their precious catch without realising what harm they have done. Trout anglers fishing their riffly habitat in an evening, might catch up to twenty or thirty in a well stocked nursery area, whilst children fishing a nursery burn in flood with a worm might catch a similar number, or even more. Few of those caught on a worm will survive, as they are hooked too far down the throat. With more and more anglers taking up the sport annually, the toll of feeding parr taken by these enthusiasts could rise to unacceptable levels.

Smolts, on their outward migration, also feed voraciously as they descend their rivers, and they too readily pounce on angler's flies, etc. In their case, however, quite apart from the mortalities which occur from the actual result of being badly hooked, there is another danger – that of losing part of their silver livery. This guanine coating which covers the whole body and skin is usually soft at this stage and comes off easily on to the angler's hand when he handles the smolt to unhook it, in a similar fashion to touching wet paint. When this happens, that part of the smolt's body where the coating is removed cannot stand erosion from sea water and many smolts perish on reaching the sea in consequence.

Parr are also a favourite diet of two mammals, namely the otter and the mink, although the former is not numerous enough to pose a real threat. However, the mink is getting more and more numerous on many river systems and may well, in years to come, become a serious threat to parr, particularly in the smaller watercourses.

Once parr take on their silver livery they become known as smolts, and shortly afterwards begin to descend their rivers at the start of their outward migration. As they wend their way surely seawards often in large shoals, they glint and glitter as they are buffetted by the current or as they negotiate sparsely watered fords and are, therefore, easily spotted from the air attracting the unwanted attention of many species of bird predators, such as the osprey, gulls and terns, as well as the more deadly diving birds. These birds gorge themselves quickly as they intercept the shoals in confined sectors of the river. Cormorants and goosanders are known to take a daily feed of between twelve and fifteen smolts or large parr; mergansers and blackheaded gulls between six and nine, and herons a dozen upwards. With an expectancy of a 10 per cent return from smolt to adult, the loss of an adult per day per bird is more than most salmon fisheries can possibly afford without showing some effect.

On their arrival in the estuaries and whilst still close inshore, bird predators continue to take a significant toll of these fish. Once again, they are sitting targets as they are both temporarily stunned by the shock to their system of the significant change in specific gravity of the sea water and caught in a completely strange environment. Cormorants, shags, gannets and many others account for a substantial toll at this stage.

In the early 1980s many bird predators of young salmonids were protected by law. These included the heron, goosander, merganser and cormorant. These, apart from the heron which is a fully protected species, can still be killed under licence. This has to be applied for and obtained from the Department of Agriculture. Even so, the NCC keeps strict control on the issue of these licences and although they used to run for a twelve month period they have now been restricted to a three month period early in the year. This means that when hatchery reared fish are released, these predators are free to decimate the nursery areas at will.

AT SEA

Although predation losses in freshwater are significant, on their arrival in the sea smolts are immediately faced with their worst adversary of all in the form of the seal. Many different species of these very large mammals predate throughout the world on all kinds of fish, and around the United Kingdom it is the grey seal which is the worst culprit, although the smaller common seal is also a serious threat to salmon stocks. Even at the smolt stage these mammals lurk in the estuaries and off the coastline and greedily decimate the smolt shoals on their outward migration, at a time when they are both numbed and mesmerised by their new surroundings. Thereafter, during their entire feeding period at sea, throughout their homeward migration, and when they return to the coastline and enter their native estuaries on the last lap of their journey, they are dogged by these predators. In recent years, with the increase in the seal population, the number of seals in estuaries has increased alarmingly, and some now follow the runs of homing salmon many miles up the rivers, well upstream of the tidal influence.

In 1914 concern was shown that the grey seal population had declined to approximately five hundred seals around the shores of the United Kingdom. In the same year the Grey Seals Protection Act, 1914, was passed through Parliament to protect these mammals as it was feared they were threatened with extinction. This Act provided a close time for killing seals during the breeding season. In 1932, this close time was further extended for the period 1 September to 31 December annually. Due not only to the provision of this Act but also to the fact that the trade of seal hunting declined owing to the lack of demand for products obtained from seals, the population of these mammals quickly escalated.

In 1959 the Government set up a Committee to review and advise on the seal population and their Report was published in 1963, estimating the population around the British Isles to be 36,000. It was advised that this population should be controlled by carrying out culls on colonies which were expanding quickly, in order to slow down this rapid increase in seal numbers. The report was strongly criticised by nature groups and in 1970 the Seal Protection Act was enacted. This confirmed the close season for grey seals from 1 September to 31 December, and introduced a close season for common seals from 1 June to 31 August. At the same time, stringent regulations were introduced as to the method of killing seals.

In 1978, a seal cull due to be carried out in Orkney was cancelled owing to pressure from nature groups. Instead, the Government ordered a fresh report on the seal situation to be conducted by the Sea Mammal Research Unit, under the auspices of the Natural Environment Research Council. In 1984, the NERC report estimated the grey seal population of the world to be 150,000 of which over 84,000 inhabited the British coastline – 74,000 of these around the Scottish shores. It is estimated that this population will increase to 100,000 in 1991 and be approximately 200,000 by early next century.

The report stated that British grey seals each ate an average of eleven pounds of fish per day. This means that the Scottish population at that time required over 132,000 tons of fish per annum. The Scottish wild salmon catch by all methods in 1986 weighed 1,251 tons. Therefore, even if only 2 per cent of the seal's diet comprised of salmon, their annual consumption of salmon would be practically double that of the total rod and net salmon fishery catch in Scotland. This figure would be substantially higher today, and there is no doubt that it is the white fish industry which bears the brunt of the damage.

This report, entitled *Interactions between Grey Seals and UK Fisheries*, based its information on the analysis of the faeces of seals, whereas previous research into the damage to salmon stocks by seals was based on the food remnants found in the actual stomachs of these mammals. The main evidence was accumulated by counting the number of otolith (ear) bones of fish species found in the faeces, and the report suggested that on this information sand eels made up a large proportion of the seal's diet. This evidence was strongly contested by white and salmon fishermen alike, because it is well known that when the grey seal eats the larger fish they strip the flesh from the bone and discard the skin, backbone, tail, fins and head. This not only means that the otoliths of the larger fish will not appear in the seal's faeces but also that, in all probability, many of the small otoliths which appear in the faeces were originally in the stomachs of the larger fish previously devoured by the seal. The Government has, therefore, ordered further research work on the subject, which is at present being carried out under the auspices of the Department of Agriculture and Fisheries Scotland Research Laboratory in Aberdeen.

All this research work, unfortunately, takes time and the seal population increases alarmingly every year. Therefore, the actual loss of revenue as a direct result of this predation, to both the white fish and salmon industry, also increases. As no white fish or salmon can be purchased for less than £1 per pound in the shops, even in 1984 after allowing a reduction for non-commercial species consumed, the cost to these industries of fish devoured by the British grey seal population would have been over £300,000,000. At the present time, this figure would be appreciably higher with the growth in the grey seal population now estimated at 90,000 and it does not take into account any fish consumed by the common seal, whose population is now estimated at 32,000. Even if part of their food did consist of sand eels, as these fish form an important part of the food chain of both salmon and white fish, any serious reduction in the sand eel population will reduce the food available for them and this is almost as damaging as the loss of the fish themselves.

With part of the human world population already starving, and certain species of fish becoming so scarce that catch quotas have had to be restricted when negotiations to fix fish quotas in the EEC and North Atlantic convention areas are undertaken, is it right that the British Government should demand one quota to sell and eat, and another to feed the seal population around the British Isles?

The main fear facing salmon conservation at the present time is the recent drastic decline in the early runs of the species. Earlier in this century, when spring runs were strong, several hundred fish at a time often entered their native estuary and ran the gauntlet of only twenty to thirty seals and most of these valuable spring fish survived to reach their river of origin. Today, spring runs have declined to such an extent that far fewer salmon enter these same estuaries at a time and these fish have to run the gauntlet of several hundred seals. It is not surprising that the numbers which reach the safety of their native rivers are now much reduced. It is quite possible that, unless the seal population decreases, this decimation of the early run fish could reach such a level that spring fish will eventually become extinct.

Apart from the seal, some species of sea fish are predators during the salmon's sea water life. These usually take the largest toll of salmon during the first six months of the period they spend at sea, when they are still relatively small in size.

CHAPTER TEN

Angling

Salmo salar is probably the most sought after freshwater game fish in the world, not only because of its size but also because of its fighting quality and strength. As the fish vary from 4 to 40 pounds, when an angler feels the long elastic pull on the end of his line, it is the thrill and anticipation as to what size of fish he has hooked that really makes the adrenalin flow, and the longer the battle the greater the expectancy as to the size of the prize. Sometimes ones wildest dreams come true and a real beauty of over 20 pounds is at last grassed, whilst at other times, although disappointment dawns when the fish turns out to be smaller than expected, the relief at landing a salmon is still none-the-less rewarding.

It is this challenge to the angling fraternity which makes salmon fishing so popular and makes many of the four million anglers in the United Kingdom alone determined to catch a salmon before they end their days.

The salmon, is now recognised as one of the most important natural resources any country can have. Not only does it draw many tourists both from home and abroad to participate in the sport of angling, but it also creates both direct and indirect employment providing a spin-off to the whole community at large. It, therefore, plays a small but none-the-less important role in the economy of rural areas where viable industries are scarce.

This anadromous species of fish feed voraciously during their early life in the river where they are born. Due, however, to a combination of the limited food supply and the short feeding period per annum, as they do not feed once the water temperature falls below 42°F, their growth rate is very slow. Even as smolts migrating to sea after two or more years of river life, they are only on average four to six inches in length. Once they enter the sea they feed voraciously and must have an extremely high food conversion rate, because even after spending only a little over a year at sea their weight gain is astounding. Even if they return as grilse their weight will have increased from a mere two and a half to five ounces as smolts when migrating to sea, to between five and seven pounds when they return after a year at sea. If they remain two or more years at sea and return as salmon, they can weigh anything from eight to forty pounds.

Having reached maturity, they feel the urge to migrate back to their rivers of origin for the sole purpose of regenerating the species. They stop feeding and begin their long journey homeward and, strange to say, discard their feeding teeth as they do so because they do not feed on their return to freshwater but live off their body fat. This strange phenomenon, in all probability, is nature's way of safeguarding the species because, if on their return to the river they were required to feed so voraciously as they did in the sea, due both to their size and the numbers returning, they would decimate fish stocks resident there. Not only would trout and coarse fish suffer, but also the progeny of their forebears and this would undoubtedly decimate the feeding fry and parr shoals within the river and in the long run jeopardise the very existence of the species.

How then, one may well ask, is it possible to catch these fascinating fish on their return to freshwater in a river system. This pertinent question is admittedly very difficult to answer with any sense of authority as it is just one of the many mysterious aspects about this fish which is completely unclear. The fact that they do take angler's lures of a wide variety of kind, colour and size throughout the season, albeit sometimes sporadically but at others very freely, is completely without challenge and, therefore, cannot be denied. What, then, is the reason for these actions when they do not take it for the purpose of feeding? Obviously, like any other fact that is unclear there are several controversial schools of thought. Some say salmon take the lure because it annoys them or angers them and they do so in the end out of sheer frustration; others say they are merely playing with it and snap at it in the process. However, there are some who firmly believe that the lure stirs a memory from their sea or freshwater feeding life and they merely act subconsciously and take it out of habit. Who is really right or wrong? It is impossible to say, but I freely admit that if I had to hazard a guess it would undoubtedly be the latter choice, unless of course unbeknown to us they do actually feed on rare exceptional occasions when a tasty morsel happens to come their way. Certainly in the case of worm fishing, a salmon, if he is given plenty of time and slack line, when he takes the worm will nearly always swallow it and this in itself must at least cast some doubt on the matter.

There is absolutely no doubt though that this unknown quantity makes the salmon's taking habits completely and utterly unpredictable, and this is one of the main reasons why salmon fishing is regarded as such a challenge by all who partake in the sport. It is quite unlike other forms of freshwater fishing because in these cases an angler can study the feeding habits of the particular species he is trying to catch as well as their movements and what they feed on. Having done so, he is reasonably assured of success once he has mastered river or still-water craft and served his apprenticeship in the art. Salmon are however not thought to be feeders in freshwater and fishing for them is an entirely different ball

Waiting to net a salmon on the River Carron.

A spring salmon safely in the net.

game where the reward is far more likely to be achieved by patience, perserverance and the ability to ring the changes instead of possessing a wealth of knowledge about its food chain. Intimate knowledge of the water one is fishing is a priceless asset either learned by years of experience or passed on to the angler by a ghillie or friend who has the necessary knowhow. In either case, the angler will know where fish will lie within each individual pool and these positions can, and often do, change drastically according to even the smallest change in water flow and can vary considerably in the spring, summer and autumn periods.

The angler will also find that although fish may lie throughout the entire length and breadth of the pool, there are often only a few specific places within that pool where they take freely. These taking places seldom vary from one year to another, unless there is a significant change in the composition of the bed of the pool, such as a stone being washed out or a deep area becoming silted up. They do, however, change appreciably as water levels in the river either rise or fall, mainly because in high water the neck of the pool becomes too fast and tumultuous, and the fish have to relinquish their lies and fall back to the mid or lower section. Similarly, in low water the tail of the pool will lack sufficient current to fish it properly and the head of the pool is then most favoured; but in high water fish running up the river will often rest as soon as they enter the pool after their exertions in ascending the more turbulent shallower water downstream and between the main holding pools. Therefore, the tail of the pool can be very productive.

In the early part of the season, due mainly to the fact that water temperatures are under 40°F, salmon favour the slower moving deep quiet pools as their habitat, or lie in the tails of faster flowing pools. However, later in the year as the temperature rises during the summer months, they spread out and can be found literally anywhere where the depth exceeds two and a half feet. Little pots or runs, large holding pools and canal-like slow moving stretches are all favoured habitats. Then in the autumn, the shallower runs and holding pools with a gravelly composition are well inhabited by the fish which have reached their destination and are in the proximity of their spawning grounds. Those still ascending the river can be found literally anywhere with reasonable depth, and they often favour the shallower gravelly glides at the tails of pools, and the shallower runs inbetween the main flows, whilst in lower flows the streamy necks of pools are favoured haunts. When the water temperature lowers as the nights grow longer and frost returns, so the fish begin to fall back into the deeper sections of the pools so much favoured in the early part of the season with similar conditions prevailing.

Now turning to the little we do know about this imponderable species taking habits. There is little doubt that at sea the salmon is an extremely voracious feeder, predating on all types of fish such as capelin, sprats, sand eels and also different types of crustacea. Another favourite diet is phytoplankton. It is then reasonable to suppose that this fishes habits are similar in most ways to those of any other predator, being most attracted to a quarry which is trying to escape from him. Certainly any experienced salmon angler will know that a lure moving away from this fish is more likely to tempt him into taking it, than a lure which is moving towards him. The old fishing adage 'always fish from the shallow into the deep' ably bears out this theory because the salmon will be lying in the deeper area of the pool, and if one casts one's lure there it is bound to swing away from his lie thereby tempting him to follow it. On other occasions, at the very end of a cast when a fly or minnow is being quickened in motion immediately prior to re-casting this is often the moment a salmon takes, or when a fly is being dragged or dibbled on the surface to simulate an insect struggling on the surface – both seem fatally attractive to this unpredictable fish.

Water temperature, air temperature and water conditions are all factors that seem to be important guides as to when a salmon will or will not take freely. But quite frankly, provided an angler has his lure in the water, there is always an outside chance that this contrary fish will take it when it crosses his path, so one can honestly never say that conditions are ever absolutely hopeless. Ideal conditions are a river dropping quietly without undue turbidity, with the air temperature 5°F to 10°F higher than that of the water. A rising river, apart from the first half hour of the initial rise, is not compatible with good taking. It is not hard to realise why water flow is important, because naturally when a river is high and settled there is far more fishable water for an angler to exploit. However, once the level falls to a low range of flow, both current velocities and water depth recede, and instead of being spread out over a wide section and area of the river, fish are confined in a far smaller section of fishable water.

What is far more difficult to understand is why the balance between air and water temperature (with the air always needing to be higher than that of the water) is seemingly so vitally important to good taking, especially with regard to fly angling. Although even 1°F or more difference is reasonable and a nil difference acceptable, when the water temperature is higher than that of the air an angler's chances are much reduced, and often fairly forlorn. All one can really say is that temperature, particularly that of the water, is a vital factor controlling many aspects of the life of this fish, and the effect on their taking habits is certainly no exception. Not only does it largely control when a salmon will or will not take, but it also has a very important bearing on what size of lure these unpredictable but fascinating creatures will take. For instance, in cold water temperatures under 40°F they rarely take a lure under two inches in length, and in these temperatures in high water flow can take much larger lures – six inches or more in length. However, once the water temperature rises to over 55°F, they favour much smaller flies from a quarter to an inch, or size 8–12, according to water flow conditions. Inbetween 40°F and 55°F they are far less particular and can take any lure from a quarter to six inches in size. A great tutor of mine in the past, who had been a ghillie for over sixty years on a prime beat of the Tweed, once said, 'only if you fish a pool first with the size of fly of your choice and then with the sublime and finally with the ridiculous have you fished it thoroughly and given the salmon a fair chance in this temperature of water range'. An old rule but one that I freely admit has held me in good stead ever since. It would seem that the most likely reason for this temperature related choice of lure is that this was the type of food they were eating in similar sea water temperature ranges during their sea feeding period.

With temperature playing such an important role in a salmon's taking habit, an angler can be guided to a small extent as to what time of day he is most likely to glean success throughout the different seasons of the year. However, weather conditions can, in this country, be very changeable and uncertain throughout the entire duration of a fishing season so even this small guide is not infallible. What he is really hoping to achieve is to be able to concentrate his fishing efforts over the most likely period when the air temperature is appreciably higher than that of the water. In the early spring and late autumn with snow melt on the hills, long duration of nightfall and the chance of night frosts, the water temperature is often at its lowest ebb, in the 34°F to 42°F range. Therefore, at these times of year, unless a hard frosty wind is blowing or an air frost is actually falling, he stands an excellent chance of finding a favourable air temperature – even when soft snow is falling the air tempeature usually warms up appreciably. Often around mid-day or in the late afternoon, before darkness falls, are the best times for fish to take – as long as no frost comes in with the dusk. But even early in the day fish can take quite freely if it is mild. This is probably the main reason why these times of year are the most productive when fish are present. In the days when early runs of salmon were strong, the spring fishing period was undoubtedly the most sought after time of the year to fish, for this very reason. Not only would an angler almost assuredly catch fish, but the gleaming shining specimen he caught was a prize worth having. Now, with spring runs declining, the pressure has swung onto the autumn season instead, when anglers know fish will be more plentiful and are likely to take more readily, making their chance of success greater. Often, however, their prize is not of the same quality as a spring run fish nor such a beautiful specimen, usually having lost its silver sheen and become reddy pink or even tartan.

During the summer months the gap between air and water temperature is far more uncertain. Winter snow on the hills has by now nearly all melted, night frosts rarely fall, and the nights are much shorter. Therefore, the water temperature has risen and is usually within the 52°F to 67°F range, according to water flow; being in the low fifties Fahrenheit in high water and appreciably higher during times of drought. It is also often very similar to the air temperature during changeable weather conditions, especially if a cold east-north east wind is blowing. At times of low flow and settled hot weather, a wise angler should give careful thought to the times of day when he fishes his water, avoiding if possible the periods when sunshine is likely to be most intense and glaring down on the surface. Early morning just after dawn, and again at dusk, are the obvious choices open to him for many different reasons.

Concerning early morning fishing, the water temperature is at its lowest point before sunrise after the cooler evening and night period; whilst the air temperature in most cases will be rising sharply as sunrise comes in. Therefore, for an appreciable period after dawn, before the water temperature also rises, the air is much warmer, giving favourable taking conditions. Climatic conditions are also good as strong cold winds are unlikely and the sun will not be beating relentlessly down onto the surface of the water as it is low in the sky. The fish are also more likely to be settling down after moving during the hours of darkness, consequently they are much more likely to take when they are resting in their lies. The first three hours after dawn can be the most productive, but provided the sun is not too strong, an angler can have a break for breakfast and then fish on at least until lunchtime with conditions in his favour. The afternoon, after 2 o'clock, can produce variable results and is much dependent upon prevailing weather conditions.

In the evening, between 6 o'clock and darkness, although the water temperature gap may not be quite so favourable, the heat of the sun begins to die and pools again become quickly shaded. Fish which have been resting in the deep water in the main body of the pool during the day, begin to feel the urge to move again in the evening, and generally move up into the fast streamy neck of the pool in preparation for their nocturnal journey. They are, therefore, again available in the best taking areas of the pool where, even in the lowest flows, there is sufficient current flow to enable the angler to exploit these areas with a good chance of success. Favourable mild conditions are usual once the wind drops, but midges and flies can frustrate and taunt even the most ardent angler as dusk approaches.

In bright sunlight, an angler must remember that on an east coast river during the morning the sun is not so likely to be glaring down into the angler's eyes as it is when it moves round in the afternoon; whilst on a west coast river the opposite applies. In the morning the sun will be shining straight down river and the glare will impede the angler's vision, whereas by the afternoon it has moved round sufficiently to be less of a problem. Most people will be well aware how difficult it is to catch a ball thrown directly into the sun, or to see anything clearly when looking straight into the glaring rays of sunshine. It is, therefore, wise for the angler to watch this point carefully, particularly in the summertime when he is using floating lines with very small flies close to the surface, and to consider how difficult it must be for fish to have any chance of seeing these tiny flies under such conditions. Many people put on all their finest tackle under these circumstances, but in actual fact this could be counter-productive. I have always found that a fly dragged on the surface is more effective in these conditions, as there is more chance of the fish being alerted by the surface movement than by a fly swung neatly and quietly on a floating line with little or no movement to alert the fish of its presence.

Many anglers believe that wind is a nuisance as it disturbs the rhythm of their casting and, at times, it even frustrates them to such a degree that they become irritable and lose their self-control. Wind is, however, one of the greatest assets for an angler because it ruffles the surface of the water and extends the amount of fishable water. This is particularly true in the lower water flow ranges, when the current flow dies quickly just below the neck of the pool and leaves a long expanse of unfishable water in the centre and tail of the pool. When the wind is blowing upstream, or downstream, this riffling wind disturbs the area of water and makes it eminently fishable, particularly by the backing-up method. An upstream wind blowing up against the current will tend to make the pool choppy with waves rolling over the surface. This is ideal for taking, whereas the same strength of wind blowing downstream will have far less effect and probably only ripple the surface lightly.

In low water flows, canal-like water or still long tails of pools can only be fished when wind ruffles the surface, but these areas are generally well populated by fish – even throughout the driest periods. If there has been a quiet spell of weather and suddenly a windy day occurs, this type of water can be very productive because the population of fish lying within these reaches may not have seen an angler's lure for some appreciable time and they often take more freely. Once again, a little careful thought or the guidance of an experienced friend or ghillie, can be a priceless asset in determining where and when an angler should fish.

The depth at which an angler pulls his lure through the water can also be of great importance and it is wise to remember that the higher a lure swings through the water, the more visible it must be to a fish lying beneath it. This is because a high object is contrasted against the lightest background available, which is always the sky – regardless of whether it is a bright or dull day. However, once the lure is fished deeper in the water, the fish then has to contrast it against the landscape, bank, or even submerged terrain and at the same time, through a wall of water which might well be turbid. This in itself makes the sunken lure that much more difficult to see clearly. An angler must also remember how the eyes of the fish are positioned in its head, with the long length of nose projecting in front of each eye. This means that something hung directly in front of or above the nose of the fish is in a blind spot as it is at the extreme extent of the vision of either eye. Therefore, an object moving towards or away from the fish is far more attractive, as it is in full view. All these points are basic, but extremely important in helping an angler to achieve success.

Regarding the actual lures which are used for salmon fishing in the early part of the season, fly fishing or spinning with a minnow or spoon are the most popular methods practised. In most cases the size used at that time is between two to six inches in length. These baits are cast downstream and traverse the width of the pool as they are quietly drawn back by either reeling or handlining. Once the lure has traversed the width of the river, it is re-cast.

Undoubtedly these objects simulate a small fish as they swing through the water in a life-like manner negotiating the various eddies and currents under the surface of the water.

Later in the season when the water warms up, spinning and fly fishing are still the most popular methods, but the size of the lure varies from ¼ inch to 2 inches in fly fishing, and ½ inch to 2 inches with minnows and spoons. Once again, if these are fished on a taut line they resemble small fish of various sizes and their movements are akin to these natural objects. However, when a small fly (between size 12 and 8, or ¼ inch to ½ inch long) is fished on a floating line, if the angler wishes he can simulate water borne invertebrates, by moving it slowly and jerking it by handlining in very short staccato movements, or allow his fly to hang completely inert in the water with no movement whatsoever. He does this by continually mending his line, so that his line and the fly are lying perpendicular to the current flow, thereby preventing any current drag on the fly.

Bait fishing, by using shrimps, prawns or worms, or fish such as sprats or minnows, although frowned upon by many of the angling fraternity, are all highly effective types of lures, especially shrimp, prawn or worm in low water conditions, and worm in rising water. The most popular way to fish these, is to allow them to rumble down the river bed projected by the current or suspended in the current flow by the use of a float at varying depths, depending on the depth of water in the pool one if fishing.

One of the most important aspects of any type of fishing is to try and simulate a type of food which is a known diet of the fish for which one is angling. Therefore, it is important for the angler to pause and think what he is tyring to imitate with his lure, and then by handline movement or rod tip control, it is up to the angler to try and simulate the movement of the creature he is trying to imitate into his lure thereby making it look life-like and attractive to his quarry.

Due to the unpredictable taking habits of *Salmo salar* and also to the fact that so much depends on climatic and water flow conditions for anglers to achieve a reasonable chance of success, rod fisheries are a highly inefficient method of culling salmon stocks. This is particularly true concerning the four seasonal components of the over-all stock of a salmon river. Mainly because each individual component of a river's stock is subjected to a different annual period of exploitation by the rod fishery. This is due not only to the different times of the season that these individual runs enter the river systems, but also to the duration of the rod angling season on different river systems throughout the United Kingdom. The rod angling season varies between thirty-four weeks on the Aberdeenshire Dee, thirty-nine weeks for the Welsh Dee and forty-three weeks for the Tweed. Therefore, on these rivers the winter run may be exploited over the entire duration of the angling season; the spring run for thirty to thirty-five weeks; the summer run for twenty to twenty-nine weeks, and the autumn run only two to eleven weeks.

The toll, therefore, taken by rods of the spring and winter runs is likely to be appreciably higher than that taken by rods of the summer run. This run also enters our river systems during the driest period of the year and an appreciable period of the twenty to twenty-nine weeks that can be exploited may, in many seasons, coincide with drought conditions quite unsuitable for angling. Consequently it is quite possible that whereas twenty per cent of the early run fish are likely to be caught by anglers, only one to five per cent of the summer run will fall victim to angling effort. This figure may well depend on weather and water conditions which prevail during the particular year in question. In seasons such as 1955, 1976 and 1989 to mention but a few of the driest summers, anglers could not exploit this run of fish for sixteen weeks, as the rivers were so dry that no salmon or grilse could ascend them. Therefore, the period when these runs could be exploited was severely curtailed during these seasons. Although these were exceptionally dry years, there are few seasons when angling during the summer period is not curtailed by drought. The autumn run, because of its late arrival in our river systems, often coincides with the closure of the rod angling season and in some cases, this run is not exploited by anglers at all. Only on rivers such as the Nith, Tweed and Fowey, where the rod fishery closes either on the 30 November or into December, does this run stand a chance of being exploited for a reasonable period. Even so, this period only lasts a mere ten to twelve weeks, and may well be much shorter if weather and water conditions are adverse for angling. The toll taken by the rod fishery of this run is, therefore, likely to be extremely low over all.

If salmon stocks do need to be culled to a level which each and every river is capable of supporting, then some method other than angling must be used.

Angling is also affected when the stable regime of the river is upset.

Not only are the number of days when optimum angling conditions usually prevail severely curtailed by a flashy regime, but also many good holding pools with angling potential are ruined if they become silted and lose their holding capacity as a result.

CHAPTER ELEVEN

Tackle

RODS

Being of the old school, I was taught to fish and brought up on wooden rods, spliced Greenheart and then more recently spliced split cane or the ferruled steel centred or ordinary cane rods. All of these were powerful heavy rods in the larger sizes, 14–17 foot, and beautifully actioned, easy to time, rods in the medium size range, 11–13 foot 6 inches.

Being a powerfully built man myself, I normally used Greenheart spliced rods with heavy zinc reels to balance them, and a No. 7 tapered kingfisher line in the spring, whilst I used a variety of the same type of rod in the summer months, ranging from 12–13 foot 6 inches, according to the size of the river I was fishing. These old Greenhearts were slow-actioned rods with extreme power and capable of overcoming most adverse weather conditions with ease. Having no dead spot at all, due to the spliced joints, they literally worked the whole way from the cork handle right up to the rod tip, and were one of the smoothest types of rod I have ever handled.

The split cane rods with steel centres were also very powerful but on the whole heavier than the well-seasoned Greenheart, and needed a heavy reel on the butt to balance them; otherwise, with a lot of weight forward, they were very hard on the angler's wrists. These powerful rods had two dead spots, where the metal ferrule joined the centre piece to the butt and to the rod tip. With the friction of casting, faults often appeared above and below each joint and, therefore, the rod was likely to break at these places especially the older second-hand ones. Also, if these rods were not looked after and varnished and rebound regularly, water could get into the heart of the rod and rust begin to eat into the steel centre. If this happened, the rod was often finished, whereas if a spliced rod did break then one merely had a new piece made and the rod was as good as new.

Shortly after the war, a firm called Sharps began to manufacture spliced split-cane rods, and these were amonst the nicest actioned wooden rods I have ever used, especially in the 12–14 foot range.

Although they also made 15–16 foot rods, these seemed to be on the whole softer actioned, and it was rare to get a good powerful rod in these sizes. From experience, I always used rods of this make made of the darker grained cane, and found this tip served me well as the rods made of the lighter grained cane were not nearly so powerful, and often soft in the centre piece with no lifting power.

For a very short time at the end of the war, metal rods did appear on the market but these were horrible to cast with and impossible to time, as they were far too springy and whippy, catapulting the fly out of the water like a rocket on the back cast.

Once glass-fibre rods came on the market, everything was transformed and these powerful rods felt like a wand in the hands of we old stagers in comparison to the heavy wooden rods we were used to. From then to the present day, with carbon fibre and boron fibre, the whole ball game has become transformed overnight and one wonders what is in store for us in the future.

Certainly there is no doubt whatsoever that these fibre rods are here to stay and also, because of the cost, wood will never return – anyway, not as we knew it. There is also absolutely no doubt that these light rods are a pleasure to fish with and whether it be children, women, men, invalids or the aged, there are rods to suit every one of us which can be fished with all day without tiring us.

At the present time rods made of these materials are costly and probably far more prone to serious breakages, as being frail and slight in appearance, they cannot stand the same abuse as rods of the past. I must admit that when I first handled these rods I was frightened to cough, let alone cast with them, they seemed so frail in my hands!

Glass-fibre rods are undoubtedly good work-horses, ideal for children and beginners to learn on prior to moving on to carbon fibre, when they have had some of their rough and ready habits smoothed over. I have found many of the 13 foot 6 inches to 15 foot glass-fibre rods a pleasure to fish with, especially the 14 foot rods. They are slow timers along the lines of the Greenheart range of wooden rods and can take power if need be without any undue repercussions. These rods are solid in their lift off especially in the centre-piece which, to my mind, is one of the most important aspects of any rod because if a rod is soft in this field, it completely mars the cast, even a strain in the centre-piece could, in the old days, entirely ruin the action of a wooden rod. I have found, however, that after continual use for several hours some glass-fibre rods can suffer from a build up of static electricity, and their casting performance deteriorates drastically from a type of fatigue, until they are lain down and rested for a while; after which time they seem to recover completely. I always use a 14 foot glass-fibre rod as my estate rod, which all and sundry can use if perchance they either have an accident with their rod or else have no suitable rod with them. This has held me in good stead for many years and is performing as well today as it ever did.

Carbon-fibre rods can be bought in practically any size or make, some whippy while others fairly stiff. All of these are again much lighter even than the glass-fibre rods as they are far slimmer than their predecessors. I, personally, do not like a whippy rod at any time because in my opinion they lack power of casting, especially in adverse conditions, as well as striking power, another point I am fanatical about. Therefore, I choose a stiffer rod in the 15–17 foot class. I find these are also relatively slow-timers along the lines of the old Greenheart and have never found any difficulty in casting with them. However, I do find that they will not readily take power or forcing in the same way as wood or glass fibre, and this to my mind can be a drawback. They are excellent for switch, roll or spey casting and because of their lightness many people, ladies included, can fish with a rod of much longer length than they would have done before. This, of course, gives them far better casting ability and, more importantly, control over the fly as well as being able to overcome adverse conditions. This is a huge added benefit to a much larger range of anglers who had, in previous times, been handicapped through their inability to be able to wield rods of that length because of the physical effort involved.

Even children can start off with 10–12 foot rods with ease, at a fairly young age.

The latest advance in carbon or boron fibre rods is the hexagraph type, shaped almost like the old split cane. These may be slightly heavier, but they are undoubtedly stronger and more powerful to handle. In my opinion they are a great step forward, and can be forced without repercussions.

The only way one can fault the modern rod on the whole concerns the reel mounting. Many makers have unfortunately restricted these housings to take a modern metal alloy reel, with small flanges. This unfortunate error means that many of the beautiful old makes of reels with the longer flanges cannot be fitted on to the modern rod. This error should be rectified as soon as possible.

I must finally stress the importance of balance. No rod can serve its master to its best ability unless it has a reel and line which suit it. A rod equipped with too light a line reduces its performance to a fraction of its real ability, whilst a rod equipped with too heavy a line will be easily strained or – even worse – broken. So anglers should beware, and always read the instructions to make sure they use the line the makers recommend for each specific rod.

Even the weight of the reel is of prime importance, as too light a reel will make the rod nose heavy and this will cause needless strain on the angler's wrists; whilst too heavy a reel will add needless weight for casting, and disturbs the balance.

REELS AND OTHER EQUIPMENT

There is little doubt that an angler's reel is one of the most important parts of his equipment, because if it is not working properly he might as well go home.

I would, therefore, always advise any angler who is equipping himself in this department not to scrimp when making this purchase. Buy the best is certainly my motto, but if you cannot afford to do so make sure that what you are buying is made by a reputable manufacturer or in other words – don't buy some cheap gimmick. This is mainly because if it jams, seizes up or some part breaks or falls off, you are left helpless.

I also always advise anglers to buy a wide spool reel. You can then fill it with 100 yards of good quality backing and the line of your choice. There is nothing more annoying than to find that the spool is just too small to take your new line, because then you are inclined to overfill the reel both to the detriment of the line and also risk the reel jamming or worse still, some part of the actual reel breaking.

Reels with interchangeable spools are very useful because you can carry alternative lines ready mounted, which you can change more or less at your will, anywhere on the river bank. However, I have always been a great fan of the old reels and in what I once called a moment of madness in the late nineteen forties, bought fifteen really high quality second-hand reels all in excellent condition, suiting both summer and spring rods, for a mere pittance. Needless to say, as it turned out, it certainly was not madness but one of the best things I have ever done as I have never had to buy a reel since. Happily these reels are in perfect condition today and all in good working order. The secret is to interfere with them as little as possible, except for oiling and normal maintenance. On some of the reels the bottom line guide is literally grooved with wear from the line under tension, having been so long in use.

Anglers should always be careful how they reel on their line, as many a fish is lost if the line snags on the drum as it makes a run and this slight hesitancy can easily wrench the hook from its mouth. A sweet smooth-running reel, plenty of line and sound backing is one of the main recipes to a successful end when a fish is being played.

An angler has a choice of carrying his other equipment in a bag on his shoulders, or wearing a coat or jacket with plenty of deep pockets, maybe even both. I mainly take my tackle bag in the boot of the car and, having checked the water level and weather conditions prevailing that day, I merely take what I think I will need out of the bag and fill the pockets of my jacket or waterproof. If I find I need something else later in the day, I can easily return to the car and get it.

A fly fisher is lucky in that what he requires is not nearly as bulky as that required by a bait fisher or spinner. All he needs to carry on his person, having first checked his water level and bearing in mind the time of year, is one box with a selection of flies of his favoured patterns in roughly the right size for the day, and another box filled on one side with much smaller sized flies and the other side with much larger sized flies to suit both the sublime or the ridiculous in case he might require them for shock tactics. Two old tobacco tins of tubes of varying sizes and types, including the long winged variety, empty film containers full of trebles of varying sizes and two small spools of nylon of different breaking strains. Personally, I never carry a net, gaff or tailer as I rely on beaching my fish at all times unless I am fishing some very difficult water with extremely high banks, etc., then I would prefer to gaff (if permitted on the river I was fishing) the fish under the chin when I had played it out completely.

In this way the angler is carrying a minimal amount of gear to hinder him. If he wishes, he can carry a thermometer in his jacket pocket and a pair of scissors round his neck on a lanyard, but in no way can he be called overloaded, even with this vast selection of gear neatly stowed away, as his entire load will be under 2 pounds in weight – equally distributed. On a fine day, he can take off his jacket and leave three out of the four boxes of flies in it at the head of the pool. He is left with less than ½ a pound's weight in his pockets.

The less one carries in the way of tackle the better because then one has more freedom to carry the fish if fortunate enough to catch any, and if not, at least one is not dressed up like Father Christmas, huffing and puffing between pools and sweating on the steep inclines with no hands free even to mop one's brow!

Another useful thing in which to carry tube flies is a plastic box with individual compartments in which vets get their supplies delivered. These have a sliding lid and are ideal for carrying tubes in as being transparent the tube of one's choice can be quickly and easily selected. These boxes, which come in two sizes, are ultra light and fit into a deep pocket easily, while each will carry up to a dozen or more tubes.

A surgical instrument which can be of great assistance is of course the surgical forceps which can be locked on to the hook and because of its long reach is invaluable. Fish hooked in the back of the throat can be quickly released without the angler getting his hands scored by its teeth. It is also a quick way to remove the hook from a kelt without undue distress to the fish which can then be returned to the water unharmed, whereas without it to unhook a kelt on a cold day can be frustrating and painful to the angler as well as sometimes fatal for the kelt.

LINES

There are so many different lines to use today one's mind boggles with the very thought of having to choose from the many varieties, amongst which are lead cored lines, fast, medium and slow sinkers, sunk tips and floating lines of various types, let alone the colour range, almost as varied as the colours in a rainbow.

I must admit I wish I could turn back the clock forty years to the days when the old dressed silk Kingfisher was almost the only fly line on the market in ranges from No. 1 to No. 7, in fact, a size to suit practically any rod made in those days. If you wished the equivalent of the modern floating line, you merely greased a size that suited your summer rod and kept the line for that specific purpose, or greased up your ordinary line when and if you wished it to float, and ungreased it when you wished to return to sunk line fishing, by running it through french chalk. I can say without doubt that in my experience these lines fitted the bill for either purpose far better than any of the modern lines today for their sole purpose. Admittedly, they needed great care and attention, but if you were willing to give them the right treatment they would serve you long and unfailing. Indeed, only last year, I had at last, to discard a No. 7 which I used for just under forty years on my 16 foot Greenheart rod, a length of service that I doubt any of the modern lines will ever have a chance of serving.

These Kingfisher lines, I would say, were on the whole medium sinkers, mainly because they were double tapered and really adequate for any method of fishing. If you wanted to fish a deep fly you merely cast square, loosed off a yard of line, and allowed your fly to swim across the pool unaided, the exact technique used by the spinner. Medium depth was attained by casting at 60° not letting off loose line and then allowing the fly to come across unaided. Whilst shallow depths were attained by casting at 45° or 60° aided by handlining, or of course, for summer fishing, greasing the line.

Certainly today the angler can choose a specialist line for whatever he wants on that day, and can carry several with him, mounted on spools which can be interchanged with the spool on his reel. To an old hand like myself, this I think is over-simplification as I feel too much time is wasted changing from one to the other, especially if fish are down, rather like taking a bait rod, a spinning rod and a fly rod on rivers where any lure is allowed. Often, the angler never gives any one lure a fair chance, as he is always thinking one of the lures on the other rods is better than the one he is using. I fully admit that in the summertime we nearly always carried a rod mounted with a greased line and a stronger rod with sunk line which we used where they were best suited, and if the elements became unfavourable, such as a gale force wind getting up, we stuck to the sunk line rod for casting power.

Even today I believe a tapered medium sinker and a good floating line are really all any angler requires, provided he uses his knowledge to diversify with either if adverse or unusual circumstances prevail. With the advent of reels with interchanging spools, he is ideally equipped, and not encumbered with a lot of unnecessary baggage.

Some people however swear by sinking tips. These admittedly, are a clever innovation of this era, and can be quickly attached to a floating line. Certainly, in order to save casting effort, they can be useful but quite frankly I do not believe they swim a fly as neatly as either a plain floater or sinking line would do, as it is really trying to compromise between the two, a thing that seldom works. I believe it fishes at more of an angle in the water than it would otherwise do. It is also more difficult to time properly in adverse conditions as with the main length of line floating and only the tip of the line sunk, it seems to lift off with a spring rather like a cork coming out of a bottle, rather than the even take off of a normal line.

Fast sinkers and lead core lines are adequate for use in big deep pools where snags are few and far between, such as the Tay in springtime or the Tweed in autumn. But quite frankly, I believe they are quite unnecessary, horrible to cast with and undoubtedly very hard on the rod unless in the hands of a very experienced angler. Other people, however, may heartily disagree!

Shooting head lines with only a short length of line and a reel filled with backing are impressive to watch, handled by an expert in well nigh perfect conditions, but a nightmare to handle in really adverse conditions with high foliage around the banks.

Whether this impressive array of lines for every possible occasion, water height, and weather condition actually helps to catch more fish, or are manufactured for the prime purpose of catching the angler himself, must be a matter of opinion.

CASTS

Long gone are the days of the old gut cast, the cast soakers and all which went with that era. Although when one looks back on those days, provided one followed the instructions to the letter they held us in good stead, and in all probability there were many more heavy fish landed on these than have, so far ever been landed on nylon.

However, the fact that they were so brittle and fragile when dry and so strong and supple when wet, was undoubtedly a worry to any angler, because during the first half an hour of the day when the long elastic pull came, one never knew whether as one tightened there would be momentary resistance on the end of the line and then the sickening ping as the cast gave, or the pleasure of an awe inspiring battle and then the reward as the fish was grassed.

Many of us cast our fly into a backwater and sat down to allow it to soak for upwards of ten minutes, on arriving at our first pool. Others meticulously took a cast soaker which was round in shape and made of aluminium fitted for the angler's pocket, with two discs of woollen blanket inside it. An hour before we ventured forth, we used to fill this narrow container with tepid water and place a 3/5 and a 5/5 Hercules cast in between the layers of wool for spring fishing, and a 8/5 and a 10/5 Hercules in it for the summer.

Then, on arrival at the river, we took our mounted cast off the rod and having replaced it with one of the soaked casts, wound it up and placed it in the soaker as a spare. We were then reasonably assured of no problems apart from if we picked up a wind knot when casting and did not notice the fact, as this was almost certainly curtains when we hooked the next fish, as few gut casts were strong enough to stand a knot.

Probably the worst period of anguish concerning casts breaking when fish were being played was the transition period between gut and nylon. I well remember an opening day at Argoed on the Welsh Dee, when my mother, father and eldest brother lost eight large fish all due to breaks when they used new American nylon casts given as a Christmas present to my father by a tenant. I can assure you that it was not safe to be on the bank of the river that day, as the annoying thing was they did not break on contact but after five to ten minutes play, and for no apparent reason. I remember about midday seeing a bundle of white cellophane packets floating past me, and knew full well these were the casts on the start of their journey back to America!

Undoubtedly, part of the problem was that these casts copied the gut casts to the letter, and were knotted every foot or so of their length, and it was these knots which always gave. About that time I was lucky enough to be given a hank of cast called Japanese J gut, the strongest thing I have ever used – once soaked. This held me in excellent stead for spring fishing for several years afterwards, and saved me many trials and tribulations which others experienced over the transitional period, and up to the time nylon casts were perfected. Even to this day, however, I never trust made up nylon casts, tapered or otherwise, but always buy level spools of nylon of different breaking strains, and if need be, make up my own taper accordingly.

In the old days, for spring fishing we used a No. 6 or No. 7 Kingfisher, tapered line, and then a length of plaited gut some four feet in length, which we called a collar, attached to the line, before finally tying the 3/5 or 5/5 gut cast leader between the collar and the heavy 6/0 to 10/0 single ironed fly. The purpose of the collar was to produce a better taper from the point of the line down to the fly for both ease of casting and wind penetration, and of course, this combination gave a far better lead to the heavy fly. I personally believe even to this day that this point is of prime importance and often completely overlooked. If it is, the angler is naturally put at a severe disadvantage and handicapped accordingly, as it is impossible for a reasonably long length of light level or tapered nylon to lead a fly that may or may not be weighted into a head wind. Often, as a result, one sees the angler's fly and point of line land in close proximity on the forward cast. If some of these anglers used a level cast of 32 pounds breaking strain in high water conditions, or a collar of three strand plaited of 20 pounds, four feet in length, and then a leader of 25 pounds, they would find a tremendous difference. Then by scaling down the breaking strain of both as the season progresses, they should find that their casting prowess is transformed, especially in windy conditons, when before it was often a nightmare.

For my part, I abhor weighted flies but freely admit that on occasions I do use them – in what I call moments of madness, and do kill fish on them. However, I feel that quite apart from maltreating my rod, I should not need to use them, nor do I enjoy fishing with them. Because of this, I seldom use a collar but instead a level cast of 32 pounds breaking strain, nine feet in length in high water during early spring, and scale down the strength of my cast thereon for the rest of the season, all according to water, weather conditions and time of season.

In the summertime I have fairly strong views as to the strength of cast I use, albeit based once again on years of experience. It must be remembered, however, that I invariably use a dropper once the water temperature rises to 42°F, and this must have a slight bearing on my choice. In rocky rugged rivers, I seldom if ever go below 12 pounds, but in smooth canal-like waters would be prepared to go to 10 pounds in low water. Below that I will not budge, except on lochs or estuaries. Both these gauges of nylon are like silk thread in comparison with the gauge of gut casts used in similar conditions in my early days, and I must admit that I do, and always will, base a lot of my judgement on lessons learnt whether rightly or wrongly; certainly they have held me in good stead and I see no reason to change. It is one thing to hook a fish and another to land it, especially without the aid of an experienced ghillie who, unfortunately, is now a luxury of the past. Those who now ply that role are often more like guides than personal assistants as, in their defence, they have many more rods to look after and more chores to attend to and cannot, therefore, always be in the right place at the right time.

With finer casts, there is always the chance of a quick turn of a fish chaffing the cast against a jagged rock, the quick slap of a heavy fish's tail on the taut cast, an unwelcome wind knot drawn too tight, too much strain in the excitement of the moment as the angler draws his fish to the landing place, or even the wrong pressure at the wrong time by the over-excited or inexperienced. Are these risks worth taking when they are largely unnecessary and can be avoided with forethought, and if a stronger cast that would have withstood these problems had been used? Certainly they are not, in my humble opinion.

What I think is just as important as the breaking strain of nylon is its texture. I far prefer the stiffer brands to the more pliable varieties which crinkle and kink as one ties on a fly, and lead it in a corkscrew fashion. The latter also fail to cut the wind and are often annoyingly blown off course at the last second, as well as being hopeless for use as a dropper leg because, being soft, they continually foul the main leader and thereby render the dropper useless.

It is only by trial and error that an angler will find one which suits him best and he certainly has a plentiful choice if he is willing to shop around.

THE CHANGING SCENE OF SALMON FLIES

In my lifetime it has been interesting to see the change that has taken place in fly tying. For almost thirty years when I was a young man flies were tied immaculately to patterns that had been handed to us from generation to generation. Admittedly during this period the odd new pattern appeared and was either named after the person who tied it, an estate or some other descriptive term. Then during the war the odd bucktail hair-winged fly appeared, so did tandem hooked flies which were really copied from and were larger editions of the old tandem sea trout fly lures.

It was not until the late forties or the early fifties, shortly after Messrs Redpath & Co. of Inverness brought out the famed Hairy Mary fly dressing, that many professional and amateur fly dressers jumped on the band wagon and started to produce an assortment of 'bastard' patterns of hair-winged flies, many of which had the authentic bodies of the old renowned patterned flies. These were more easily tied and cheaper to produce. Many of them were very effective and some were then named. Probably the most renowned were the Stoats Tail and Silver Stoat.

Waddington then brought out his lure type Waddington patterned flies, many of which were styled on the old renowned favoured pattern flies. Almost immediately the Parker Major tube flies with heavy leaded spinning-type mounts and lighter smaller tubes from the same maker heralded the arrival of numerous types of tube flies, many of which were poorly dressed and mainly tied to a plastic body which was often too light, with no form of anchorage for the treble. This led to the treble catching the gut above the tube during the cast and rendered not only the cast, but if it went unnoticed many other casts, quite useless.

Since then many modifications have greatly improved the effectiveness of the tube flies, many of which are fitted with a plastic glove that now anchors and stablises the treble hook. Aluminium and brass tubes for these flies to be tied to are fitted with a plastic liner to prevent the gut, passing through the tube, from becoming frayed, now give a variance of weighting to these tube flies to combat any water conditions that might prevail. Waddington flies also benefitted from some of these modifications. Unfortunately, the old patterned flies, which were a work of art, are fast disappearing and it is now doubtful whether in another twenty years there will be many fly tiers left with the knowledge and experience to tie these beautiful specimens of the past. There is no doubt that labour and material costs are partly to blame for these famous old patterns being priced out of the market and any that are on the market today are generally of far poorer quality compared with the pre- and post-war specimens, with only a fraction of the minute detail and far fewer feathers making up the dressing of the wing.

One of the most effective modifications to tube flies was the Long Winged Variety such as the Collie and the Tadpole, whereby the wing overlapped the body and hook by almost twice the latter's length. Whatever the reason there is no doubt that its movement in the water is devastatingly attractive to fish and will move them when no other fly will.

The final innovation that has become very popular is the long shanked treble hook which is named after the inventor Esmond Drury. Many late spring and summer patterned flies are tied on these strong shanks and they are proving to be excellent hookers of fish.

It is very interesting to compare the present flies with those of the past, both with regard to their hooking efficiency and their ability to attract fish. Also to weigh up the pros and cons of the multitude of different lures that can be part of an anglers' armoury. Do they really enable us to kill more fish than we used to on the old single hooked patterns? Personally I have my doubts about both these points but with certain reservations.

In the old days for early spring fishing in high water conditions we used single iron flies 6/0 to 10/0. These were aptly named meathooks!

There is absolutely no doubt that these were really excellent lures and would kill fish very freely, with the wide replica of different patterned wings of all colours and various types of bodies, we were well equipped to contend with any circumstances. The weight of fly could also be varied according to the size of iron the fly was dressed on, with the old Dee iron light and sharp in comparison with the heavy wide gape hooked varieties. The only problem was that we required heavy 15–16 foot rods of either Greenheart or steel centred split cane to not only cast them but also to drive the hook home. The latter point being of the utmost importance as from point of hook to point of barb on some irons was nearly half an inch in length. The hook had to be literally driven home.

On many occasions I have seen the hook driven down through the fish's chin, out through the roof of its mouth or slap through the hinge and these fish seldom escaped, there rarely being any leverage with a single iron hook. It was only those that had not been struck properly that were liable to be lost.

In modern times under the same conditions we are armed with tubes or Waddingtons of every shape, size and colour as well as those of the long-tailed winged varieties. However, many of these are, in the main, sadly lacking in body variation which I personally regard as of the utmost importance and I firmly believe many of us suffer badly from this loss under certain conditions.

Our rods are, on the whole, much lighter but still have tremendous power and these rods, 13 feet to 17 feet 6 inches, are mostly capable of casting even the heaviest brass tube an adequate distance. Invariably, however, all but a few of us are using trebles because we fish with tubes or Waddingtons, although admittedly these do not need to be driven home with the same power as the old ironed flies. I am adamant that we lose far more fish on them and I can only assume that this is due entirely to leverage on the fish's jaw by the hooks that are not fully embedded in its mouth. Generally this takes place when only one leg of the treble has taken hold. Naturally when two or more legs are firmly set in the mouth losses are far less but strange to say this is often the exception and not the rule.

In the summertime once again the angler of the past had a tremendous range of different colour sizes of fly with a wide variation of hackles and bodies to choose from, and varying in size from No. 10 to 2/0. It is interesting to note that at this time of year most of the famous varieties had no jungle cock feathers inserted on either side of the eye of the fly, as did most of the spring patterns. There is no doubt that these represented the eyes of a fish which these cold-water patterns were meant to imitate whilst summer patterns represented plankton or waterborne invertebrates and therefore did not require eyes. All of these established patterns were dressed in every minute detail, even down to the tiniest sizes.

The irons varied tremendously in shape, size and weight but in the smaller sizes below No. 6 one had a choice of either the ordinary or long shanked hooks, both in double and single hooks. These in my opinion were excellent hookers of fish and I always favoured the Tilson long shank hooks when available, especially for low water fishing.

At the present time during the summer months many of the old pattern single and double hooked flies are still used dressed on the old types of iron. But as well as this variety, tubes, Waddingtons, and Esmond Drury flies dressed on long shanks add greatly to the choice of lure that the angler has at his command.

There is no doubt that tubes do add significantly to the angler's repertoire as these have a different action when fished in low water conditions and cannot be simulated by flies dressed on ordinary irons. The small size, 12–16 trebles, seem to be better hookers than those used in the spring size 4–8.

Esmond Drury flies are excellent in medium and high water flows but in my opinion are too heavy for grease line fishing in low water conditions, when I still prefer to fish Tilson Hook single iron flies or a small tube. Long winged flies such as Munro Killers, Tadpoles and Collies are effective in all heights of water and can be fished in grossly exaggerated sizes in comparison to normal flies, even in the lowest water flow. When fish move to this type of fly they often take them in a most voracious manner, quite unlike their normal behaviour. It would seem, therefore, that these particular flies simulate a favoured diet found during their sea life.

Once again flies used in the autumn are a mixture of those used in the spring and summer, according to the weather and water conditions that prevail. As the water temperatures drop in the late autumn so the big spring flies come back into their own.

CHAPTER TWELVE

Fishing Methods

FLY FISHING FOR SALMON

This is probably the most practised and also the most popular method of salmon fishing, and is used universally in its many varied and diverse forms. It is also one of the most difficult to learn and master properly! Most anglers have to serve a long and often frustrating apprenticeship before they become proficient in all the different techniques of a fascinating art.

Although this particular method is named fly fishing, no one using it can really believe that the varied assortment of flies of widely differing size and colour used bear the slightest resemblance to the fly in its literal form. Therefore, when he sets out to fish, the angler should bear this point firmly in mind and instead of just casting out his line and allowing it to traverse the width of the river at its own free will, or at the discretion of the current flow in the pool he is fishing. He should pause briefly and decide what creature or object he wishes his fly to simulate as it swims through the water.

Unlike most other methods of fishing, where an angler is trying to simulate a fish or some other specific form of bait, the fly fisher is capable of employing a multi-purpose role and simulating a variety of different natural foods such as fish, water borne invertebrates, insects in distress or plankton, merely by employing a different means of presentation and/or imitating the movement of these creatures by transmitting their natural life-like movements into his lure, either by rod tip or handline control. By doing so, the angler is far more likely to stir a memory from the salmon's feeding period at sea or as a juvenile in fresh water before migrating to sea and can, therefore, tempt the fish into making a mistake by taking his fly. These different techniques warrant further explanation.

In the early part of the season, from January to April, for many years fly fishing had been regarded as a pretty good waste of time by most anglers who looked upon spinning as the most efficient and productive method of catching salmon during this time. There is little doubt that this method does have many advantages over fly fishing when rivers are swollen and running high, due to a seasonal combination of rainfall and snow melt.

This is mainly because this method required less effort to overcome the inclement weather conditions, and also is an easy way of covering a greater area of water due to the casting ability of spinning equipment. It is, however, very interesting to note that the rivers whose rod angling season opens earliest in the year on 11 January happen to be in Sutherland, in the north of Scotland, and on these particular rivers by proprietor's agreement, angling throughout the entire season is by fly only. It is also worth noting that spring catches on some of these rivers, such as the Naver, Helmsdale, Brora and the Kyle of Sutherland, are amongst the best in the United Kingdom. Therefore, this goes a long way to counteract the argument that fly fishing for salmon in the springtime is an inefficient method. It is sufficient to say that for all and sundry who wish to use this method, provided they use large flies and a strong rod with sinking line, there is every chance of catching a salmon in the spring. It is, however, more effort, and the water they are able to cover is admittedly slightly inhibited, but many would agree that in spite of these obvious disadvantages on some of the larger rivers, it is infinitely more pleasurable to the purist to have a cast with a fly rod.

During the early part of the season, with low water temperatures and high water flows the norm, a wise angler chooses a fly two to six inches in length if it is a tube, and 4/0 to 10/0 if he is using an old single-iron patterned fly; all according to the weather and water conditions on the particular day. The angler is, therefore, left in no doubt whatsoever as to what he is trying to simulate with that size of fly; it could only be one thing and that is a fish of one type or another. Therefore, first and foremost, he must try as best he can to imitate the life-like movements of a fish into his fly, in order to make it look as tempting and attractive to his quarry as possible.

Today, the fly fisherman is blessed with the equipment to enable him to fish his fly at whatever depth he wishes. Either by using a sunk line or fast sinking line with or without a brass tube fly or weighted Waddington, he is able to fish his fly deep, whilst if he wishes to fish at moderate depth, he uses a slow sinking or intermediary line with a single ironed fly or aluminium tube. Again, if he wishes to fish a fly closer to the surface he then fishes with a sunk tip line or full floater and a fly to suit these. The depth at which his fly is fishing can be further regulated both by the angle at which he casts his fly into the river as well as the speed at which he moves his fly by handlining or pulling in his line. If he wishes to fish it deeper, he casts square across the river and, at the same time lowers his rod and, if he wishes, looses off a yard of line to give the fly time to grip the water, and then handlines only sufficiently to keep in contact with it; whilst if he wishes to fish shallower, he casts at an angle down and across the current and then handlines at moderate speed. It is by either rod tip or handline control that he can transmit the swimming action of a fish

Pool Morrail on the River Carron, a famed fly pool.

into his fly by varying its movement through the water, either speeding it up and making it dart or alternatively slowing it down. The angler must, however, be aware that the deeper he fishes his fly the less visible it becomes to the fish as it is no longer contrasted against the sky, but instead against the much darker background either of the landscape or an underwater bank, often through a considerable wall of turbid water. Also, if a salmon moves but does not take the fly if it is being fished close to the surface, the fish will almost inevitably leave a tell-tale blemish or boil on the surface – commonly known as a rise in angling terms – as the fish turns away from the fly. However, when the fly is fished deeper and this happens, the angler is quite oblivious to the fact he has moved a fish because there is unlikely to be a surface movement to alert him.

As the temperature of water in the river rises through the low 40°F range and into the mid-50°F range, salmon have a preference for a much smaller sized fly, fished much closer to the surface in most ranges of water flow. Therefore, the angler should gradually reduce the size of the fly he fishes accordingly; until he is down to size nine to twelve in single or double hooked patterns, or a quarter to half inch tube flies once the water temperature rises to a level in excess of 55°F. The only real exception to this useful rule is when he is fishing General Practitioner or Shrimp flies, which by their very nature are significantly larger. During the transition period from large flies of two inches or more down to half inch tubes or similar size ironed flies, it is highly probable that for the most time the angler is still simulating a fish; therefore, he must still continue to fish his fly in a similar fashion by imitating its natural movements. Once, however, he has reduced the fly size to below half an inch in length, by altering the method of presentation of his fly, he can simulate waterborne invertebrates, insects in distress and the vegetative plankton, or if he so wishes, still continue to simulate a fish.

If he wishes to simulate waterborne invertebrates, he should choose a drab dull coloured fly such as a Stoat's Tail, March Brown, Lady Caroline, etc., use a full floating or sunk tip line and move the fly across the surface in short pulls of a staccato nature, creating a short sharp movement, followed by a period of little movement. This method can be effective both in streamy and dead water, provided the latter is ruffled by wind. When fishing dead water it is best to cast square across the wind and hand line in draws of two to three inches, by almost tweaking the fly in the water.

If he wishes to simulate plankton, the angler must remember that this is not a living creature, but instead a vegetation. It must, therefore, be allowed to hang inert, without drag, in the current. The angler can only achieve this imitation by using a full floating line and casting at 45° down and across current. Immediately the fly lands on the surface he must mend his line, by lifting his rod tip to flip his line so that it lies parallel to the current flow immediately up and down current in direct line with the fly. He must allow it to lie in that position without movement. If his line begins to show the slightest sign of drag, he must immediately mend again to correct its alignment with the fly. When he is fishing pools that have a smooth even surface, the number of times he has to mend his line as the fly traverses the width of the river, will be far less numerous than when he is fishing a pool with uneven buffeting surface currents, in which case he might have to mend and remend five to eight times during the fishing out of one single cast.

This method was first devised and perfected with great effect during the late spring and early summer by A. H. E. Wood of Cairnton on the Aberdeenshire Dee. Once again, he advocated the use of drab flies such as the Lady Caroline, Blue Charm, Sweep and Logie among others. He was also a great believer in either holding his rod tip high and lowering it as the fish took, in order to give it momentary slack line before he lifted it again to set the hooks firmly in the fish's mouth, or holding a loop of a yard or two of slack line in his hand, which he allowed to run through his fingers as the fish took, before raising his rod tip to make a firm connection.

If the angler wishes to imitate an insect in distress, he achieves this by simulating the movements of a fly or larger insect which has been blown onto the surface of the water and is struggling to get airborne once more before it drowns, either by dragging his tail fly or dropper on the surface of the water. When he uses a dropper, he dibbles this on the surface in much the same manner as a trout fisherman, when fishing from a boat, drags his top dropper up on the surface of the waves. It is best to use a fairly long rod so that the angler has sufficient rod tip control to lift his dropper up to flutter on the fast surface at the neck of a pool, and he can only fish in this manner with a short line. A slightly heavier tail fly is a benefit as this acts as an anchor and thereby allows the dropper fly to flutter on the surface in a pendulum fashion.

In low water flows this method can only be used in the fast rippling water at the head of a pool in a streamy narrow run, or in pots and rocky gutters, which are often unfishable by any other method. The angler starts with a short line, casting almost square to the current and as soon as the flies land on the water, he raises his rod tip sufficiently to allow his dropper to brush the surface and keeps it teetering on top of the ripple as it traverses the pool. By controlling his flies with the rod tip the angler can slow down or quicken up their progress, allowing them to pause briefly at the far side of the current, behind a boil in the water or where he thinks fish are most likely to be lying in the pool. Once he has sufficient line out to cover his fishable water, it often pays to make three or four casts from each stance before moving on down the pool three or four steps, and then repeating the performance. Fish that are attracted by the movement of the dropper often come slowly up to it and literally suck it off the surface, head and tail on to it as they move upstream, or occasionally they make a big splash as they jump at it. In all cases, therefore, the angler must steel himself not to strike too soon, but instead quietly lower his rod as the fish comes to the fly and allow it time to turn before he finally tightens to set the hook.

When he drags the tail fly on the surface, this method is better suited to medium river flows, or in confined streamy pools. The angler should use a larger double hooked fly or a one to two inch tube, and once again he controls the fly with his rod tip and raises the fly so that its hooks are just trailing on the surface as soon as it lands on the water. He should then work it quietly against the current, bouncing on the ripples as it traverses the width of the pool, in exactly the same manner as that used when dibbling with a dropper. As soon as the current flow begins to slacken, this method is no use as there is insufficient resistance to keep the fly buoyant on the surface. Both these methods will attract fish when all else has failed. They can also be very effective on days of relentless sunshine and in sections of the river which are boulder strewn and which could not be exploited properly by any other means.

In flatter, quieter pools with insufficient current velocities to enable these methods to be used, and angler can make his fly bobble on the surface by using the riffling hitch method. He must use a floating line and a long leader, and put a half hitch round the body of the fly, so that instead of swimming gracefully through the water, the fly is pulled onto the surface by either drag from the current or a handline movement by the angler. This is also a fascinating method of fishing which can be very productive at times. Its main advantage over the dibbling methods is the fact that it can be used throughout the entire width and length of a pool, in any height of water, as it does not rely either on rod tip control or current flow to make it buoyant on the surface.

In the autumn, with the ever increasing hours of night coinciding with cooler and wetter weather conditions, the water temperatures in the river usually fall steadily. As they do, the fly angler has once again to change his tactics, and slowly return to the techniques he used in the springtime. By mid-October and sometimes earlier, in cold wet years, he may find that he is having to use two to six inch flies, similar to those he used in February and March, and of course, simulate a fish instead of the other variations. He may, however, find that at this time of year fish are lying in the shallower gravelly pools and runs which were not often inhabited during the early part of the season. Therefore, in most cases he may not have to fish the fly as deep as he did then. During these later months of the year, orange or reddish coloured flies seem to be particularly effective.

SPINNING

Apart from fly fishing this is undoubtedly the most popular method of salmon angling. In fact, it would probably be fair to say that during the early and late months of the season it is the method which is most used on rivers throughout the United Kingdom. There are, however, exceptions such as the river Tweed, where it is banned during certain seasons, such as 1 to 14 February and 15 September to 30 November, and in this case the ban is enforced by law. In other cases, for instance in the north east of Scotland, in the Kyle of Sutherland area and further north, by proprietor's agreement fishing is by fly only throughout the season. On other rivers a similar rule is applied during certain seasons or months of the year.

For some strange reason, for many many years it has always been considered that spinning is a far more effective method of catching salmon in the spring time than fly fishing. This old adage is one that has been passed down from one generation of anglers to the next. Whether more fish would take a minnow or other spinning lure in preference to a fly or lure presented on a fly rod, must be a matter of question. However, what cannot be questioned or denied, is that it is a method that is ideally suited to early and late season fishing, when rivers are likely to be swollen by either heavy rainfall and/or snow melt, and when the fish are often found in the wider sections of these river systems – particularly in their lower reaches. This is mainly because the spinning rod and reel is designed to enable an angler to cast his lure a much greater distance than is possible with a fly rod and reel.

This fact in itself is of prime importance, but another very important factor is the simplicity of this method of angling. Spinning equipment both past and present has been devised so efficiently that it has been possible for a complete novice in the art to learn how to handle it and become proficient in its use within a matter of hours rather than days, whereas the novice taking up fly fishing may take several years to achieve the same standard of efficiency.

The third, and no less important advantage of spinning in relation to fly fishing, is that a shorter rod is usually required and there is no necessity for bank clearance upstream or behind the angler to enable him to cast out his minnow or lure, as is the case in fly fishing. This is because the minnow is wound up just below the tip of the rod before each cast is made. Then, with either a side swing up and outwards, or a quick overhead flip, the minnow is projected and angled towards its intended destination across or down river. This enables the angler to fish from an extremely confined space such as a tree lined bank, out of a wood, or in front of a cliff, without any undue restriction to his freedom of cast: in most cases, places the fly fisher would not even contemplate fishing regardless of whether he could roll or spey cast or not.

All these obvious, basic points are a great temptation for both the experienced and inexperienced anglers when they set out to fish, especially if it is a river they have never been to before. It cuts out all the worries and doubts as to what length of fly rod he will need, does he require a floating line, sunk line or sunk tip, what size of fly shall he take, does he need chest waders, etc. Instead, he merely puts in a spinning rod, a reel with a spare spool, an assortment of spinning lures and his choice of waders. If he is wise (or a pessimist) he will take a spare rod and reel, just in case! Provided the beat allows spinning, there is much less worry, much less bulk and a good assurance of catching a fish – provided there are any in the river!

There are many large rivers in the country with slow moving pools or tails to the pools, some heavily wooded or tree lined and others of extreme width, which cannot be properly exploited by the fly angler, unless he is able to fish from a boat, in all heights of water. In fact, even the spinner has got to take advantage of this help at certain times and during some conditions. Many rivers such as the Tay, Tweed, Welsh and Aberdeenshire Dee, and Wye amongst others have many many beats that are better suited to and can be more usefully exploited by spinning than fly fishing, particularly in the higher and medium levels of water flow that usually prevail both early and late in the season, not only due to the width of the river but also to the lack of velocity of water flow in the lower sections of the long and varied character of many of the holding pools. This latter point is very important, as once the current velocity of a pool dies there is insufficient movement to enable a fly fisherman to work his fly across the width of the pool, and then, unless there is a wind ruffling the surface and he backs up the pool, it is virtually not worth fishing. However, this lack of current flow in no way handicaps the angler who is spinning because he merely casts either across the width of the pool or angles his cast across and downstream thereby injecting the necessary impetus into his minnow to enable it to traverse the width of the pool, counteracting the lack of current in the process. Even in the lowest flows when the deeper centre and tail sections of most long pools are virtually still and motionless, the spinner can still be productive provided the angler adjusts his speed of retrieve by winding more quickly to suit these conditions and thereby counteract the lack of flow.

The angler spinning any pool must adjust the weight of the spinner by adding weight on the line entirely according to the velocity of water flow that prevails in the pool because the depth at which the spinner traverses the pool can be of the utmost importance and can alter according to the season of the year. He can also vary this and increase or reduce the depth that the spinner fishes by adjusting the angle of cast, either by casting squarer and delaying the retrieve or by casting at a narrower angle down and across and speeding up the retrieve. With the modern, light monofilament line now being the norm, he gets very little advantage from this source to help him regulate the depth at which his lure fishes. A fly fisherman on the other hand can vary the weight and density of the line he uses as one means of achieving this important aspect. If he wishes to fish deep he fishes a fast or slow sinking line, if he wishes to fish shallower he puts on an intermediary line or a sunk tip, and if he wishes to fish the fly just below the surface – a floating line. Advantages I am sure that would be welcomed sometimes by the spinner.

It is very interesting to look back over the last fifty years or so and see how spinning lures and their weighting have gone through radical changes and phases. Early in the century, especially in the springtime, natural sprats dyed gold or fished in their natural state (silver) were probably the most favoured. These were mounted on a spinning flight with a weighted pin; with two separate treble hooks in tandem attached to the flight on a short length of plaited wire or gut. The leaded pin was pushed into the mouth of the sprat so that the lead was lodged in its throat and the flight positioned just to the front of the head of the sprat, the tandem hooks were then pinned onto the body of the sprat and laced on with either thread or fine flexible wire. If further weighting was required, a suitably sized torpedo shaped weight was attached to the cast the requisite distance above the sprat. Even today there is little doubt that this bait is as effective as ever, but many people are put off using it, because it is a messy business to mount them and carry both the sprats and the necessary equipment. Anglers therefore much prefer to use artificial lures. In the days when many of the artificial minnows were made of shaped canvas, and hand painted to resemble parr or trout natural baits were considered better. Most were either gold, green/silver or blue/silver. These had a leaded pin of varying weight enclosed in the body with a flight and hooks attached at the head and fixed to the body. Seldom was extra weight required.

In the late 1830s to 1950s minnows began to be produced from various types of metal. These were turned on a lathe into torpedo shaped tubes, fins were soldered on just behind the thicker head on either side to act as the flight and propel the minnow through the water. A treble hook attached to a swivel by plaited wire passed through the minnow attached to the gut or wire trace. In most cases the aperture through the minnow was quite large, therefore it was necessary to place a bead, usually red in colour, on the hook mounting just in front of the hooks to prevent them being drawn too far into the aperture thereby masking them. Some of these minnows were made of copper or brass, whilst others, known as Devons, were made of a lighter metal alloy. In most cases they were all heavier than their predecessors and apart from some Devons needed little extra weight elsewhere on the cast. These minnows varied in colour from gold, gold and red, silver, blue and silver, silver and red, black and orange, to brown and gold. The last two were much favoured in the spring and autumn whilst blue and silver were usually more effective in the summer.

During the late 1950s there was again a shift from these heavier minnows back to a lighter variety of wooden minnows, usually made of balsa wood with a metal liner to house the hook mounting. Others were made of a synthetic wood substance, moulded around metal liners of various weights. These minnows also had a similar hook mounting with bead and swivel attached, as was used on the Devons. Even to this day, this latter type of minnow, or the Devon, are amongst the most popular forms of spinning lure.

In recent years spoons have become very popular. These are made of various shapes and sizes and different weights. The colours are very similar to those of the minnows; copper and gold, and black being popular in the spring, whilst copper and silver, silver and blue and silver can all be useful during later months. Many of these lures derive from either Scandinavian or French origin, and there is no doubt whatsoever that they are gaining in popularity with anglers in this country all the time. The Mepps and Toby spoons are both much in favour at present.

The tendency now to use slightly lighter minnows instead of the much heavier ones that were used during the middle part of the century, allows the minnow to fish at a depth where it can be silhouetted against the sky. In other words, it is in the fish's window contrasted against the lighter background, whereas if it was fished at a greater depth where the fish themselves are lying in the pool, it would either have to be contrasted against the landscape or the underwater bank: in either case, a darker background than the sky, this contrast also having to be made through a wall of turbid water. Therefore, the angler who fishes his minnow at the greater depth often reduces the fish's chance of a clear vision of a lure presented in this manner.

In the early part of the year, water temperatures are normally at the lowest, often in the range of 36°F to 42°F whilst flows in the river are usually on the high side, either swollen as a result of heavy rainfall or snow melt from the high catchment; or a combination of both. Early running fish are mainly confined to the lower or middle sections of the river where the width of the river is likely to be significantly broader than that of the upper reaches. Under these conditions most of the fish will be lying at a reasonable depth in the quieter, slow flowing sections of the holding pools or in higher flows in the quiet lulls at the edge of the main current where they are baffled from the relentless current velocities further out in the river.

Under these conditions, the spinner should arm himself with a good strong rod, a fixed spool reel mounted with 150 to 200 yards of good strong monofilament line and an assortment of favourite minnows of various sizes, from 3 inches downwards, or sprats if he prefers to use them. In higher water flows he will probably select his largest minnow and search the quieter sections of the pools, either fishing the water he can cover across the full width of the pool or in very high flows the quieter water close to his own bank. In these heights, fishing well out into the river, it often pays to cast square across the current and as soon as the minnow lands on the water loose off a few yards of line so that the minnow has time to grip the water and sink quietly to a reasonable depth before the current catches it, or the line, and swings across. Having done so, the angler should keep his rod tip fairly low and wind very quietly just sufficient to keep in contact with his lure as it traverses the width of the pool. Once it has reached the nearside of the pool he should wind in quietly, and recast.

As water flows drop, the river will reduce significantly in width; pools then become much more clearly defined and water velocities are materially lower: therefore, fish will be able to lie in comfort over a much wider section of the pool. The spinner must then be guided by the water temperature and weather conditions that prevail on each day as to what size of minnow to use and also at what depth he wishes the lure to fish. When temperatures remain low, he should use a large minnow, fish it reasonably deep and retrieve it quietly. However, as temperatures rise he should first of all try a slightly smaller minnow, two to two and a half inches in length, and fish this at an angle downstream and across, and at the same time retrieve the minnow slightly quicker. If this fails, he can change to a large minnow and fish it squarer and retrieve it more slowly.

The angler must always remember that he is trying to simulate a fish when he is spinning, therefore, it is wise to try and make his minnow act in a life-like manner, as it moves through the water. He should try to transmit life-like movements into the lure by varying its pace, sometimes quickening and then slowing down its movement as it traverses the width of the pool instead of merely bringing it across in one monotonous, continuous movement.

In the early part of the season, when temperatures are below 40°F fish on the whole do not like to make quick movements and only do so if they are forced to. Therefore, some people believe that the Toby spoon is not so effective under these conditions, due entirely to the fact that it moves erratically through the water as it dives and rises when encountering various buffeting eddies and underwater currents, causing fish to move quickly if they wish to intercept it. These anglers prefer to use minnows during January, February and March, and then begin to use spoons as the water temperatures rise in April. This of course, like many similar points in angling, is controversial and I honestly believe that it is best not to be too dogmatic about anything in this field. If fish are not taking what I am presenting to them, I then ring the changes and am prepared to offer them the full range of my armoury in the hope that something will take their fancy and lead them into making a mistake. I would, therefore, prefer to offer them a spoon as a last resort and thereby let them decide for themselves whether they wish to take it or not!

Once mid-April or May arrives, rainfall often decreases and snow reservoirs on the mountainous catchment get smaller. River flows then begin to reduce significantly. It is at this time of year that the majority of anglers take out their fly rods and stow away their spinning tackle for re-use later in the year. It is also the time of year that on some rivers, by proprietor's agreement, a fly only rule comes into being – except when the river is flowing at a high water level. On the beats that do allow spinning, however, those who wish to spin in any water level still do have a good chance, provided they use either small minnows or Mepps spoons in the lower water flows and similar medium sized lures when the river flow is higher. In the lower flow ranges, fish can either be taken in the necks of the holding pools or towards the tails. In the faster areas, it often pays to cast at a 45°F angle down and across, and retrieve at moderate pace, whilst in the slacker areas a cast slightly upstream or square across the pool with a fast retrieve can be productive. In the higher flows, a square cast or one angled downstream with a moderate pace retrieve seems most productive. Toby spoons can be very effective during the summer months, both in high and low water flows, whilst Mepps spoons can often be equally productive and, in spite of the fact that they are usually much smaller than Toby spoons, they can also be used throughout the full range of water flow. At this time of year extra weight is seldom if ever required and, in fact, it is better to use, whenever possible, lighter lures than one would use during the earlier part of the season.

In the autumn on rivers, apart from the Tweed where spinning is not allowed after 14 September, or on other rivers that have a similar local agreement, spinning once again becomes a popular form of fishing. This is mainly due to the fact that this season of the year usually sees a return to heavier rainfall and at the same time, water temperatures in the rivers begin to fall significantly due to the longer nights and also the return of night frosts and generally cooler weather conditions. Rivers often become swollen again, for longer periods, and with the arrival of the autumn run, the wider longer pools, especially in the lower reaches of the rivers, again become well stocked with fish.

At this time of year, minnows, spoons and other recognised lures can be productive and the spinner has a wide choice. It is nearly always prudent for the angler to choose a lure that he has confidence in and if that particular lure does not prove successful, then he should ring the changes in the hope that he will find one that will. His method of presentation is very similar to that employed in the spring. Basically in the higher ranges of flow he should cast square across the current and reel in more slowly as he retrieves his lure, whilst in the lower ranges he should angle his cast across the downstream, and reel in slightly faster. Of course, this may need to be adjusted according to the configuration of each individual pool fished.

HARLING

This form of fishing is not common to most rivers, and was really devised and used exclusively for many years on the River Tay, the largest salmon river in Scotland.

Harling is specifically designed to overcome the problem of being unable to cover the entire width of a very wide stretch of water efficiently, where this is quite impossible to achieve by an angler fishing from either bank. The water may be too deep to allow him to wade out and thereby overcome the problem, or the banks may be too heavily wooded to enable him to have sufficient casting clearance. This method is mainly used in high water flows, when there are no hazards or obstructions to impede the free and uninhibited use of a boat. It is, therefore, most popular during the periods from January to April, and again from August to the end of the season when water levels are likely to be swollen by either rainfall or snow melt on the catchment.

In the past a clinker built boat was rowed by the ghillie, with the angler or anglers sitting with their backs to him in the stern of the boat, their rods either held in their hand or placed with the butt on the floor of the boat and the rod resting against its gunnels, with the line and lure trailing out behind. The ghillie would start at the head of the fishable water and row quietly up against the current at an angle across the river. Once he reached a point close to the other bank, he would turn the boat and re-cross to the side he had first come from, gauging the speed of the boat so that he held it into the current without moving upstream or downstream. Having crossed and re-crossed the width of the pool, thereby allowing his angler's lures to cover the entire width of the fishable water thoroughly, he would then allow the boat to drop downstream a few yards and repeat the performance as many times as he needed to fish out the length of the pool.

If an angler hooked a fish, the other rods in the boat were wound in, and the ghillie usually rowed quietly to the bank, whereupon the angler played the fish out whilst he sat in the boat. If perchance, the fish became wild and moved either up or downstream too far, the ghillie pushed off the boat and followed it and re-landed once it had settled down again.

Nowadays, the boat is seldom propelled by oars but by an outboard motor. The ghillie sits in the stern and controls the motor whilst the angler or anglers sit in the centre or bow of the boat. Sometimes in this case it is no longer necessary to land whilst playing a fish but instead the boat remains out in the river whilst the fish is being played and once it is played out it is netted from the boat.

Sometimes up to four rods, each mounted with a different lure, are used at one time when a pool is being fished in this manner. In the early part of the year a variety of minnows, spoons or the Kynoch Killer are the most favoured lures, whilst later in the year some anglers still prefer to fish these lures, others believing that flies fished on a fly rod are equally effective.

There is no doubt that when the river is high this method of fishing covers the water more thoroughly than any other method, and in some cases it is the only means of achieving this. However, many anglers find it very boring as they are doing absolutely nothing but sitting in a boat waiting for a fish to seize one of the lures being towed behind the boat. They then merely lift the rod and hopefully land the fish.

LOCH FISHING

There are many lochs sited either at the head or elsewhere on the course of many of the river systems frequented by salmon. Therefore, these lochs are often inhabited for various periods by the fish as they ascend the rivers, and during that time they can be exploited by anglers. Particularly on the west coast of Scotland and in the islands off that coast, due to their narrow catchments, the lochs are often to be found only a short distance from the sea. Fish will run quickly into the lochs and remain there for long periods; often in fact, until they are ripe and ready to spawn. On the east coast, however, due to the much greater lengths of the river systems, the lochs are normally sited a greater distance up river, with the exception of Lochs Ness and Brora, both of which are sited low down their river systems. Many of the lochs on the east coast river systems are of much greater size and depth than is the norm on the west coast, although, again there are some exceptions on the west coast, such as Lochs Awe, Assynt and Lomond.

Although some lochs can be fished from the shore, anglers are dependent on wind and weather conditions being suitable to enable them to successfully exploit the water properly. Anglers are, therefore, much more mobile if they fish lochs from a boat, because they are able to take full advantage of whatever conditions happen to prevail by manoeuvering their boat accordingly.

For fly fishing, depth of water is of the utmost importance, fish rarely take a fly in depths over ten feet; depths ranging from two feet six inches to eight feet are the optimum for this method. Therefore, shallower bays and banks, or ridges, out in the loch are amongst the most productive places. The shallower sections are often to be found around the shore line or islands offshore, although high ridges can also be located a considerable distance into the loch with nothing to denote their presence. Intimate knowledge of the loch's topography is extremely helpful and the aid of an experienced ghillie with that knowledge can be invaluable, if the angler does not have this knowledge. In modern times, however, with experienced ghillies scarce, anglers can overcome this problem to a certain extent by obtaining an echo sounder and charting the shallow areas himself. If he spends a little time exploring the loch before he starts fishing using the sounder, he will at least know that he is fishing over productive water instead of wasting endless time fishing over a deep area where his chances of catching a fish are, to say the least, forlorn.

There is no doubt that for fly fishing the ideal situation is when there is one angler in a boat accompanied by a ghillie with intimate knowledge of the loch. The ghillie will know exactly which banks or bays are best suited to every wind, and therefore, regardless of which direction it blows from he will know where best to go. He will also know over a wide variable range of water levels in the loch, which banks or areas are best suited to the height that prevails on any particular day. There is then no time wasted in choosing where to fish; he will make for the best places straight away.

Having reached the fishing area, the ghillie will position the angler in the stern of the boat with his back to him and then row quietly as he holds the boat into the wind, so that the angler can comb every nook and cranny of the banks over a wide arc, as he gently drifts over them. If he moves a fish that does not take, the ghillie can quietly pull the boat up wind and allow the angler to come over it again. If he hooks a fish, the ghillie can gently row up wind away from the bank so that the unfished water is left undisturbed whilst the fish is played and landed. When fishing a bank close inshore, the ghillie can row quietly into and across the wind at an angle, so that every inch of this area can be covered meticulously without haste. Therefore, regardless of the strength of the wind, the boat is never allowed to drift too quickly over the best water.

If, however, there are two anglers in the boat with an experienced ghillie, although no time will be wasted fishing worthless water, the best places cannot be covered and fished quite as thoroughly, mainly because the boat has to be positioned square onto the wind and allowed to drift quietly down wind in order that the anglers sitting either in the stern or bow can both cover the water with a similar chance of success. The speed of the drift over the fishable water cannot be controlled by the ghillie but

Pool Morrail on the River Carron.

Old barrage at the exit to Loch Buidhe.

instead is controlled by the strength of wind blowing on that day. This naturally lessens the efficiency and thoroughness of how each drift can be exploited.

Early in the season, from January to March, the fly angler has a very limited chance of success, unless he trolls a large tube fly or weighted Waddington behind the boat, but in April and particularly during May, his chances of success vastly increase as the water temperature in the loch rises to the high 40°F or low 50°F ranges. It is best to use a twelve foot rod and an intermediary or sunk tip line; only in rough or very cold weather should the angler resort to a slow sinker. His cast should be fifteen to twenty pounds breaking strain, again according to conditions and in particular, the size of fly which he is using. Fly size will depend mainly once again on weather conditions, but the level of water in the loch is also an important factor to bear in mind. In mild conditions, with moderate wind and low loch levels, flies size three to nine or tubes a half inch to one inch are often the norm. However, on very windy, cold days with high loch levels, size 2 to 2/0 flies or tubes one and a half to two inches in length would be preferable.

Of all these factors at any time of year wind is probably the most important when fishing for salmon in a loch. Within reason the stronger the wind, the more chance there is of catching salmon on a fly. A six inch wave is acceptable, but stronger winds with troughs between the waves is ideal, provided in all cases it is a steady wind and not blustery, with 'cats paws' racing across the surface. Salmon can be caught in lighter winds on occasions, but mainly in the late evening or early morning.

The angler should cast out a reasonably long line at this time of year and draw his fly back towards him by handlining, gauging the speed of this handline movement entirely according to the speed at which his boat is drifting down towards the fly. If he mistimes this movement the fly will merely lie on the surface or sink, instead of 'swimming' in a life-like manner through the water. Once again, the single angler in a boat with a ghillie has a huge advantage as he can cover a large arc of water to the right, behind and to the left of the boat in alternate casts, whilst the ghillie holds the boat into the wind. The speed at which the boat is moving down towards the fly is then significantly diminished and the speed of retrieve is much easier to time. The angler can also fish the less productive water quickly and efficiently by side casting as the ghillie quietly rows into the wind. To achieve this, the angler again sits in the stern with his back to his ghillie and casts square across the wind and allows the fly to swing in an arc round behind the boat, whereupon he recasts.

When fishing a loch and a salmon moves to a fly it often leaves a tell-tale blemish on the surface, which is known in angling terms as a 'boil' or 'rise'. The angler must then delay his strike until he either feels the fish or has given it sufficient time to take before striking. I always count three slowly and if I have not felt the fish by then strike automatically in case it has come towards me as it takes. It is surprising how often, by adopting this method, the fish is securely hooked without feeling any contact beforehand. If the angler feels the fish before he sees any movement on the surface, the fish has taken his fly deep and he must, therefore, strike straight away.

Later in the year and during the summer months, when I am loch fishing for salmon I much prefer to use a single handed rod of ten feet to ten feet six inches, with a three fly cast, the same as I would when fishing for brown trout or seatrout. I almost invariably use size eight seatrout flies, and occasionally a small tube fly on the tail fly position. My cast varies according to conditions, from ten to fifteen pounds breaking strain. On a rough day I use a sunk line and on a mild day a floating line. My method is exactly the same as that practised earlier in the season, casting out a long line in the colder weather conditions, or when there is a light wind, and drawing my flies back toward me either by handlining or by use of rod tip control. However, in milder conditions I believe in using a much shorter line and lifting my top dropper onto the surface as soon as my flies land on the water, so that it literally bounces on top of the waves controlled almost entirely by rod tip control.

Fly patterns are really a matter of the angler's own preference and it is prudent for an angler to first and foremost fish with flies that he has confidence in himself. Of course, if the loch he is fishing has its own special favourites, he is always wise to purchase a few of these to have as a standby if he requires them.

Early in the season, I have always found the Willie Gunn, Munro Killer, Stoat's Tail, Thunder and Lightning, Mar Lodge and Sweep effective; to name but a few. Later in the season, when I revert to trout flies, I prefer to use on the tail an Invicta, Greenwell or Butcher; in the centre a Grouse and Claret or Green, or a Peter Ross; and on the bob a Black Pennel, Soldier Palmer or Goat's Toe. In very rough weather I often use a Worm fly on the tail and a Loch Ordie on the bob. There are, however, many other good flies both new and old, that do the job equally well.

Both fly fishing and spinning can be exercised from the bank, but I have said earlier that the shore angler is far more inhibited and mainly dependent on an offshore wind, or wind blowing parallel to the shoreline, to be able to exploit his water effectively. Waders can be a significant advantage if the loch happens to have a shallow shoreline, but those who wear body waders and wade in deep often do more harm than good, as they disturb their fish. It is far better to wade at knee height or mid-thigh at the most. For a shore fly fisherman a longer rod than he would use in the boat is often an advantage, fourteen to fifteen feet is probably the most useful.

Areas where a burn enters the loch, close to an outlet, off headlands or promontories or in bays, are the best places to concentrate on. The former, particularly in the later part of the season if it is a spawning burn or area, as salmon will congregate around these burns, until they are ripe and ready to lay their eggs, before ascending them.

Spinning can also be exercised from a boat, but those wishing to use this method usually troll their lures behind a boat powered by an outboard or else rowed by a companion, rather than spinning their lure from the boat. By this means they are able to cover a far greater expanse of water and often have more chance of picking up a taking fish. Depth of water is not so important for either trolling or spinning, nor is there the same need for an adequate wind and fish will take these lures sometimes in deep water with little wind to ruffle the surface, or when it is too blustery for fly fishing. Minnows, spoons or Kynock Killers are useful lures, with their size largely dependent on the conditions prevailing as well as the season of the year. In the early spring, with cooler water and air temperatures, a large lure is the norm, whilst during the summer small Mepps spinners or minnows can be more effective.

PRAWN AND NATURAL MINNOW FISHING

PRAWN FISHING

There are four ways of fishing the prawn, each of which can be very effective on their day. These are rambling or trotting, floating, sink and draw and spinning. The first three methods are normally used when the river is low but you can spin with a prawn very effectively when the river is high. Which method used is up to you, but the character of the pool you are fishing does really determine which is the most effective.

To start with I will take the trotting or rambling prawn as this method is the most exciting and can be used either on a fly rod of between twelve and fourteen feet in length, or a spinning rod. I would recommend that a rod of over twelve feet in length is used as this does give the angler more control over the prawn as it rambles down the stream. First of all the prawn has to be mounted on an ordinary bait hook size 1–1/0 with a nylon or wire trace attached. The best prawns are good red ones and I prefer those with red eggs between their legs. Straighten out the prawn, attach the bait needle to the loop of the hook trace, and thread the bait needle through the head of the prawn, pass it carefully along the fleshy back so that it comes out in the centre of the tail between the fins. Draw the trace through the body until the bait hook is lodged securely in the head of the prawn. You then bind the body of the prawn securely to the shank of the bait hook. You should do this either with pink silk, or better still very light copper wire, because if this is not done the body of the prawn will break up as you cast and as good natural prawns are extremely expensive this is wasteful. When you bind the prawn to the bait hook be careful to place the bindings between each set of legs so that they stand out and are not compressed against the side of the prawn by the binding material. Some people prefer to use a long pin as well as the shank of the bait hook to make certain that the body of the prawn is straight when it is being fished, but I have always found that a long shanked bait hook is perfectly adequate.

When the prawn is mounted (and it is a good idea to mount two or three before you start fishing) attach the trace to your line with about four feet of nylon if you are fishing with a fly rod or, if fishing with a spinning rod, tie the trace directly to the spinning line. Sometimes if you are fishing very fast flowing water it pays to have a small weight, preferably a spiral lead attached about three feet from the prawn. Start at the top of your pool about ten yards down from the head and then lob the prawn upstream into the neck of the current entering the pool. As the prawn comes down towards you raise the tip of your rod or draw in line so that you are always in immediate contact with the prawn and then, as the prawn rolls past, either release line or lower the rod tip to allow the prawn to move freely down the pool without dragging. Once the prawn has fished itself out and starts to drag then hand line in quietly and recast. In theory this method allows the prawn to swing and gyrate in the eddies of the current as it goes downstream, stabilised by the weight of the prawn and/or the weight attached to the line which is positioned to give the prawn depth and to regulate its movement in the water. Always keep in constant touch with the prawn so that it does not snag on the bottom and you can only do this by hand lining or raising the tip of your rod. If a fish takes and the prawn stops then you must strike immediately, and if you have too much drowned line then you will obviously miss your fish.

There is no doubt that a long rod is extremely helpful when fishing the rambling or trotting prawn because it gives you more direct control. I also think that the weight of the fly line stabilises the movement of the prawn in the water far more effectively than the lighter monofilament mounted on the modern spinning reel.

Try four to six casts from each position and then move downstream three or four yards at a time, and repeat this until you have fished out the streamy part of the pool. Once you get to the slower part of the pool this method is really less effective but if you wish to continue into the slacker current then you should remove the weight if you are using one. Ideally this method works best in narrow, streamy pools or cambered pools where the current bears in strongly on one bank. It is also very effective in small pots and rocky pools but it does not work so well in a pool which has a wide broad head or in wide, slow moving pools. Any pool which has a high bank or one where you can stand a distance above the water is well suited to this method of fishing because this enables you to have a better control over your bait, but this is by no means essential and I have, on occasions, used the rambling or trotting prawn very effectively when I have been wading fairly deep at the head of a run. The head of the Summer-house pool on the Argoed side of the Welsh Dee was ideal for this type of fishing.

THE FLOAT-FISHED PRAWN

This method is probably best suited to the older type of spinning rod of around ten to eleven feet in length but you can use a normal fly rod perfectly adequately. Mount the prawn in the same way as for the rambling or trotting prawn and attach a small weight about three feet up the line from the prawn, attach a float four to eight feet above the prawn, this distance will vary according to the depth of the water that you are fishing.

It is an advantage to grease the line for about twenty yards between the float and the rod so that it sits on the surface of the water and does not become drowned. This allows you to strike quickly if a fish takes, and it also stops the drowned line from dragging the float itself. Start at the top of the pool using the same tactics as you would fishing a rambling prawn, lobbing the prawn up into the head of the pool, then as the prawn comes past let the line run off the reel and allow the float to carry it down the pool. I let the prawn float down about twenty or thirty yards before checking it and then wind in very slowly. If you are fishing a wide pool start off by letting the float come down the near side of the pool first and then cast across the centre and then to the far side so that the prawn is shown to all the fish in the pool, regardless of where they are lying, over its entire width. When a salmon takes the prawn the float will bob on the surface and may be pulled across the current or upstream, or even on occasions downstream. When this happens you should pay out slack line and wait until the float is pulled below the surface before striking, otherwise you may pull the prawn out of the fish's mouth. I have often watched a salmon taking a floating prawn and very often it holds the prawn crossways in its mouth and plays with it before taking it properly. This is when the float bobs across the surface and therefore you should be patient and wait until the float actually plunges below the water before striking.

You should be careful to calculate the proper depth at which your prawn should fish as salmon rarely lie directly on the bottom of the pool and if your prawn is too deep you may actually be swimming it below where the fish are lying. To start with I would set my prawn at a depth of four feet, unless I knew the water well, and then gradually fish it deeper if

I had no success at that depth. I would say, however, that it is rarely necessary to set your float higher than eight feet above the prawn. A pool where there is a backwater, which the floated prawn can glide around in, can be a very effective taking place for this method of fishing.

SINK AND DRAW

I have always found it best to mount the prawn on an ordinary spinning mount with the spinning flight removed. Again, choose a good red prawn (preferably red eggs), then straighten it out and insert the pin of the mount between the fins at the tail of the prawn and along the fleshy part of its back. Once the prawn is straight then the hooks can be placed carefully between the legs and underneath its head then bound in position with either cotton or copper wire. The head of the prawn faces down the line and you should attach a good weight, preferably a spiral one, about four feet above the prawn on the line.

The sink and draw method works best, however, in a narrow deep pool, or a pool where the fish are lying in deep water beside a rocky ledge close to the bank, and it is not nearly so effective in shallower wide pools. Start fishing just above the deep water in the pool and stand about five yards above where the fish lie, and then cast across the pool square to the current. When your prawn hits the water keep your rod tip low for about half a minute to allow the prawn time to sink, and then crisply raise the tip about six feet then lower it again slowly. Continue this motion until the prawn has worked its way to the side of the pool at which time you should reel in and cast again. When you raise the tip of your rod you make the prawn shoot to the surface and it then falls slowly back into the depths of the pool dragged down by the weight. As it does this it gyrates gracefully in the eddies and currents. Fish which take the prawn fished in this way normally take it as it falls back into the depths or just as it begins to move once more to the surface. If you feel any pull or feel the prawn hesitate strike immediately, as fish are very inclined to snap at the prawn when it is fished in this way which is why it is mounted on treble hooks. This method can be deadly when other techniques fail and I can only imagine that the salmon is attracted by the quick movement of the prawn as it is being drawn to the surface.

It is an advantage to fish the sink and draw prawn with a fairly long rod and this is particularly true when the fish are lying against a rock ledge or a steep bank, as you can hold the bait the correct distance across the river just beyond where the fish are lying without snagging the prawn on a ledge. Pay particular attention to the distance that you place the weight above the prawn and this is just as important as the size of the weight you use. The size of the weight must be governed by the strength of the current in the pool you are fishing. The closer you place the weight to the prawn the more you curtail the prawn's movement in the water as it drops back into the depths of the pool. I have often seen a fisherman be successful immediately he moves his weight a foot or so further away from the prawn. Always be prepared to experiment with this and very often the small adjustment can make the difference between success and failure.

That famous fisherman, the late Captain Hughes-Parry, used the sink and draw method of fishing a prawn with great effect on the Slaughter-house pool of the Welsh Dee.

THE SPINNING PRAWN

This is exactly the same as any other method of spinning and you do not need to adopt any special tactics. Mount the prawn with the head down the line on an ordinary sprat tackle inserting the pin between the fins of the tail and then sliding the tackle into place along the back of the prawn. This straightens out the body of the prawn, you then bind the hooks on to the body using copper wire or cotton. I have heard some fishermen say that the legs of the prawn should be bound against the body as this makes the bait more streamlined, but I personally believe in placing the binding between the legs so that they stand out, even for this method of fishing. This does mean that the prawn wallows about in the water as it is being spun and I feel that this attracts fish and makes the bait more effective. This is rather akin to spinning for Salmo ferox or cannibal trout in lochs with a natural bait, when you should place the flight in the shoulder of the small trout and not through its head to produce this wallowing motion. Use the spinning prawn in medium or low water, or use it in high water provided that the river is not too coloured. It is probably most effective in still wide pools or in the glide of the tail of a big pool. I used a spinning prawn on the Welsh Dee with great success from opening day which in the past was 15 March until the end of May. Some of my friends used second quality prawns, that is ones without eggs or those with black eggs, when they fished the spinning prawn but I would recommend that you use the best quality prawns available and do, if you can, use those with eggs.

I know that prawn fishing is a very controversial subject and many anglers believe that it should be banned. It is, however, a highly skilled method of fishing and, if it is not abused, it can be a useful addition to any angler's armoury as it often allows him to kill fish in stretches of water or parts of pools which would be impossible to fish in any other way, unless he was spinning.

It is a fact that it very seldom pays to persevere with this bait. Fish either take it straightaway or completely disregard it and therefore a few casts with a prawn using the method best adapted to a particular pool is quite sufficient to find out whether the fish are going to take the prawn that particular day or whether you should go home or resort to some other method of fishing.

I am sure that many people will be puzzled by the importance I attach to fishing with prawns which have eggs between their legs. When I started fishing as a boy I was always told by my tutors that you should use prawns with eggs and I was puzzled why this should be. Now, after long experience, I am as convinced as they of the importance of this and rightly or wrongly I put forward the theory that as the prawn is buffeted by the currents as it drifts down the river, these eggs are dislodged. They float down in the water, and salmon scent them and often home into the prawn by following the eggs to the prawn itself.

This theory may sound a bit far-fetched, but I am positive that it is correct. For example, in the wood on the right bank of the Major pool on the Welsh Dee there were two places ideally suited to fishing the floating prawn. One was immediately above a projecting buttress of rock close to the bank and below this buttress was one of the main lies in the pool. No fisherman could work a prawn down to this lie because once it passed the buttress it was no longer within sight. This meant that you had to swim the prawn down above the rock buttress and then cast again when the float reached the projection. This was a section of the pool where fish seldom lay. However, when you fished this river with the floating prawn very often you caught a fish, and this usually occurred on the third or fourth cast. As there was a high bank above the river you could watch the fish in the main lie when the angler started fishing. Very often after one or two casts the fish in that lie become alert, and then move up slightly before swimming around the buttress and following a weaving course until they saw the prawn which they then took.

Another place was below the buttress at a small promontory we called 'Taylor's Stance'. From here we used to cast the prawn upstream and let it float down to the pool below where we stood. Here it got caught in the small backwater and the float circled around this little bay until we lifted the prawn up to cast again. Often, I could watch fish following down the exact line that the prawn had taken just moments before turning in at the bottom of the backwater and gulping the prawn as they came back upstream. There is no doubt that in both these places the fish were following the scent that the prawn had left in the water as they could not possibly see it, and I firmly believe that this scent is provided by the eggs as they get washed out by the current. Certainly I have always found that a prawn without eggs was far less effective and I would go so far as to say that it is virtually useless, unless it is used for spinning in high water.

THE SHRIMP

Shrimp fishing is identical to fishing with a prawn in every detail, and mounting the shrimp is exactly the same. It works best during the summer when the rivers are low and the temperature is high and the period from the beginning of May until the end of September is the best time. I have always found that the rambling and floating methods of fishing with shrimp are by far the most successful and on numerous occasions I have found that shrimp will work when the prawn has failed, although I always believe in trying prawn first and never the other way about.

When rivers are low and water temperatures high, bait fishers will find that they kill four fish on the shrimp to every one on the prawn, but here I am speaking of the natural prawn and in recent years those prawns dyed deep purple in colour have proved very successful, particularly in the summer months. So successful have they become that the day of the shrimp may well be over.

THE NATURAL MINNOW

This is the last natural bait that can be used for salmon fishing and I think that it is best when fished with the sink and draw method. It is, of course, a well known bait to use for big wily old trout, but it can kill salmon that have become stale in pools after a prolonged spell of low water and it is worth trying, as a last resort, when all other baits have failed. Mount the minnow by passing a bait needle attached to a hook trace through the mouth of the minnow, down through the body, and out beside the tail. Fold a piece of lead or lead wire around the shank of the hook and then pull the hook into the mouth of the minnow so that the lead and shank lodge in its throat and the hook and barb lie outside its mouth against the gill casing. No further weighting up the line should be necessary.

Cast out the bait and work it in exactly the same way as you would a sink and draw prawn. Concentrate on those areas of the pool where the main lies are sited and also the necks of the pool but surprisingly if a fish takes do not strike immediately, but pay out line in exactly the same way you would if you were worming. This allows the salmon plenty of time to gorge the bait and eventually you can strike crisply when you judge the time to be ripe.

All these methods of fishing with natural baits are not only very effective but also highly skilled. There is no doubt that a great deal of the art lies in the ability of the angler to mount and present the bait properly, and when you are fishing it is of the utmost importance to show the bait free of drag. There is, however, one proviso to this – salmon do sometimes take when you are reeling in to cast again. You should therefore always concentrate right up to the time when the bait leaves the water. The only other point I would make is that you should be careful not to handle the natural bait when your hands are covered with fly repellent, as salmon have a very acute sense of smell, and I think this is a mistake even when you are fishing with an artificial fly.

I have always been slightly perplexed why fishing with these natural baits, worm, shrimp and prawn is frowned upon when spinning with gold and silver sprats has always been accepted by most anglers without question. I cannot see any logical reason for such a differentiation and would say that of all baits, including all forms of spinning, the worm, fished properly, is the most harmless. It not only disturbs a pool the least but is the one bait which rarely, if ever, foul hooks a fish.

WORM FISHING

This interesting form of fishing for salmon is, on the whole, despised by many who for some unknown reason seem to believe that it is rather an underhand method of taking these unpredictable fish. However, few can deny that if it is practised correctly it is probably one of the most artistic and difficult forms of fishing for any angler to accomplish, as well as being one of the most effective.

There are two entirely different methods of worm fishing quite apart from the many different means of presenting the worm to salmon. In the first case, this involves using a single red worm either mounted on a Stewart tackle with three small hooks in line ahead each attached to the other by a small length of gut, two facing forwards and the centre one backwards, or mounted on a single bait hook. This method is very similar to that used by the trout angler. In the second case, two or three large lobworms are used, all threaded on one single bait hook size 1 or 2 for preference. There is no doubt that these widely different methods can both be very productive on their day, but they are so dissimilar in appearance that it is worth while pausing and considering this point.

When using the single worm there is no doubt that this will stir a memory of the fishes freshwater feeding phase when it was a parr in the river before migrating to sea and, therefore, the reason for the salmon taking this is quite understandable. However, the other method is more difficult to explain because two or three lobworms fished together form quite a large lure and certainly not one that would reasonably represent a worm in its literal form. Therefore, what does the salmon believe it is? We can only conjecture about this, but it would be reasonable to suppose that it might simulate some creature that forms part of their stable diet at sea. This in all probability could be a small octopus, squid or similar sea creature found during their meanderings in the oceans.

It is also interesting to note that when fishing either of these methods, when the worm is mounted on a single hook it is wise not to strike when the fish takes but instead to feed out line. This is to ensure that the fish does not feel any resistance as he makes contact, at the same time to give him time to take it properly, as at first they can be very tentative in their approach to these baits. Often their attitude as they take is almost playful and resembles that of a cat catching a mouse. First of all they catch it, then almost immediately they blow it out of their mouth, then they take it again and roll it around their mouth and may repeat this process several times before either discarding it completely or more probably devouring it. Naturally, if the angler does choose to strike during the first stages of this performance, there is every likelihood of him pulling the worm out of the fish's mouth or away from the fish with little or no chance of hooking it. On initial contact the angler will feel a sharp tug-tug on his line and then he should immediately allow a loop of line to slip through his fingers allowing the line to go slack, this should be repeated if there is further tapping and tugging. Only when he feels a firm continuous pull should he strike. It can be up to 30 inches of line that is taken or even more before this happens so he must be patient and steel himself not to react too soon or all will be lost. Only when the angler is using a single worm on Stewart tackle is it permissable to strike on contact and even then I would say his chances of a firm contact are no more than 60 per cent. But there again, if he delays, the chances are that when the fish is rolling the bait in his mouth he is almost bound to make contact with either one or other of the hooks, whereupon the fish will immediately discard it. This, in my opinion, is the disadvantage of using more than one hook when fishing the worm.

Another very unusual feature of this type of fishing, is the fact that when a salmon takes the worm properly, having been given time by the angler, almost invariably the fish is hooked in the gullet or further down. This, in itself, must throw at least some doubt on the fact that salmon never feed on their return to fresh water, otherwise this unusual aspect of worm fishing is extremely difficult to explain.

The single worm method can be effective under almost any height of water flow with one of the most favoured being a rising river beginning to show or already having turbidity in it. This again is understandable as this is when one would obviously expect worms and insects to be washed into the river from the surface of the land and is regarded as the optimum condition for worming for trout. Not quite so explainable is that worming is also a reasonably productive method in dead low water and it is under these conditions that it is a real art, true accomplishment requiring an expert's touch.

The expert nearly always prefers to use a fly rod for fishing the single worm by the rambling method, because this longer rod gives him far more control over his worm as it trundles along the river bed than he would have when using a shorter spinning rod. This form of fishing is used when the angler can gain access to an area where fish are lying reasonably close to the bank, or where he is able to wade out to fish. It really depends on the speed of the current and/or the water height whether he has to use a weight, and if so, how heavy it should be, but if he does this it should be attached some 18 inches to 2 feet above his worm. Normally, one or two small lead shot are sufficient. Having positioned himself just below the neck of a streamy pool, the angler should draw off a loop of some five to ten yards of line and quietly lob his worm upstream by swinging his rod upwards and slightly outwards, and allowing the slack line to run through his fingers as it is drawn out by the impetus of his cast. As soon as his worm lands on the water he should give it time to sink and then raise his rod quietly upwards, to allow for the fact that his worm is coming down current towards him, and at the same time he should hand line in quietly, in order to gain contact with the worm. By doing this it is easy to keep the rod tip in complete contact with the worm as it trundles along the river bed; if it hesitates or stops the rod tip should be raised slowly and if it has been taken by a fish the angler will feel the tell tale tug-tug on the line, whilst if it is the bottom of the river bed he will feel a solid tremor. In the first case, he must immediately release a loop of slack line from the loose line which he has been drawing in in order to give the fish time to take the worm solidly, whilst in the second case he merely lifts his rod tip higher, which should release the worm and allow it to trundle on downstream. As the worm comes opposite the angler, in theory the rod should be held high and nearly all the spare line should be in his hand. As it passes him the angler should then lower his rod and pay out slack line to allow it to continue downstream until it reaches the point when the line between the worm and the rod tip is taut and no slack line remains. This is the end of his cast. The angler then hand lines in and recasts upstream in exactly the same manner repeating the performance several times from the same position. He then moves downstream ten yards to a new stance.

If the angler does not raise his rod tip sufficiently or fails to handline in fast enough as the worm floats down towards him, it is almost inevitable that this will snag the worm on the river bed. It is essential, therefore, for the angler to get the feel of this procedure and it often pays dividends to practise with a small weight and no hook on the line. By doing so, he will soon get used to getting the feel of the weight with his rod tip, recognise when it gets lodged on the bottom and learn how to release it when it does so. This will also save him endless frustration when he puts it into practise in good fishing conditions.

In very high water flows, he should concentrate on quiet areas close to the bank where there is a lull or eddy just at the side of the current, or in a backwater. He should in the latter case, keep contact with the worm by use of his rod tip in exactly the manner I have described, and instead of allowing it to trundle downstream and past him, merely allow it to swing round and round the circumference of the backwater.

In low water conditions, he should concentrate on runs, gutters and pots as well as the short streamy necks of the main pools. In these conditions he should cast his line as if he was fly fishing, flicking the bait as far upstream as possible and keeping contact with it as before. A long rod is essential, to enable long and accurate casting and to be able to control the worm's passage around and past prominent boulders in what is often a rock strewn river course. These are the testing conditions that require the expert touch, and this technique can only be perfected by long experience. Under these conditions even light weights are seldom required and this lessens the chance of the worm becoming snagged. As the small red dung worm is usually soft and brittle, it often breaks off the hook as it is cast out. A useful tip to prevent this happening is to dig these worms several days before they are required and place them in a container with powdered red brick and soil mixed together. Their skins become rubbery and much tougher, without harming them in any way.

Another method of fishing the single worm is to use a float, and merely trot it down the pool. The distance between the float and the worm entirely depends on the depth of water the angler is fishing, and can vary from 2 to 5 feet. This method is very similar to that already mentioned, with the worm being cast upstream and then allowed to drift down towards the angler and then on down past him.

For this method it is not essential to use a fly rod because the float, if set at the correct depth keeps the worm suspended above the river bed and this in itself should reduce the chances of snagging on all but stones or rocks which protrude high above the river bed. It is prudent, however, to grease the line between the rod tip and the float so that this section of the line never becomes drowned, but instead floats on the surface. Alternatively, if a fly rod is being used the angler can use a floating line. The obvious advantage of this method over the rambling one is that the worm can be floated down any section of the entire width of river in most depths of water and is not confined to the near section, where the rambling worm can only be controlled by the rod tip. Its disadvantage, however, is that it is floating some distance above the river bed and fish have to move out of their lies to take it, whereas the rambling worm bumping along the bed of the river or a short distance above it, searches every nook and cranny where fish may be lying.

When a fish takes, the float begins to teeter and bob on the surface, and the angler should then pay out line as before, and only strike when the float actually plunges below the surface and disappears from sight. If the float stops and drags on the surface without an erratic motion, the angler will know that he is snagged.

Weighting is all according to the current flow which prevails in each pool that the angler fishes. Sometimes it is necessary to place a medium weight 2 to 3 feet above the worm, whilst at other times only the lightest of weights are required. In very low water, fishing fast runs and torrential sections it is difficult to control a float properly as it becomes drowned by the velocity and is, therefore, not nearly as effective as the rambling method.

Now turning to worm fishing with the larger lobworms. It is best not to thread these worms right over the entire hook, but instead impale them in the centre so that their ends dangle free either side of the hook, thereby simulating a creature with tentacles. These can be fished effectively in the same manner as the single worm either by rambling them or floating them down a pool, as previously described. They can also be very deadly when fished on what is known as the sink-and-draw method. A medium weight should be placed some 3 feet above the worm. The worm should then be cast out square across the river, and allowed to sink. The angler keeps the point of his rod low as soon as the worm lands on the water for maybe 10 seconds and then the rod tip is raised crisply about 6 feet upwards, and then lowered quietly again. This motion should be continued until the bait has worked its way to the nearside of the pool, at which time the angler should reel in and re-cast in similar fashion. When the angler raises his rod tip quickly the bait shoots towards the surface, he then lowers it again quietly; it sinks back into the depths dragged down by the weight of his cast. As the worms move they tremor and gyrate gracefully in the current and eddies in a most life-like manner and are, therefore, very attractive to any fish lying in the pool. Fish generally take these worms either just as they move towards the surface, or just as they begin to fall back into the depth. If the angler feels any pull or hesitation, he must immediately feed out line to give the salmon time to take properly, then strike. This method can be particularly effective at times of low flow when fish are confined to the main holding pools, and will often take when all other methods of worm fishing and other modes of fishing have failed.

The lobworm method of fishing seems to favour either a rising, turbid river or dead low water, the latter even when there is bright sunshine and clear blue skies, particularly during the month of May, but it can be a useful alternate string to an angler's bow in any water conditions. Most anglers will find, however, that on the whole it either works or does not work, and if nothing happens after twenty minutes to half an hour it is seldom worth persisting with, but instead try another lure or fly, and then return to it later in the day. If, however, the fish are going to take they generally do so straight away and then usually for an appreciable period.

Small pots and runs in rocky gorges, necks of streamy pools and the shallower, fast flowing runs are all useful places in low water flows, whilst backwater eddies and quiet lulls at the side of the main current are useful areas in high spate flows.

Ledgering, with the worm anchored to the river bed by weights and the worm free to gyrate in the current can kill fish, but is a most boring and monotonous method and in my opinion not a very rewarding form of fishing. It is far better for the angler to go out and search for his fish, rather than sit down on the bank and expect the fish to come to him.

To sum up briefly, always use good lively worms, preferably with hard tough skins. Always keep in contact with the worm whilst it is fishing by using rod tip control, otherwise you will be continually frustrated by hooking the bottom and being snagged, quite apart from the wasteful loss of tackle. Especially in low water, approach the water with stealth and try to avoid erratic movements. Always, if possible, keep the worm moving quietly, guided by the pace of the current, and avoid any drag on the line and thence the worm. If during the summer months the angler does not follow this advice, he is very likely to be pestered by eels taking his worms. Use a medium sized single hook for preference.

CHAPTER THIRTEEN

Nets and Traps

For very many centuries various types of netting and trapping methods have been acknowledged means of exploiting salmon stocks. In fact, the earliest records of the industry show that salmon were being caught by these means as long ago as the thirteenth century. Basically, however, in those days salmon were primarily looked upon as an easy source of food, which had a very high nutritional value. These stocks could be easily exploited as they ascended the river systems, by different forms of crude traps and baskets placed in strategic places on the coast, estuaries and parts of the rivers, such as falls. As time progressed so the various forms of traps became more scientifically constructed and by the seventeenth century many of them had been diversified into wide ranging forms of net and trap fisheries, some of which are still operated both on the coastline and within river estuaries, even in the present day.

In Scotland, for example, under the 1863 to 1868 Salmon Fishery (Scotland) Acts, both rod and net fisheries were far more strictly controlled. Not only were open and close seasons strictly defined, but also fishery districts were formed, many of which were administered by its own District Fishery Board. Every district had estuary limits delineated and an area of coastline was allocated to each district. The annual close time imposed for net fishing was set at 168 days, except for the River Tweed where it was 153 days, and in addition a weekly close time was imposed. The actual dates of the annual close time varied from district to district, mainly according to when fish spawned within the rivers in that district. The weekly close time did not vary from district to district, but this period has been extended from time to time over the years since the legislation came into effect.

The methods of net fishing within a district were also strictly controlled. Within estuary limits net and coble was the only method permitted, whereas seaward of these limits within the district, fixed engines such as bag nets, fly nets, poke nets and beach seine netting (the term used for net and coble fishing practised outside estuary limits) are all allowable means of netting.

The net and coble method requires a boat carrying the net to move out into the river as it sets the net and then returns to the shore, having completed a semi-circular movement. A fisherman on the shore must keep hold of the end of the net, which has to be kept in motion relative to the water while fishing. The construction of the net must also show that it is designed to encircle fish and not merely to enmesh them.

Beyond estuary limits, the most common form of fixed engine used in Scotland is either the bag net or stake (fly) net. The bag net is defined as a net extending seawards from the shore, suspended by floats and anchored in a fixed position. It consists of a trap made of netting towards which fish are directed by a netting leader. The purpose of the leader is to direct fish towards and into the trap. One end of the leader is fixed firmly either to the shore or seabed whilst the other is attached to the trap. The leader must be made of material which is clearly visible in order that it can be clearly shown to lead fish into the trap, and is not there for the purpose of catching fish by enmeshing them.

The fly, or stake net, is a net fixed to the foreshore by stakes extending seawards. It is a curtain of netting set vertically on stakes driven into the foreshore, and this acts as a leader to direct salmon towards and into traps made of netting placed at intervals along its length. Once again the netting leader is there for the purpose of leading fish into the trap, and not in itself for the purpose of enmeshing fish. The only form of trap allowable within a river system is a cruive, which is rarely used and then only by owners who hold cruive charter rights passed down through the centuries. The cruive dyke is formed by a stone built weir across the width of the river, with one or more apertures or boxes formed in the weir through which the water flow passes downstream and which fish could ascend. The cruive is fished either by forming a trap upstream of each aperture or box into which the fish swim or alternatively by placing slats in the boxes set close enough together to allow the water to flow through but at the same time prevent the passage of fish. The fish, therefore, are forced to congregate in the pool downstream which is then netted at intervals. Probably the best example of a well preserved cruive dyke exists today on the Beauly river in Inverness-shire, although it is no longer operated.

Restrictions controlling the duration of the netting season and netting methods also regulate net fisheries in other parts of the UK, but these differ considerably from those imposed in Scotland.

For nearly a hundred years after the 1868 legislation, salmon stocks in Scotland went from strength to strength and for a period in the 1950s Scotland alone was catching more Atlantic salmon than any other nation. It was not until drift net fishing and net fishing on the high seas began to escalate in the 1960s, followed shortly afterwards by the outbreak of UDN disease in Eire and the UK in the late 1960s, that these catches began to decline steadily over the next twenty to thirty years.

There is no doubt that the innovation of synthetic nylon fibre netting such as monofilament was the main factor which heralded the revival and escalation of drift net fishing for salmon. Once this practically invisible type of netting replaced the old traditional hemp netting, the efficiency of this type of fishery vastly improved. In particular, the fact that it was barely visible to fish made it nearly as effective in daylight hours as it was at night, which was a significant advantage over its predecessor, because hemp was too easily seen by fish in the daytime to be of worthwhile use. Another substantial advantage of nylon is that it is light and far less bulky than hemp. It was, therefore, far easier to handle and much longer lengths of netting could easily be carried on board the fishing boats.

This led to an immediate expansion of the traditional drift net fishery on the north east coast of England off the Northumbrian and Yorkshire coasts, and also of the Irish drift net fishery. At the same time, a similar fishery started up off the east coast of Scotland. Due to the rapid development of this latter fishery, there were fears that salmon stocks might be endangered. A committee, under the Chairmanship of Lord Hunter, set up to review the law relating to salmon and trout fisheries in Scotland, was asked to give priority to this subject. In a report published in July 1963 the committee recommended a prohibition of drift net fishing reinforced by a ban on the landing of drift net caught fish in Scotland. The Government acted quickly and implemented this by introducing the appropriate Orders. These have been renewed and the ban on drifting off the Scottish shores is still in force.

Unfortunately, however, the drift net fisheries off the north east coast of England and the Irish drift net fishery were not similarly dealt with and these fisheries continue to intercept salmon returning from their feeding grounds at sea to their rivers of origin in Scotland, England, Wales and Ireland and are, therefore, indiscrimate fisheries predating on stocks from many different river systems. The revival of the English and Irish drift net fisheries coincided with the start of the high seas net fishery off the coast of Greenland. I have covered the history of net and long line fisheries on the high seas and also the matter of interceptory net fisheries elsewhere in this book and will not go further into these subjects here.

In the 1970s legislation further tightened the ban on net fisheries that enmeshed fish by banning all forms of gill or hang nets for catching salmon in Scotland. This strengthened the ban on drift net fisheries, prevented hang nets being set off headlands and also prohibited panels of monofilament net being used in the leaders attached to fixed engines such as bag and fly nets. This type of net is set hanging vertically in the water suspended by floats, its mesh being sufficiently large to enable the head of the fish to pass through, but too small to allow the rest of the body to follow. When the fish tries to turn round or withdraw, the mesh traps the fish behind the gills. In its struggle to escape, the flesh of the fish is usually bruised and its skin is either descaled behind the shoulder or maybe cut. Therefore, the quality of the catch caught in these fisheries is of considerably lower quality than those caught either by net and coble or fixed engine methods. Any fish that die and fall out of the net or escape badly wounded, become carrion on the bottom of the sea and those which are wounded but manage to reach their native river may become a disease risk. Hang, or gill net fisheries can be termed, for these very reasons, a wasteful form of fishery.

There is little doubt that net fisheries do play an integral and essential part in Atlantic salmon fisheries management, provided they are controlled properly; mainly because they are required to cull runs of fish returning to their rivers of origin to the numbers the river is capable of supporting. Naturally, this must include accommodation and both seeding and rearing. It is, however, very important that the right balance between netting cull, rod catch and spawning escapement is achieved.

In the Hunter Committee's report of 1965 it was recommended that all fixed engine stations outside estuary limits should be phased out, and those within estuary limits reduced to a single netting point or fish trap within the estuary of each river system. However, no Government has seen fit to implement these recommendations since the report was published. There is no doubt that these recommendations were made in order that salmon stocks could be culled in a more controlled and scientific manner as they return to their own river of origin, instead of being intercepted on the coastline as they search for the entrance to their native river.

Nearly twenty years later, in 1985, the Atlantic Salmon Conservation Trust was set up with the prime purpose of trying to implement the Hunter Committee recommendations by different means. This was by purchasing both coastal and estuary net stations in the open market, and then closing these stations down. Many stations on the coastline of the Moray Firth in the vicinity of the Ness, Nairn, Findhorn and Spey; off the mouths of the Dee and Don, and also around the coast and estuary of the Tweed, were dealt with in this manner. During the same period, the Government extended the compulsory weekend net slap period for netting to sixty hours, in order to further reduce netting effort and conserve salmon stocks. It must remain to be seen whether these actions, taken in order to conserve salmon stocks, actually produce the results for which they were carried out. With *Salmo salar*'s approximate five year cycle, it will be some considerable time before these results can be evaluated rationally.

However, in recent years, mainly due to a combination of factors such as the decline in salmon stocks, rising labour and operating costs and large consignments of farmed fish flooding the market, many net fisheries have become unviable economically. This had led to a number of these fisheries being closed down voluntarily and this in itself has led to a significant reduction in coastal and estuary salmon net fishery effort throughout the UK. Whether these further steps to curtail netting were really necessary is naturally controversial.

In 1989 and 1990 a consortium of nations spear-headed by Iceland, has been looking into the possibility of buying off both the Greenland drift net and the Faroese long-line salmon fisheries on a long term basis. If these bold steps come to fruition and are backed by all nations which stand to gain by this project, there is little doubt that the money paid in compensation to the relevant fishermen will have been well spent, especially in the case of the Greenland fishery. This will release large numbers of multi-sea-winter fish and allow these precious components of the overall salmon stocks to return to their native rivers in both Europe and North America. In the Faroes, not only the fish caught as part of the quota in the fishery, but also many other immature fish caught and then returned to the sea, many of which are damaged and die afterwards, will all be free to return to their rivers of origin.

If, because of this enterprise, these two commercially indiscriminate fisheries on feeding grounds at sea are closed down, not only will this probably lead to the balance of seasonal salmon runs being again restored, but also it could well lead to the eventual end to all indiscriminate interceptory drift net fisheries that predate on stocks of *Salmo salar*.

There is no doubt that if this step could be achieved, it would not only quickly restore the balance of salmon runs returning to their native rivers, but also enable scientific research projects on the subject to be carried out more easily and with a greater degree of accuracy.

Salmon ranching is a new form of commercial net or trap fishery that has been successfully developed in countries such as Iceland. Small rivers and large burns that do not have the necessary commodities to support salmon stocks of their own are chosen and developed for this purpose. Salmon ova and fry are then reared on to the parr and smolt stage in hatcheries close by. On some occasions the water supply for the hatchery is drawn from these watecourses. The parr and smolts are then released into these rivers or burns, and migrate to sea when the time comes. On their return as adults they are either trapped or netted at the mouth of the river. Those that are required for regeneration purposes are kept in tanks in the hatchery until they are ripe for stripping, whilst the rest of the catch is marketed. This self-supporting little industry can be a very lucrative form of salmon fishery. Unfortunately, salmon ranching in this country would be unlikely to be a viable concern, because the drift net fisheries off the English and Irish coasts would inevitably deplete fish stocks returning. Therefore, until all drift fisheries are closed down, further development of this new commercial industry is not possible in the foreseeable future.

CHAPTER FOURTEEN

Poaching

Salmon poaching in different forms has been going on for centuries, but until this century it was generally a case of 'one for the pot' to feed the family, rather than on a commercial scale. In the past, various forms of cleeks, gaffs and spears were favoured, either to poach fish in pots near falls or at night from a boat with a light thrown onto the surface of the water from a burning tarred torch. Others preferred to make crude traps out of wire or net pools surreptitiously. In those days the poacher took only what he required and prided himself on his ability to leave behind no trace of his activities or damage to either property or his quarry.

It was not until early in this century that better transportation gave not only mobility to the poacher, but also an easier means of disposing of his catch. This eventually led to commercial poaching becoming a profitable form of livelihood, or at least a means of supplementing income. The risk involved often added to the challenge of this lucrative pastime.

In pre-war days commercial poaching raids on rivers were largely confined to netting activities or sniggering at falls, but an odd explosive raid did take place, mainly when the deeper, rocky holding pools were the chosen target. After the war, however, when food was still scarce, more ruthless poachers began to use poison such as cymag in order to further their cause by increasing their catch. This form of poaching, particularly in the early stages, often created indiscriminate destruction, mainly because few people who used cymag realised its power and too large a charge was applied. Often this resulted in more fish being killed than could be handled by the users, and as a result many fish were left behind to rot at the bottom of pools, whilst many more salmon fry and parr and other freshwater species that inhabited the affected area, were killed in the raid. Even the fish fauna and vegetation in these sections of the river were destroyed.

Even in the present day poison poaching is still practised and can seriously affect salmon stocks in the rivers for some considerable time in the future after the raid has taken place, frequently causing unacceptable pressures on declining salmon stocks.

With the advent of nylon replacing hemp as the material nets were made of, net poaching became far more favoured. This was mainly because it was light and, therefore, long lengths could be carried and handled with far more ease and stealth. The use of this method has escalated drastically, both at sea, in the estuaries and also in the main river systems. Nylon netting is readily available at a reasonable cost and can be used either as a set net or as a sweep net.

In spite of much heavier fines and sentences being levied by the courts in recent years, there are many people who are still willing to take the risk and partake in this nefarious activity for their own personal gain. Many work in gangs and use sophisticated methods, both at sea and in fresh water. Even with the reduction in the value of their catch as a result of farmed fish flooding the market, their will and enthusiasm to carry out their illegal work seldom wanes. Unfortunately, this means that fishery managers are forced to spend large sums of money to combat poaching, which otherwise could have been spent on research, hatcheries and river improvement works to maintain and improve salmon stocks. Increased river watching staff, transport and equipment to counter these more organised sophisticated methods of poaching are a drain on funds which could be far better deployed to conserve the species. Unfortunately, however, pressure on salmon stocks from this illegal activity has escalated to such a degree in the last twenty years, that there is no alternative but to take such courses of action.

After the fish have survived rigours and dangers both at sea and in fresh water over nearly five years of life and have returned to their native rivers as mature adults ready and able to regenerate the species when the time comes in the autumn, no river can possibly afford to lose them literally at the eleventh hour of their life by this means.

CHAPTER FIFTEEN

Atlantic Salmon in Other Countries

The Atlantic salmon is indigenous to most rivers in Europe, Scandinavia, the east coast of North America, and Iceland, where these rivers border the Atlantic seaboard. In some areas they have thrived better than others, but in the main, where salmon stocks have declined, it has been almost entirely due to carelessness, bad land use or polllution by mankind.

In many countries in Europe and North America, the construction of dams across the full width of rivers to provide water power for a variety of uses has, during the last few centuries, been primarily responsible for the decline of salmon stocks in many of the prime salmon rivers. Such dams, especially those built in earlier times, had no fish pass facilities incorporated within them and the ascent of this migratory species was either completely debarred or largely impeded. Accordingly they could not reach their vital destination – the breeding ground. Due entirely to this simple fact, salmon stocks in the rivers were virtually destroyed.

In many other countries, pollution in different forms has been primarily responsible for the decline of salmon stocks or, in some of the worst cases, the local extinction of the species. In North America, mercury pollution from the timber trade, spraying of forests against pests and the mining industry, have all played their part in retarding salmon stocks on their breeding grounds. Localised industrial pollution has also created problems by reducing water qualities to unacceptable levels in some rivers.

In Europe, industrial pollution has been so intensive in certain areas, that salmon stocks have been completely destroyed. In other areas, particularly in France, waste materials from the dairy industry have created serious problems, retarding fish fauna and causing fish kills, which has caused salmon stocks to decline.

In Scandinavia, whilst some rivers have suffered localised pollution from the countries own industries, by far the worst problem has been the fallout of acid rain produced by the intensive industrial areas in neighbouring countries. This has seriously reduced the pH value of many rivers to such an extent that the value is below the level in which salmonides can survive and in some rivers and lakes, especially in the south of Norway salmon stocks have either seriously declined or in extreme cases become extinct.

In all these countries, since the last war, tremendous efforts have been made to rehabilitate salmon stocks in many of the affected rivers in order to try and redress the present decline. This has entailed –

1. Research in order to pin-point the problems.
2. Reduction of pollution and improvement of water quality.
3. Installation of fish passes, on both existing and new dams.
4. Restoration works, such as the founding of artificial spawning channels, and the stabilising of river banks.
5. Building of hatcheries and propagation programmes.

In spite of this large investment in an attempt to improve salmon stocks, the progress towards recovery in most cases has been slow. Although there is little doubt that salmon are a very resilient species, it would seem that one of the main reasons for this could be that once they have lost their predominance on both feeding and spawning areas to other species, it is very difficult to re-establish that predominance and thrive as they did in the past. Some countries do still have salmon stocks in many of their rivers and these provide good fishing.

EIRE

Salmon fishing in Eire is comparable with that of the UK. As it is also an island and not a mainland nation, instead of having several very large rivers it has numerous smaller rivers draining widely different sizes of catchment. Many of these produce prolific runs of fish throughout the spring, summer and early autumn, all of which are capable of providing excellent sport for anglers.

Although some of the major salmon rivers, such as the Blackwater, suffered very badly as a result of the outbreak of UDN in the late 1960s and temporarily lost their famous runs of spring fish, these runs are now well on their way to recovery. Both spring and summer runs, the latter including a large proportion of grilse, are at the present time drawing anglers both at home and abroad to partake of the sport; surrounded in most cases by a serene landscape and breath-taking scenery with its ever changing lights, regardless of weather conditions. These anglers can all find a fishery to suit the method of fishing they prefer best whether it is fishing a river or a lough or even both, from either boat or bank.

Amongst the many fisheries are the Foyle in the north, the Corrib and

Shannon in the west, the Lee and Blackwater to the south, and the Boyne to the east, all of which produce an adequate supply of both salmon and grilse of various sizes and weights.

SPAIN

Not many people realise that Atlantic salmon frequent rivers quite so far south, nevertheless there are several useful salmon rivers in the north of Spain, such as the Cares and the Dava. These rivers, set in beautiful surroundings do still have an early run of fish and can, like all other salmon rivers, provide good sport on their day. The relevant authorities are striving very hard both to maintain and improve this useful salmon fishery.

FRANCE

At one time France had some of the best salmon fishing in Europe, and rivers discharging into the Channel and to the south abounded with salmon. Many of the fish entered the rivers early in the season and were, therefore, present to be exploited by anglers over a long period of the season. Due to a combination of pollution, impeded access and competition from various species of freshwater fish, salmon stocks in some rivers have shown a marked decline, although others, particularly those in Brittany, still have an adequate stock and can afford good sport for anglers. These attractive rivers of various lengths and character are useful for all methods of angling and some well suited to fly fishing. Due to the importance of this natural resource, the French government has in recent years not only promoted both research and stricter legislation in order to restore salmon stocks to their former strength, but has also been prominent on the international front in furthering the conservation of Atlantic salmon stocks. Some of the best known salmon rivers are the Loire, Allier, Elle, Elorn and Le Trieux.

NORWAY

This country, in the northern hemisphere, has not only been regarded as having some of the best salmon fishing in the world, but also the size of its Atlantic salmon draws anglers form all over the world to partake in the sport.

Due to the long hard winters, with the heavy winter snow fall clinging to the high mountainous terrain well on into the early summer, the salmon fishing season is severely curtailed in duration in comparison to that in others parts of Europe. Late May to mid-September is the norm, with June, July and August undoubtedly the best months. Therefore, the main angling season is only fourteen to sixteen weeks long compared to that of the Tweed which extends to forty-three weeks.

Due to the short feeding season for juveniles in these great rivers because of the cold climate, parr normally remain feeding in the rivers for two to five years, and in some cases in the north of the country they are seven years old before they smolt. The smolts normally leave their rivers during the period May to July, with the earlier runs taking place in the rivers in the south of the country.

Throughout the country, most of the rivers are relatively short and in some cases steep, with the water levels swollen by snow melt throughout the early part of the season. Many of the pools are, therefore, very deep and fast flowing and often the angler has to get his lure beneath the fast flowing surface currents to where the fish are lying. Once he hooks a fish he not only has to contend with the force of the current but also with the strength of his quarry. In some cases this strength can be formidable as, in the larger rivers, fish of twenty to fifty pounds in weight are quite common, and often the norm. Unless, therefore, he is firm with his fish once he hooks it, the fish will play him rather than he play the fish. There are many excellent rivers throughout the length of Norway that provide excellent sport for all methods of angling. The angler has a wide choice if he wishes to fish one of the larger rivers with a good chance of catching a real monster of forty pounds or more. He can on the other hand fish a river with prolific grilse runs and a smaller class of sporting fish. No matter where he chooses to fish, he will be faced with a great challenge and exciting expectation in beautiful surroundings.

To name but a few of the most prolific salmon rivers, there are to the north the Tana on the Norwegian–Finnish border, and the Alta and Laksley which are amongst the most famous rivers for big fish. The Alta has also always had the reputation of being one of the best rivers for fly fishing. In mid-Norway, the Namsen, Gaula and Surna have an excellent reputation, whilst in the south the Laerdal and the Numedalslagen are both good rivers where fish can often be caught earlier in the season than in northern rivers.

It is reputed that the Duke of Westminster landed thirty-three fish in one day, averaging twenty-four pounds on the Alta in the mid–1920s. Other individual daily catches were even larger on the same river during the last century.

ICELAND

Another island nation which can provide excellent salmon fishing on its numerous small rivers. In many cases, these short rivers are akin to those found on the west coast of Ireland or Scotland. Again, because it is sited well to the north these rivers only enjoy a relatively short angling season, mainly from late June to early September, but undoubtedly July and August are the best months. Many of the fish caught are grilse, but the angler does also have the chance to catch salmon of eight to fifteen pounds in weight and the odd heavier fish can be taken. These rivers have a wealth of pools of wide and varied character, ideally suited to fly fishing. Anglers from far and wide are drawn to this well managed and maintained salmon fishery.

Many of the best rivers are grouped on the west coast around the capital Reykjavik, or along the north coast of the island. There are other rivers that are glacier fed, but most of these have water carrying high turbidity levels and are accordingly, not suitable for the species.

THE UNITED STATES OF AMERICA

Atlantic salmon stocks are, of course, confined to the east coast rivers of the USA. They were severely impeded in their ascent of certain rivers when the country was being developed, mainly because the importance of the salmon was not then recognised: dams to provide water power were built across numerous salmon rivers, which debarred fish from their breeding grounds. As a result, the species became extinct in many rivers and dwindled to a fraction of its former strength in others. More recently great efforts have been made to restore salmon runs to rivers that have not been inhabited by the species for many years and at the same time, strengthen the runs in the rivers where they still exist.

Rivers such as the Penabscot, Sheepscot, Naraguagus and the Connecticut, in the states of Maine and Massachusetts are amongst the best known in the present day for providing good angling. Once again the fishing season is of short duration, mainly confined to a twelve to fourteen week season between June and early September

Fly fishing from a canoe or punt is a popular method on some of the wider, slower stretches of these rivers. It is also interesting to note that dry fly fishing for salmon is a very popular method of angling and is at times extremely productive, whereas this method of fly fishing is seldom practised on rivers in Europe. Even when anglers do try to practise the American technique of dry fly fishing in this country, it seldom works effectively, but it must be admitted that methods such as dibbling or using the riffling hitch, which could be termed a compromise, are growing in popularity all the time. Single handed rods are often used to good effect for salmon fishing on many sectors of these rivers. Not only are they ideal for dry fly fishing, but also as the season is so much later in opening than it is in the UK, most of the tackle required is similar to that used during the summer months in this country. Therefore, floating lines and small flies are the norm.

Methods of fishing are, on the whole, more strictly controlled and in many cases restrictions on the size of catch an angler may take are imposed.

CANADA

For very many years the numerous rivers of New Brunswick, Quebec and Newfoundland swarmed with countless salmon and this nation was, therefore, by far the biggest producer. A larger share of salmon was caught here than in any of the other countries where the species was indigenous. Unfortunately, however, pollution from the mining and timber industries and the spraying of forest pests throughout the years has put an unacceptable pressure on these stocks and Canada's salmon stocks have showed a marked decline in line with European countries which have similar problems.

During this century, however, government and state authorities have done everything in their power both at home and on the international front to ensure that everything possible has been done to conserve salmon stocks at sea and in the rivers. Stringent regulations have been imposed to curb indiscriminate net fisheries, restrict angling catches and, at the same time, curtail poaching activities. Every endeavour has been made to clean up existing pollution and prevent new sources of pollution thus safeguarding the ecology of many rivers which are faced with widely different problems.

Once again, in Canada the angling season is much shorter than that in Europe and much more in line with the season in Scandinavia, Iceland or the United States, namely, from June to early September. Strangely enough, however, the first onslaught by anglers occurs as soon as the ice has broken exploiting the 'black fish' or kelts, and very soon afterwards both grilse and salmon enter the rivers and their attention is then turned in that direction. Again, much of this fishing can be undertaken with shorter rods, floating lines and small flies. Often on some of the more renowned rivers or beats, anglers are flown out to fishing lodges, where they are looked after extremely well, and then taken out to their alloted beats. Usually they are given their own guide, who takes them out in a canoe, or other type of craft, from which they can easily cover the water with a single handed rod, or one of their choice. Each angler is limited to what he can keep, and the rest of the fish are returned to the water. On other waters, anglers may fish from the bank from whence they can cover their pools efficiently.

Many of the rivers of various lengths and widths are liable to significant change from time to time; mainly due to the heavy movement and pressure of the ice when it breaks up once the thaw sets in after a long, hard winter. These ice flows often gouge large runnels and grooves in the gravel and river bed, which can form narrow channels to provide ideal resting places for fish, where they often take readily during the angling season. Even though salmon stocks have shown such a marked decline, many of the Canadian rivers still provide some of the best and most productive sport that salmon anglers can obtain anywhere.

It would be quite impossible to name more than a fraction of the best rivers because they are so numerous, but amongst them are the Miramechie, and Restigouche in New Brunswick; the Moisie, Godabout, Matane, Cascapedia in Quebec and the West Arm Brook and Big Salmon River in Newfoundland. All have great reputations, and no list of Canadian rivers would be complete without mentioning the St John. Of these the Moisie probably has the heaviest fish, some of which run up to thirty to forty pounds.

Further Reading

ADAMS, J., 1923, *Salmon and Trout Angling*, Hutchinson

ASHLEY-COOPER, J., 1988, *A Salmon Fisher's Odyssey*, Whitherby

ASHLEY-COOPER. J., *A Line on Salmon*

BALFOUR, H., 1978, *Folk, Fish and Fun*, Terence Dalton Ltd

BALFOUR-KINNEAR, G. P. R., 1937, *Flying Salmon*, Longmans

BALFOUR-KINNEAR, G. P. R., 1938, *Spinning Salmon*, Longmand

BALFOUR-KINNEAR, G. P. R., 1963 *More About Trout and Salmon*, Longmans

CHAYTOR, A. H., 1910, *Letters to Salmon-fishers' Sons*, Murray

CROSSLEY, A., 1939, *The Floating-line for Salmon and Sea Trout*, Methuen

FALKUS, H., 1984 *Salmon Fishing*

GILBERT, H. A., 1929, *The Tale of a Wye Fisherman*

GRAESSER, N. W., 1982, *Fly Fishing for Salmon*, Boydell and Brewer

GRAESSER, N. W., 1987, *Advanced Salmon Fishing*, Boydell and Brewer

GRAESSER, N. W., 1989, *Finer Points of Salmon Fishing*, Boydell and Brewer

GREY, L. R. N., *Torridge Fishery*, Nicholas Kaye

HUGHES-PARRY, *A Salmon Fisher's Methods*

HUNTER, W. A., 1926 et seq. *Fisherman's Pie: an angling symposium*, A. & C. Black

HUTTON, J. A., 1920, *Rod Fishing for Salmon on the Wye*, Fishing Gazette

HUTTON, J. E., 1930, *Fishing Ways and Fishing Days*

JONES, J. W., 1959, *The Salmon*, Collins

MENZIES, W. J. M., 1925, *The Salmon – Its Life Story*, W. Blackwood

MILLS, D. H., 1989 *Ecology and Management of Atlantic Salmon*, Chapman Hall

MILLS, D. H. & GRAESSER, N., 1981 *Salmon Rivers of Scotland*, Cassells

OGLESBY, A., 1971, *Salmon*, Queen Anne Press

OGLESBY, A., 1988, *Reeling In*, The Crowood Press

RIGHYNI, R. V., 1965, *Salmon Taking Times*, Macdonald

RIGHYNI, R. V., 1973, *Advanced Salmon Fishing*, Macdonald

RUDD, G. F., See Scott

SCOTT, JOCK, (RUDD, G. F.) 1933, *Art of Salmon-fishing*, Witherby

SCOTT, JOCK, (RUDD, G. F.) 1935, *Greased Line Fishing for Salmon*, Seeley Service Ltd

TAVERNER, E., 1930, *Lonsdale Library Salmon Fishing*

WOOD, I., 1957, *My Way with Salmon*, Allen & Unwin